GUIDES
AS EASY AS IT GE

The Common Core Standards

WITHDRAWN

by Jared T. Bigham, EdD

ALPHA
A member of Penguin Group (USA) Inc.

ALPHA BOOKS

Published by Penguin Group (USA) Inc.

Penguin Group (USA) Inc., 375 Hudson Street, New York, New York 10014, USA • Penguin Group (Canada), 90 Eglinton Avenue East, Suite 700, Toronto, Ontario M4P 2Y3, Canada (a division of Pearson Penguin Canada Inc.) • Penguin Books Ltd., 80 Strand, London WC2R 0RL, England • Penguin Ireland, 25 St. Stephen's Green, Dublin 2, Ireland (a division of Penguin Books Ltd.) • Penguin Group (Australia), 250 Camberwell Road, Camberwell, Victoria 3124, Australia (a division of Pearson Australia Group Pty. Ltd.) • Penguin Books India Pvt. Ltd., 11 Community Centre, Panchsheel Park, New Delhi—110 017, India • Penguin Group (NZ), 67 Apollo Drive, Rosedale, North Shore, Auckland 1311, New Zealand (a division of Pearson New Zealand Ltd.) • Penguin Books (South Africa) (Pty.) Ltd., 24 Sturdee Avenue, Rosebank, Johannesburg 2196, South Africa • Penguin Books Ltd., Registered Offices: 80 Strand, London WC2R 0RL, England

International Standard Book Number: 978-1-61564-732-3
Library of Congress Catalog Card Number: 2014945994

17 16 15   8 7 6 5 4 3 2 1

Interpretation of the printing code: The rightmost number of the first series of numbers is the year of the book's printing; the rightmost number of the second series of numbers is the number of the book's printing. For example, a printing code of 15-1 shows that the first printing occurred in 2015.

Printed in the United States of America

Note: This publication contains the opinions and ideas of its author. It is intended to provide helpful and informative material on the subject matter covered. It is sold with the understanding that the author and publisher are not engaged in rendering professional services in the book. If the reader requires personal assistance or advice, a competent professional should be consulted. The author and publisher specifically disclaim any responsibility for any liability, loss, or risk, personal or otherwise, which is incurred as a consequence, directly or indirectly, of the use and application of any of the contents of this book.

Most Alpha books are available at special quantity discounts for bulk purchases for sales promotions, premiums, fund-raising, or educational use. Special books, or book excerpts, can also be created to fit specific needs. For details, write: Special Markets, Alpha Books, 375 Hudson Street, New York, NY 10014.

Publisher: *Mike Sanders*
Executive Managing Editor: *Billy Fields*
Executive Acquisitions Editor: *Lori Cates Hand*
Development Editor: *Ann Barton*
Production Editor: *Jana M. Stefanciosa*

Cover Designer: *Laura Merriman*
Book Designer: *William Thomas*
Indexer: *Celia McCoy*
Layout: *Brian Massey*
Proofreader: *Claudia Bell*

Contents

Appendixes

Introduction

The Common Core State Standards have become an important topic across our country because they impact our most prized possession as parents and our most valuable resource as a nation: our children. The discussion around Common Core has moved from the classroom, schools, and other education circles to the forefront of many other political and social conversations.

There is a great deal of information out there on Common Core, especially in the opinion columns and blogosphere, so it can be a challenge to separate fact from fiction. It can also be a challenge to filter out the rhetoric that has nothing to do with education at all.

This book seeks to give a historical perspective on how Common Core came into being as a concept, how it was developed, and how it has been implemented across the country. It also seeks to give a simple nuts and bolts look at what the standards actually are at each grade level and you as a parent can support the standards in order to help prepare your child for life after high school.

How This Book Is Organized

Part 1, How Did We Get Here?, deals with the historical events that led to the idea of a common set of standards. It outlines the major players involved in the initial discussions about the Common Core and the steps that were taken to develop the standards. This section also discusses how states have successfully implemented the standards and why some states retreated from implementation. Finally, this section looks at how the Common Core is changing the way students are taught.

Part 2, The Literacy Standards, takes a look at the English Language Arts standards. The standards are broken down by grade level and by topic, with clear summaries of the expectations at each grade. Each ELA chapter includes examples of complex texts appropriate for the grade range as well as tips for helping to support your child's learning at home. The final chapter in this part looks at the literacy standards for history, social studies, and technical subjects.

Part 3, The Math Standards, explains the math standards for each grade. Since math is an intimidating subject for many people, an effort was made to simplify what students would be expected to know at each grade level. There are also techniques presented that you can use to support your child as they progress through the math standards each year.

Part 4, Assessments, Implementation, and Moving Forward, is a look at where things stand across the country after four years of using the Common Core in schools. This section covers some of the lessons learned during implementation, and looks ahead to the next steps for the Common Core. You'll also learn about the assessments that will be used to measure learning based on Common Core standards, and how they will be administered.

Extras

The five different sidebars in this book are designed to highlight additional insight by explaining key terms or giving advice on how to support the learning of the standards.

COLLEGE AND CAREER READINESS

This sidebar highlights the college and career readiness skills supported in the anchor standards, which are the broader skills students are expected to master by the time they graduate.

DEFINITION

Key terms to help you understand the important concepts found in Common Core.

DID YOU KNOW?

Interesting education facts and information about the Common Core.

KEYS TO THE CORE

Tips for how you can support your child's education and help them succeed with the Common Core.

TAKE CARE

These sidebars address some of the common misconceptions about the Common Core, as well as pitfalls to avoid when working with your child.

Acknowledgments

I would like to thank my family for their support through the process of writing this book and God for the energy at the end of many long days and weekends to soldier on when sleep called. I apologize to my children Cade, Maleia, and Sydney for the missed adventures while daddy was locked away in his office, and I thank my unbelievable wife, Jess, for her considerable knowledge and assistance with putting together the material. I thank my parents and grandfather for babysitting when I needed "quiet." Finally, I thank Lori Hand for her patience with me and encouragement through this project.

Special thanks also to Shannon Reed for her excellent work in writing the chapters covering the math standards.

Trademarks

All terms mentioned in this book that are known to be or are suspected of being trademarks or service marks have been appropriately capitalized. Alpha Books and Penguin Group (USA) Inc. cannot attest to the accuracy of this information. Use of a term in this book should not be regarded as affecting the validity of any trademark or service mark.

How Did We Get Here?

This section looks at the history of education policy in the United States and explains how the events of the past have influenced the development of the Common Core standards. The myths surrounding Common Core will be dispelled, and we'll take a hard look at how states have implemented the standards. This section wraps up by explaining how your child's work might look different from the way you learned in school.

History and Development of the Common Core

If you're reading this book, you've probably encountered the Common Core standards recently and want to know more. Maybe your child has come home with new learning objectives based on the Common Core, or maybe you've heard about the standards in the news and are interested in understanding why they exist and how they shape education in the United States.

Though public discussion of the Common Core has only recently become prevalent, gaining the attention of many parents and other groups, the development and implementation of the standards has been a lengthy and ongoing process. This five-year project has involved experts and feedback groups from around the country, and did not recently spring into being as some people mistakenly believe. In fact, I have spoken at several forums on Common Core where parents are surprised to learn that Common Core standards have been used in their children's classroom for two or more years.

In This Chapter

- The history of education standards in the United States
- The Common Core standards defined
- How the Common Core discussion began
- The development of the standards

The concept of education standards is nothing new. In fact, states have used standards to guide teaching and assess learning in their schools for over three decades.

You may be wondering, if standards have been in use for such a long time, why all the fuss about the Common Core? This is a great question. Part of the answer lies in the fact that states have never been able to agree on the most important things to teach or when to teach them. Part of the answer also lies in understanding the opposition to any kind of national education movement that is perceived to originate in a top-down manner from the federal government. This chapter will begin to address this question by explaining what education standards are, as well as how and when the Common Core standards were developed.

What Are the Common Core Standards?

Before a discussion on Common Core can begin, it's important to define what a standard is and, just as important, what it is not. Standards are learning expectations for students at each grade level that explain what a student should know to be ready to move to the next grade. For decades, different states have used different sets of standards to inform the curriculum and assessments used in their schools.

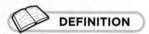 **DEFINITION**

Standards are the clearly defined statements of the knowledge and skills students should have at each grade that prepares them for the next grade.

The Common Core standards are a specific set of expectations for math and English/language arts (ELA) designed to be used on a national level for students in all grades (kindergarten through grade 12). Although some people think there are Common Core standards for other academic subject areas, such as science and social studies, this is not the case. In fact, at the time of this publication, there are no discussions or plans to develop Common Core standards for any other subjects other than math and ELA. However, the standards do support other subject areas through the emphasis on literacy and writing.

 DID YOU KNOW?

English/language arts is often referred to as ELA. This includes the study of reading, writing, and grammar.

Cross-Curricular Expectations

Reading and writing across the curriculum in multiple subjects is not a new concept, but with the Common Core standards, expectations for students are raised as they read more complex texts in their history, science, and technical classes. There is also an emphasis on reading historical texts, like the Gettysburg Address, so that students can discuss these types of documents in English and history classes. Students might also read an article from a scientific journal as part of an English assignment that is later discussed in their science class.

Again, the type of cooperation between subjects isn't a new concept, but keeping a consistent level of higher expectations in each class through the ELA standards is something that has not been previously implemented. There will be a more in-depth look at how Common Core supports other subjects in later chapters.

The Difference Between Standards and Curriculum

Knowing what Common Core is *not* is an important aspect to understanding the standards. Even though Common Core standards state in precise terms what students should learn at each grade level, *how* students should learn the standards is left up to the states, districts, or schools. This is called the *curriculum*. Often people confuse standards and curriculum, or they assume they are the same thing. It is important to note that the standards can be the same across a state, but how the standards are taught through the curriculum can vary from district to district or even from school to school.

 **DEFINITION**

> **Curriculum** refers to the textbooks, materials, instructional techniques, and other resources used to teach standards.

Many teachers have favorite themes they like to use to teach standards in their classroom and create units of study around these themes. For instance, a fourth grade teacher who is particularly interested in Native American culture and history might create English and math lessons related to this topic. This theme is part of the curriculum, but not the standards. Other fourth grade teachers might teach the same English and math skills using a different theme.

Keep in mind that textbooks and other classroom materials are part of the curriculum, not the standards. Although some materials say that they are aligned to the Common Core, this is not reflective of the standards themselves but of a particular company's method for teaching the standards. Some negative press that Common Core has received in the conventional media and social media has been the result of questionable curriculum decisions in teaching the standards or just plain poor teaching. As a result, Common Core has been found guilty by association.

This distinction between standards and curriculum is also important to keep in mind as some opponents of Common Core say it limits teachers' flexibility and creativity. The irony is that we have consistently had standards in our schools for over three decades, but when people hear the word "common," they sometimes unfairly associate it with the way teachers teach, instead of what they are teaching.

For example, the addition concept "$15 + 10 = 25$" is the same in Vermont as it is in Nevada. However, a teacher in Nevada has the flexibility to teach this concept differently than a teacher in Vermont if they choose. The point is that the students learn the concept. Some teachers prefer games to teach, and others might prefer using manipulatives or visuals. It's getting the student to learn that is the goal, and the approach is left to the discretion of the teacher. The teaching approach is the curriculum, and the standard is the goal of the teaching.

A clearer way to put it might be that a standard is a destination where teachers want students to be at the end of a lesson. How students get to that destination is up to the school and teacher. They might take a car, bus, motorcycle, plane, or walk, but ultimately, it's getting everyone there that is important.

This may seem like a lot of examples on the difference between standards and curriculum, but this is a key concept to understand moving forward as questions of state autonomy and federal intrusion come into play.

How the Conversation About Common Standards Began

The idea of national standards was often referred to as the "third rail" of education policy because, like the third rail of a subway track, if a person touched this issue, he or she died a political death. Any time the word "national" was used in discussions around standards, it made some people think more about words like "sameness" rather than "consistent" or "foundation." This is an important distinction since there is a big difference between trying to make students the same and making sure all students are consistently taught the foundational skills they need at each grade level to be successful when they graduate.

Often, when the topic of national standards was brought up, it became more of a discussion on politics rather than academic equity for students. This was due in large part because these early discussions on national standards were initiated by federal leaders in a very top-down approach to addressing the issue. Even though the concept of states teaching the same core content and skills at each grade level was the goal that was ultimately reached in the creation of Common Core, it mattered greatly in many people's minds that these early failed efforts were led by the federal government.

However, by 2006, the outlook of state leaders across the country was beginning to change as the vast differences in state standards were highlighted through reforms initiated by No Child Left Behind (NCLB), an act that began in 2001. Through NCLB, states were compelled by the federal government to develop their own high standards and their own state standardized tests to assess those standards. This led to fifty different interpretations as to what students should know at each grade level, when they should know it, and how it should be assessed. It was also the first time that each state's achievement was given deliberate attention on a national scale.

 DID YOU KNOW?

No Child Left Behind (NCLB) was a federal program that promoted standards-based reform aimed at increasing the academic success of disadvantaged students. One of the primary goals was for states to create high academic standards and assessments aligned to these standards.

Through NCLB, states were put on the path of common goals for the first time. Though reaching those goals was given complete flexibility and authority at the state level, it was the first time states were at least working toward the same outcomes. The most notable of these was: 100 percent of students would graduate high school by 2014. This meant that, eventually, nearly 100 percent of students would have to pass the state standardized assessments at each grade level. Though almost every state's standards and assessments were different, state leaders were having conversations about common goals and achievement goals. This led to broader conversations within and among states on professional development, curriculum, assessment, and resources like never before. NCLB galvanized states in a positive way in that they now had common goals and challenges that brought them to the discussion table.

A Need for National Standards

When students began taking standardized state assessments along with national assessments such as the ACT, the SAT, and the National Assessment of Educational Progress (NAEP), it quickly became apparent that individual states had very different ideas about what constituted key knowledge and key skills. In some states, 80 percent or more of the students would score high enough on their state assessment to be considered *college and career ready*. However, when these same students took a national assessment like ACT, less than 20 percent of the students would achieve the necessary score to enter college or an industry training program. This disparity in state level achievement versus achievement on national assessments instigated some awkward conversations within and among states. It also begged some questions, including:

1. What are the basic skills and knowledge students should be taught as a foundation?

2. When and in what order should students be taught certain skills or knowledge?

3. Are there certain skills and knowledge students must have to be college and career ready?

4. How can we assess these skills and knowledge in a way that gives a true reflection of student learning?

 **DEFINITION**

> **College and career ready** means that a student who graduates high school can enter college or a career training program without having to take remedial courses that don't count toward his or her degree.

In 2006, with the current differences in state-created standards, assessments, and achievement in mind, state leaders felt more comfortable with reengaging a conversation around a common set of standards on which states could agree. This was not the first time this conversation had been started; however, it was the first time state leaders felt like they could seriously discuss it without committing professional suicide. It was also the first time the discussion was solely led by state leaders, rather than the leaders within the federal government. As mentioned earlier, NCLB caused every state's achievement to be reported and studied, so some state leaders felt that reaching a consensus on what standards should be taught would help level the playing field.

There was also an issue in many states of simply having too many standards. Some states had over 100 standards in each subject area, beginning as early as third grade. With this many standards, isolating what should be taught and when could get confusing, so the idea of fewer and clearer standards was raised early in the discussion.

Early Discussions

The former governor of North Carolina, James B. Hunt, Jr., hosted a meeting for a small group of education leaders in June of 2006 to discuss the idea of a common set of standards that could be used by each state. In September of 2006, another meeting was hosted by an organization called Excellent Education. This organization was led by Hunt's friend, former governor of West Virginia, Bob Wise. This meeting was attended by education policy and advocacy groups, including the Thomas B. Fordham Institute, the Education Trust, and the Aspen Institute. The purpose of the meeting was to discuss if the time was right to develop common standards for all states. In the end, all parties agreed that some important factors supported the need for common standards:

1. U.S. students faced serious global economic competition for jobs.

2. There were dramatic differences in achievement on state level assessments compared to national assessments.

3. As a whole, U.S. students were being blown away by students from other countries on international math and science tests. The countries that outperformed the United States were all alike in one way; they had common standards across their nation instead of regional or state standards.

With these factors in mind, the James B. Hunt, Jr. Institute for Educational Leadership and Policy began a three-year movement for common standards across the nation. All those committed to the idea felt that the key component for success was ensuring that the process was state-led and not controlled by the federal government. In fact, they understood that any participation or influence by the federal government would have a negative impact on the movement.

The leaders of the movement then recruited the help of two key organizations who each saw the value in common standards for each state: the National Governor's Association (NGA) and the Council of Chief State School Officers (CCSSO). These two organizations added legitimacy and the necessary individual state leadership the movement's leaders were looking for.

 DID YOU KNOW?

The Council of Chief State School Officers (CCSSO) is composed of the state commissioners of education for each state. In some states, this person is called the State Superintendent of Education or Secretary of Education.

Creating the Standards

From 2006 to 2009, the movement's leaders conducted research and convened multiple meetings until there was sufficient support from state leaders and education policy organizations to develop the standards. At this time, it became important to formalize the effort in a written agreement among states. This was to show that the movement was state-led and that there was agreement as to how the development process would proceed. By August of 2009, governors and commissioners of education from forty-eight states signed a *memorandum of understanding* (MOU) committing to the development of common standards.

 **DEFINITION**

> A **memorandum of understanding** is a document that individuals or groups sign to show they are committed to a cause. They are usually not legally binding and do not involve money. They are often used as a formal agreement on a plan or process for a project or partnership.

Texas and Alaska were the only two states at the time that chose not to be involved in the project. As of the publication of this book, 43 states, the District of Columbia, the Department of Defense Education Activity, and the territories of Guam, American Samoa, the U.S. Virgin Islands, and the Northern Mariana Islands all have adopted Common Core standards. An updated, interactive map of the participating states and territories can be found at corestandards.org/standards-in-your-state/.

This was the first time so many states had come together and formalized action steps to create the common standards. Past attempts at creating common standards had not made it much past acknowledging they were needed. These states made the important leap from discussion to action.

Input from Work Teams

An important idea that the leaders of the movement wanted to promote was that standards should be fewer in number, easy to understand, and higher in expectations. Therefore, one of the main pitfalls they wanted to avoid was a problem that developers of state standards had continually run into in the past: too many cooks in the kitchen and no parameters within which to work. As mentioned earlier, many states had over 100 standards in each subject area, starting in the lower grades. This was largely because there were so many people in the development process who contributed favorite topics, even if they had no relevance to college and career readiness. This resulted in long lists of information that were turned into standards and became almost impossible to cover with any quality in a school year.

With this in mind, the leaders of the movement wanted to make sure the standards contained no "fluff" and only focused on the knowledge and skills students needed to be college and career ready; therefore, they recruited the help of representatives from five organizations to define the parameters the writers would use to create the standards. In essence, they would create a guideline to guarantee the idea of fewer, more appropriate standards was maintained. The five organizations were the State Higher Education Executive Officers, the College Board, Achieve, ACT, and the National Association of State Boards of Education.

Once the parameters for writing the standards were outlined, separate *work teams* for math and ELA were created. Each team consisted of experts from across the country who were involved with universities, departments of education, K-12 public education, and education policy organizations. The English/language arts work team had 51 members, and was led by David Coleman, the President of Student Achievement Partners, and Susan Pimental, founder of StandardsWork. The math work team had 50 members and was led by Jason Zimba, Professor of Mathematics and Physics at Bennington College, William McCallum, Professor of Mathematics at the University of Arizona, and Philip Daro of America's Choice.

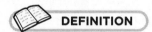 **DEFINITION**

> **Work teams** were the two groups of experts created for math and English/language arts to write the Common Core standards. They would write draft portions of the standards and then submit them to feedback groups for review.

Some states like California, Georgia, Massachusetts, Minnesota, Colorado, and Florida were recognized to already have quality standards in place, so those states were asked to recommend members for the work teams. This helped create state buy-in, as well as making sure some of the best educational minds in the country were a part of the development process. A full list of the work team members can be found in Appendix D.

Input from Feedback Groups

As the work teams produced drafts of the standards, they presented them to *feedback groups* for comment and direction.

 **DEFINITION**

> **Feedback groups** were experts from around the country who would review draft portions of the standards as the work teams wrote them and make recommendations to help guide the work teams.

There were 22 members of the math feedback group and twelve members of the ELA feedback group. These two groups included experts from universities, K-12 public education teachers, and industry leaders. University leaders were asked to ensure the standards met any minimum expectations that colleges set in order for students to enter their institutions. Teachers could offer advice from their unique perspectives on how it might look to actually teach those standards, and business leaders were able to give opinions on what skills employers in major business sectors needed students to master. This was a critical part to making sure the standards truly prepared students to be college and career ready.

Getting feedback from people who were actually working, hiring, and teaching in the field gave credibility to the development process. In the past, standards had usually been developed by a single group and then handed down to teachers with no input or reflection through the process. Teachers and stakeholder leaders might be on the team creating the standards, but the feedback often didn't come until the project was complete and the standards were being taught.

In contrast, the Common Core standards were created as a living document that went through revisions based on feedback from experts in each field. The standards were also posted online for public comment and feedback for several weeks. The feedback from all these different sources took place during development, instead of after the fact as had been the case with previous creations of standards. A full list of the Feedback Group members can be found in Appendix D.

The Least You Need To Know

- Standards are the clear statements of what a student should know at each grade level. How standards are taught is the decision of school districts.

- Individual state standards led to pronounced discrepancies between students' performance on state and national level assessments, which highlighted the need for common standards.

- The movement for and development of Common Core standards was a lengthy process that did not happen overnight.

- The development of Common Core standards was a state-led movement. The writers of the standards were experts from across the country, and experts from the field gave the writers feedback as the standards were written.

Myths vs. Facts of Common Core

In my professional role, I often find that when I'm asked to be on a discussion panel or speak to a group of education stakeholders, I spend a great deal of time dispelling myths about the Common Core standards. Depending on the group to which I'm presenting, I often make an effort to cover some of the myths I hear most often before the question and answer time even begins. With that in mind, this chapter provides explanations and facts regarding some of the most common myths and misconceptions about the standards.

In This Chapter

- Some common misperceptions regarding the Common Core standards

- A balanced look at the facts about the Common Core

- The information you need to evaluate claims about the Common Core

A State or Federal Movement?

Myth: The Common Core State Standards represent an effort to nationalize education.

Fact: There is a difference between nationalizing education and each state operating from an agreed-upon set of standards that promote the minimum students should know at each grade level. In other words, Common Core is a multistate agreement rather than a hostile takeover.

Myth: The federal government is dictating how states must teach.

Fact: The Elementary and Secondary Education Act of 1965 forbids the federal government from mandating to states how to teach, what to teach, or what resources to use in instruction at the state and local level.

Myth: Common Core was not a state-led movement.

Fact: The development of Common Core standards has been state led from start to finish. It was individual state leaders who first made the call to action to address the differences in each state's standards. Forty-eight states originally chose to adopt the standards, with no mandate from the federal government. The fact that there are states that still have not adopted or fully adopted Common Core standards is evidence that it is a state decision.

Myth: States that adopt the Common Core standards can teach only those standards and nothing more.

Fact: In order to be considered a Common Core state, states must agree to teach all the standards listed without altering or removing any of them. However, states can add an additional 15 percent to the standards if they choose. This gives states, districts, and schools a great deal of flexibility in creating a learning experience that is also reflective of their regional culture or interests by adding additional standards.

Myth: The federal government will require a national test based on the Common Core that all students must take.

Fact: There is no national test required by the federal government that all students must take. In reality, states that have adopted Common Core standards have the freedom to create their own test, form a *consortium* and create a test together, or purchase a test from a third-party vendor. About half the states that have adopted Common Core have joined either the PARCC or Smarter Balanced consortiums, about 25 percent have created their own test, and about 25 percent have purchased a test from a third-party vendor.

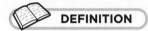

DEFINITION

A **consortium** is a group of states that have banded together to produce a Common Core-aligned assessment. Joining forces lowers the individual cost of assessment development for each state and allows student scores to be compared across multiple states. PARCC and Smarter Balanced are two of the largest consortiums.

Myth: The Common Core standards and the tests that go with them will be used by the federal government to create a database that contains information on all our children.

Fact: States have always collected school and district data and a minimal amount of individual student data. However, the Family Educational Rights and Privacy Act (FERPA) prevents the federal government or any other entity from obtaining personal information or data that would identify an individual student.

Myth: The federal government persuaded states to adopt Common Core standards through the Race to the Top grant.

Fact: Applying for the Race to the Top grant was optional for states. If states chose to apply for the grant, points could be awarded for adopting college and career ready standards, but there was no requirement to specifically adopt Common Core standards. As further evidence, some states won Race to the Top grant funding and did not adopt Common Core standards.

DID YOU KNOW?

Race to the Top was a $4.35 billion competitive grant program created by the federal government in July 2009. The grant encouraged states to create innovative ways to improve low-performing schools and implement more accountability. States received awards ranging from $17 million to $700 million.

Can Teachers Teach the Way They Want?

Myth: Common Core standards force teachers to teach a certain way.

Fact: Teachers are free to teach as they see fit. Common Core only establishes what students should know to be college and career ready. How the teacher teaches the standards is completely up to him or her.

Myth: There is a required reading list for Common Core English/language arts standards, and some of the books have questionable material.

Fact: There is no required reading list within the Common Core standards. There is an appendix that accompanies the standards (called Appendix B) that provides a list of example passages from books to demonstrate the level of reading complexity students should master at each grade level. These are short passages taken from many different books, and there is no questionable material in these passages. Some states or school districts have put together required reading lists as part of their curriculum, and some people mistakenly assume that these lists are a part of the standards.

Myth: Because of Common Core standards, teachers must teach to the test.

Fact: Actually, tests based on previous state standards encouraged teachers to "teach to the test" much more than Common Core standards do. Most state standards were based a great deal on content that students had to memorize or, at the least, be able to identify. The tests in these states assessed students on how well they could recall this information, and they relied on multiple-choice questions.

Common Core standards do have content knowledge that must be assessed, but there are added skill components that students have previously not been tested on. Most tests aligned to Common Core do not rely just on multiple-choice questions, but will also have sections where students write answers, give explanations, and even manipulate graphs and diagrams. This means that teachers are not teaching students just to recall or identify information, but they are also teaching students skills to use in applying that information. Therefore, this type of assessment does not lend itself well to "teaching to the test."

Myth: Students are forced to use many steps to answer simple math problems, such as 32 − 14, instead of simply giving the answer.

Fact: Unfortunately, bad teaching methods or steps to solving a problem taken out of context sometimes give Common Core a bad name. I have seen such math problems held up as negative examples by those who oppose Common Core. The reality is that the standard that relates to this problem simply states that students need to know two-digit subtraction. It does not say (nor do any of the other standards say) how to teach the standard. This is where the distinction between standards (what to teach) and curriculum (how to teach) becomes an important factor.

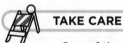 **TAKE CARE**

One of the biggest myths is that Common Core puts a stranglehold on how teachers teach. In reality, teachers enjoy greater flexibility than ever before with fewer standards to cover. Teachers are also free to use any materials or resources they or the school district feel are helpful.

Myth: Teachers are forced to teach all students the same in a one-size-fits-all way that doesn't allow for differences in abilities or individuality.

Fact: Common Core standards actually allow teachers more flexibility in their teaching methods because they have the ability to spend more time on each concept. The teachers must still meet the individual needs of the students as they have always done, and there is greater room to highlight the interests and individuality of the students with the emphasis Common Core puts on critical thinking and expression of ideas. This is in stark contrast to many states' old standards that were based largely on memorization.

Myth: The Common Core Standards do away with most fiction literature and focus on nonfiction and informational texts.

Fact: Part of the weakness in most state standards was that there was too much emphasis on fiction literature and almost no attention given to nonfiction works. Common Core standards strike a good balance between the two. The nonfiction works and *informational texts* that Common Core suggests are a mix of historical documents like the Gettysburg Address and the U.S. Constitution, as well as current informational texts like scientific journals.

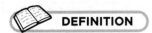 **DEFINITION**

> An **informational text** is a specific kind of nonfiction that is used to present or explain information. Examples include articles, speeches, instructional manuals, or memoirs.

Are the Standards Rigorous Enough?

Myth: Common Core is a dumbing down of our standards.

Fact: Common Core standards are much more demanding standards and set higher expectations for learning than the previous standards for most states in our country. States that had great standards prior to Common Core were used as models during development, so these states' standards were improved on even more.

Myth: The current state standards are good enough for students.

Fact: ACT reported that almost three-fourths of the students enrolling in a college or university are not scoring high enough to show they are prepared for the level of work required by first-year courses. This indicates that individual state standards were not doing enough to get students ready for college. It also means students have to take one or more remedial courses that don't count for credit, which is a loss of time and money for the student.

Myth: States have had rigorous assessments with high expectations for years.

Fact: Based on pre-Common Core tests in each state, only one state, Massachusetts, had a literacy test as rigorous as the eighth grade NAEP assessment, and no state had a fourth grade test that is equivalent to the NAEP assessment.

Myth: Common Core does not support the memorization of multiplication tables or key concepts in English/language arts.

Fact: Though there is less emphasis on memorization than there was in many previous state standards, Common Core standards do not do away with this skill. The Common Core standards still require important foundational information like multiplication tables and parts of speech to be memorized, but there is not as much attention given to memorizing bits of trivia. More time and emphasis is placed on things like critical thinking skills and problem solving.

Myth: The Common Core is an effort by big industries to produce graduates to work in production or manufacturing jobs.

Fact: The skills necessary to work in many of today's manufacturing jobs are similar to the skills needed to be successful in college, so Common Core does not limit students to certain careers after graduation. It actually gives students more options and opportunities when they graduate by supporting them in college and career readiness.

Myth: Common Core math standards focus more on students explaining their thinking than getting the right answer to a problem or question.

Fact: The right answer is still the right answer. Common Core standards do emphasize understanding a concept and being able to explain the process behind a concept, such as adding fractions, but in the end, students still have to get the right answer. This means that students are supported in learning not only the *what* when given a calculation problem but also the *why* and the *how*. This is a new and higher expectation for many students who have been learning under previous standards, but it is this move beyond filling in a blank on a math worksheet that helps students develop the critical thinking skills colleges and businesses are looking for.

Myth: No teachers were involved in developing the standards, so there is a gap between the standards and what educators in the classroom feel is important.

Fact: Classroom teachers were involved in the writing of the standards, as well as the feedback groups that analyzed the standards during multiple phases of development. Teachers from across the country were also encouraged to give feedback in an open survey at the draft release of the standards in early 2010 before the standards were finalized.

Myth: Common Core is supposed to prepare students for college, but that college is only a nonselective community college and not a four-year university with higher standards.

Fact: Common Core standards set high expectations and were influenced by the standards of some of the highest-performing countries in the world. They were also developed with the help of well-known professors from respected universities across the country who wanted to make sure students could enter a two- or four-year college prepared to begin credit-bearing work immediately.

 DID YOU KNOW?

Since the first international assessments were given comparing student achievement in K-12 education in multiple countries, the United States has never ranked first in any subject. The flipside of this is that our universities and colleges have ranked first in the world for many decades, and students from around the world are eager to attend them.

Myth: Common Core standards are not as good as those used by top-performing countries.

Fact: The developers of the Common Core standards analyzed the standards of top-performing countries and looked for similarities. The standards that were shared by several top-performing countries were used to help inform the creation of Common Core.

Myth: Common Core standards are not "field tested."

Fact: Standards are never field tested. What some people mistakenly associate with field testing of standards is actually the teaching methods that are used to teach standards or the curriculum that is used. Standards themselves are developed based on the skills and content knowledge that the writers feel are important for preparing students. The effectiveness of instructional methods and materials is what is typically examined.

Myth: Common Core math standards do not teach algebra concepts until high school.

Fact: The Common Core math standards introduce concepts necessary for algebra in grades K-7. Students have the skills and content knowledge needed to take Algebra I in eighth grade if districts or schools make that decision in their course sequencing.

Myth: Common Core focuses on teaching students skills instead of important content knowledge.

Fact: Common Core does teach students important skills such as critical thinking, problem solving, and expressing ideas, but there is still a great deal of emphasis placed on specific content knowledge at each grade level. There is less emphasis on small, trivia-type facts and more emphasis on foundational content. This content ranges from analyzing well-known fables in lower grades to historical documents like the Constitution of the United States in upper grades.

Myth: The Common Core standards are not research based; they are based on experimental ideas that have not been tested.

Fact: The developers of the Common Core were very intentional in modeling the standards after countries and states that had a history of high performance and achievement, as well as the informed opinion of experts from around the nation who had experience writing quality standards. None of the standards were pulled from thin air. They were created with a combination of guidance from people working in the field that studied the outcomes students needed for success after high school and modeling from countries that consistently outperformed the United States on national assessments.

Myth: Common Core standards cover too much material.

Fact: Under the Common Core, there are actually fewer standards at each grade level than there were under many state standards. This allows teachers to spend more time on each concept instead of trying to cram large amounts of information into students' heads and quickly move to another topic.

Myth: Common Core will force students to choose a career path as early as elementary or middle school.

Fact: There is no tracking in Common Core. In fact, when standards are learned well, students should graduate with multiple opportunities to pursue a college degree or enter a career field.

Will Transitioning to the Common Core Disrupt Schools?

Myth: Changing standards adds confusion in the schools and is a great burden on teachers and administrators.

Fact: Changing, adding to, or modifying standards has been a common practice in most states well before the introduction of the Common Core. It is not unusual for teachers and administrators to see several standards changes or modifications over the course of their career. While it can be initially disruptive, proper implementation can greatly mitigate the disturbance.

Myth: Common Core standards are forcing schools to spend a lot of extra money on computers and internet access so they can give new tests based on the Common Core.

Fact: There is some truth to this, since most Common Core assessments that are being created will be given online. However, the minimum technology requirements to give these tests are no more than what twenty-first century schools should have in place to support student learning. Upgrading technology is an expense that most schools will have to take on at some point, regardless of what standards are used.

 DID YOU KNOW?

A typical smartphone has more computing capability than the technology used by NASA to put a man on the moon. This means providing students access to technology and using it in meaningful ways is no longer a neat gimmick for schools, but a vital part of the curriculum.

Myth: The Common Core will decrease competition among textbook and instructional resource companies, and cause textbooks to become more expensive.

Fact: The Common Core actually helps to level the playing field among textbook companies and companies that develop educational resources. When all 50 states had different standards, only the largest companies could afford to create state-specific materials. By creating a common set of core standards that the majority of states have adopted, smaller companies can now enter the market with materials that are relevant in most states. This will encourage competition to produce the highest-quality resources.

Myth: There are Common Core standards for all subjects.

Fact: There are only Common Core standards for English/language arts and math. Some states have provided training for teachers in other subject areas like history, science, and technical classes to build connections between these courses and math and English/language arts. For example, there is a natural support structure in place for history and ELA when studying historical documents like the Gettysburg Address as Common Core suggests.

Myth: Common Core standards are a new idea that has recently hit the education scene.

Fact: The first serious discussions and planning around a state-led effort to create common standards took place in 2006 and resulted in the Common Core standards in early 2010.

 DID YOU KNOW?

NAEP (National Assessment of Educational Progress) is considered the nation's report card. It is administered every two years to a sampling of fourth and eighth graders from each state in core subject areas. It is the longest-running evaluation of student achievement in the United States. It has been administered for almost three decades.

Myth: Students will no longer be taught cursive because it is not in the Common Core standards.

Fact: Most states have never had a standard that specifically addresses cursive writing. However, almost all schools have taught cursive writing as a skill without the requirement of a standard, and they have the freedom to continue to do so.

Myth: Private schools, faith-based schools, charter schools, and home schools will have to adopt Common Core standards.

Fact: No state is required to adopt Common Core standards. If a state does adopt Common Core standards, no private school system within that state is required to adopt the standards. Private, faith-based, charter, and home schools still have complete autonomy and flexibility to adopt the standards they choose. The only exception might be the charter school guidelines in some states, but this is still a state decision.

Myth: Common Core standards are all students need to be college and career ready.

Fact: Having appropriate knowledge and skills in math and English/language arts is one of the most important factors of college and career success because these skills and knowledge are used in almost every other subject area in some way. However, a student still needs a well-rounded education that includes science, history, humanities, and technical classes, etc.

Myth: Implementing Common Core is costing states, districts, and schools a lot of extra money for training and new resources.

Fact: The initial implementation of Common Core might cost some states or districts additional funds, but this is not out of the ordinary when states make a standards or curriculum change, which happens quite often. However, in the long run, the cost of materials should actually go down since vendors are not having to create 50 different sets of materials that are specific to each state.

Also, teachers get new training every year, whether or not there is a standards change. As a matter of fact, most states require a minimum number of days that teachers must spend in professional development during the summer. One of the major positives of Common Core is that districts and states can work together on training and the creation or purchase of resources since they are teaching the same foundational skills. This will also save money in the long term.

Myth: Common Core tests will cost states much more than they are currently spending.

Fact: This actually depends on the state. The two test consortiums that are developing tests specifically for Common Core are Smarter Balance and PARCC. Smarter Balanced estimates their test will cost approximately $23 per student, and PARCC estimates their test will cost $29 per student. This is cheaper than about half the states in those consortia are paying right now.

Myth: There is no need to create new tests for Common Core. The ones states have now should be fine. It's the standards that matter.

Fact: It is critical that the tests that students take at the end of the year align with the skills, content, and critical thinking they are learning in class. Schools, districts, and states can't get an accurate picture of the effectiveness of their assessments if they are not aligned with what and how students are learning.

 KEYS TO THE CORE

If you are a parent and you have any questions about your district's approach to Common Core, the materials being used, or the work your child is bringing home, don't hesitate to contact the school to discuss your questions. This is the best way to fully address any questions or concerns you might have.

The Least You Need To Know

- There are many myths that accompany the development and implementation of Common Core, so be sure to do your research before believing everything you hear or read.

- The creation of the Common Core standards was a thoughtful process that was informed by expert opinion and analysis.

- It is important to always bring any myth back to the standards as a litmus test. If a myth doesn't involve student achievement or specifically the standards, it's probably political in nature.

- The best source to myth bust is with your child's teacher or principal. Go straight to the source of the instruction to help you calm any doubts you may have from negative things you read or hear.

What Makes the Common Core Standards Unique?

The history of what we know as education standards in the United States goes back only a little more than three decades. Before this reform gained widespread acceptance, standards were more or less defined by course offerings, not actual learning objectives within a course. For example, a state might mandate how many math, science, English, and history courses students must take in high school, but the specific learning outcomes were left to the school or teacher.

In the past half century, there have been movements for state standards and even attempts at national standards. Some of these efforts bore fruit at the state level, but national standards, or common standards that all states agreed on, never gained enough traction to get past moderate development. This chapter looks at these different movements to help get a better understanding of how Common Core came to be and why it is still a political hot potato for some groups.

In This Chapter

- The history of education standards in the United States

- How standards have changed over time and why

- How the Common Core brings consistency for some mobile students

- How the Common Core compares to standards in other countries

- The importance of college and career readiness

The History of State Standards

If you ask any educator who has had a History of Education course in college or was in school in 1958, they will probably point back to the Russian launch of Sputnik as a standards reform movement. In reality, nothing really changed with our standards at that time; there was just a renewed focus on math and science classes and additional funding given to public education. There were no academic benchmarks set. It was basically a patriotic reaction to Russia getting an object into space first. However, this moment in our educational history did set a precedent. It was the first nationwide reaction that focused on the quality of our education system.

Reactionary Changes in Standards

In 1983, the federal Department of Education released a report called *A Nation at Risk*. This report warned of a declining American education system. In response to this report, the Department of Education created five recommendations for fixing the problem. One of these recommendations was for states to adopt or create more rigorous standards that could be measured. This report did prompt reform in most states in the coming years to create new standards or at least revise their current standards. This report was also cited in years to come as a reflective look at where we were in 1983 and the progress or lack of progress that was made on a national scale. Every time our students scored poorly on international assessments or there was a negative achievement statistic that was brought to light, this report was mentioned, and a great deal of finger pointing took place.

The next reactionary movement in standards came in 1989 when President George H. Bush convened a meeting of all state governors for only the third time in U.S. history. The meeting was prompted by global economic competition, and the country's leaders wanted to assert some responsibility in supporting education, while also preserving local control. One of the recommendations that came from the meeting was support for standards and tests that measured them. The meeting received more attention than the recommendations that came from the meeting. There were no real action steps that were put into place, and the well-intentioned ideas never gained traction or much publicity. As with previous efforts at improved standards and common standards, the idea died on the vine before any real steps were taken toward development.

Proactive Changes in Standards

The next phase in the standards movement was all about being proactive and trying to impact education through reform. The first serious attempt at a national set of standards came in 1993 when Secretary of Education Lamar Alexander supported the creation of the National Council on Education Standards and Testing (NCEST). The council's purpose was to provide direction on a plan for the development of national standards and tests to assess them. The council did produce a report, but the whole undertaking died a martyr's death in the ever-growing standards movement.

Not to be deterred by others' previous failed attempts at impacting America's education system, in 1994 President Bill Clinton signed the Goals 2000: Educate America Act. This act created a council that was charged with certifying state and national standards. This council could not legally approve or reject standards, but they could give their blessing as to their quality. Once again, politics played a role in the process, and the provision to create the council was repealed. However, Goals 2000 did provide funding in the form of grants for states to create standards, and over 40 states received funding for this process.

The federal government wasn't done with standards, though. That same year Goals 2000 was enacted, the reauthorization of the Elementary and Secondary Education Act (ESEA) had a huge impact on the standards movement.

 DID YOU KNOW?

The Elementary and Secondary Education Act was originally passed by President Lyndon B. Johnson's administration. It is the most far-reaching federal involvement in public education. The act funds training for teachers and instructional materials in hopes of decreasing achievement gaps between students of poverty and their peers.

In order to receive federal funding for education within the reauthorization of this act, states had to meet certain requirements in developing standards and tests to assess them. This prompted the largest-scale standards revamping in our nation to date. Fifteen states had created new standards by 1996, and 49 states had created them by 2000. This was a huge leap for a nation that basically had no real emphasis on standards a decade before.

In 1996, an education summit was again convened with the nation's governors to discuss the need for raising academic standards state by state. The governors met again in 1999 with the same goal in mind; however, one of the most far-reaching federal efforts to impact standards and achievement was yet to come.

In 2001, the No Child Left Behind Act (NCLB) was passed by the George W. Bush administration. This legislation supported sweeping reforms in standards-based education and accountability tied to testing in third grade through eighth grade and once in high school. The resulting differences in state standards, assessments, and achievement on the assessments helped support the coming Common Core movement.

 DID YOU KNOW?

No Child Left Behind has had its share of detractors through the years. One positive aspect all educators and stakeholders can agree on is that it highlighted the achievement gaps between students who scored well on assessments and minority sub-groups that were consistently lagging behind.

"Fewer, Clearer, Higher"

In 2007, Jason Zimba and David Coleman (leaders of the math and ELA work teams, respectively) published a groundbreaking paper on the importance of quality standards titled "Math and Science Standards That Are Fewer, Clearer, Higher to Raise Achievement at All Levels." This paper was one of the pebbles that started the avalanche toward common standards, and the phrase from the title "fewer, clearer, higher" was a prominent theme throughout the discussions and development of the Common Core standards, which were completed in June of 2010.

Fewer Standards

At the time that the Common Core standards were being developed, most states had a large number of standards for multiple subjects, all of which were expected to be covered in a year. This often led to a disjointed curriculum and presented a great challenge for teachers. As accountability increased for teachers based on standardized test scores, the idea of using fewer standards began to gain popularity with mainstream educators. They liked the idea of being able to spend more time teaching key concepts. Most educators complained that their state standards were "a mile wide and an inch deep," or in other words, they only skimmed the surface of many topics without being able to go in depth with important content and skills.

A good analogy for this is to think about a person wanting to study the ocean floor. If they used a mask and snorkel, they could paddle for miles at the surface getting a broad view of the environment below. In contrast, a person in scuba gear might be limited in the distance they could travel, but he or she could go all the way to the bottom of the ocean floor and spend time studying the environment at a closer view to understand it better.

Believe it or not, the idea of fewer standards met with resistance from some education experts because they felt it was a dumbing down of the expectations if students were covering less material. The focus rested much more on the quantity of standards versus the quality of standards.

Clearer Standards

The idea of clear standards might seem like a no-brainer, but it hasn't always been the case for many states. For instance, states would use vague statements that could be left up to interpretation. States would also have standards that overlapped from grade level to grade level, or they might even skip a grade level and pop up again. In other cases, a standard might be a stand-alone concept or skill that did not relate to any of the other standards preceding it or following it.

Clearer standards, as promoted in Common Core, build on each other from grade level to grade level, so that the knowledge and skills a student learns in one grade prepare them for the next grade and so on. There is not a great deal of overlap, and each standard is in place for the specific purpose of preparing students for a future standard. This stairstep approach of clear, defined learning objectives that build on each other ultimately leads to a graduate that is ready for college or the work force.

Higher Standards

"Higher standards" is an easy sell from a public relations standpoint. Who wants to be against higher standards? As I have traveled my home state and across the country speaking about Common Core, I have heard this phrase many times: "Of course I'm for higher standards, but...." The explanations that usually follow have nothing to do with standards, but it shows that, usually, every stakeholder will vocally support higher standards. It's all the things that come with higher standards that cause people to take issue from a political, personal, or philosophical front.

So what does "higher" mean? Actually, it means several things. First, it means that more than just rote memorization will be expected. There is an emphasis on critical thinking and problem solving. It goes back to the earlier discussion on being able to do something with information beyond just answering the *what*. You also must be able to answer the *why* and *how*.

It also means that you don't just answer questions based on opinion or give subjective answers. Students are taught to support their answers with evidence from a text or by explaining their thinking. This support often comes in the form of more writing than has been emphasized in the past or by being able to give a visual representation in math.

KEYS TO THE CORE

Good questions are as important as answers in the Common Core. Challenging questions lead students into higher-order thinking and extend their learning.

The final piece to a higher standard's puzzle is college and career readiness. This is a deliberate focus on skills in K-12 that build on each other with the idea that when students graduate, they will be successful in entry-level college courses or an industrial training program. This means students can be trained for a job in an industry that is prosperous in order to make a livable wage, or that they do not have to take remedial courses that do not count for credit at a college or university.

In the end, it also means that a high school diploma has real value and enables students to have options when deciding what they want to do with their lives because of the knowledge and skill sets they possess. It also means that a diploma has the same value no matter from what state it is issued. This is an important factor as some graduates from states with better standards and educational systems held a decided advantage over states with less rigorous standards.

The Unifying Factor of Common Core

As a principal at both an elementary school and a high school in the corner of my state, I had the unique perspective of a border educator. My schools were within rock-throwing distance of two state lines, so we had a revolving door of students coming and going. The thing I noticed before the common standards issue ever made it into my circle was that depending on the grade level, time of year, and state from which they were coming, students might be ahead, behind, or not even in the same galaxy as the other students in their class.

I reasoned it couldn't be the quality of the school districts, because sometimes our students were ahead of transfer students and sometimes they were behind them. We had our share of students who also moved across "the line," and invariably I would run into them or their parents at the grocery store or at a ballgame, and they would tell me how much further ahead our school was or how far behind our school was. It was frustrating because there was no rhyme or reason to the differences.

Parents should have confidence that no matter where their child goes to school, they will be taught the same foundational skills and content at each grade level. The curriculums might look different, but the learning expectations should remain the same. Educators should also be able to share this same expectation. It shouldn't matter what time of year or from which state a student transfers into a teacher's class. The teacher should be able to teach with the confidence that the same grade level learning outcomes have been taught. There should not be time spent trying to catch a student up with the rest of the class, or a student shouldn't have to spend time twiddling their thumbs waiting on his or her new peers to catch up.

Transient Students

One of the positive factors of Common Core is the ability for parents to know that if they move their child from one state to another, they should be on pace wherever they enroll. This element of supporting transient students often does not get the attention it deserves, but it is an expectation that was not even considered before Common Core. In hindsight, the fact that students could not move from one state to another and expect to be at the same level as their peers in a new school should have set off alarm bells and helped instigate action long before now.

Military Families

One of the most mobile student groups are the children of military families. Most children of military families will change schools six to nine times before they graduate. I spoke with an officer this past year who said his family had moved ten times in his career so far, and each time they moved it was impossible to say whether his daughter would be ahead, behind, or on pace with the students in the school she transferred to.

Military families often don't have the option to move in the summer, so students can be transferred to a new school midyear or even at the end of a school year. You can imagine the value military families place on consistency, so Common Core gives these families hope that no matter where they might move or what time of year they move, their children will receive the same quality of education.

This consistency also applies when families are stationed overseas. The Department of Defense Education Activity (DoDEA) also adopted Common Core standards for all the schools in its system, so all schools run by the DoDEA in the United States and abroad are using Common Core standards.

DID YOU KNOW?

The U.S. military is a big supporter of Common Core for reasons of college and career readiness. It is estimated that 30 percent of high school graduates can't pass the entrance exam to join the armed forces. Besides supporting recruitment, the military also values the critical thinking and problem solving components of Common Core.

The Common Core and International Standards

A phrase that is often used in discussions about the development of Common Core is "internationally benchmarked." This phrase causes many people outside of education to scratch their heads because it sounds more like graffiti at a bus stop than a comparison of top-performing countries. Nonetheless, this phrase is used often to describe the effort that was made to make sure the Common Core standards are equal to those used by the countries that outperform U.S. students on international tests.

At the time Common Core was being developed, it was not hard to find countries that were beating the United States academically. On most international assessments given in the past decade, the United States has failed to make it into the top 20 of participating countries in math or science. However, countries like Finland, Singapore, Taiwan, South Korea, and Sweden were, and still are, consistently ranked at the top every year. One similarity of these high-performing countries? Common standards.

TAKE CARE

The United States' lagging performance on international assessments is not entirely due to lower standards. There are other factors that contribute, such as the noble effort to educate all students. And keep in mind that U.S. universities are still ranked the highest in the world and there is a long line of international students attempting to gain acceptance to them. However, the United States has a long way to go with the K-12 system.

Some people take exception when it is claimed Common Core was internationally benchmarked. Depending on your definition, it can mean doing an in-depth analysis of other countries' standards, or it can mean that other countries' standards were studied and used as guides to make sure Common Core would be of equal quality and expectation. Either way, the standards of the highest-performing countries in the world definitely informed the development of Common Core, even if the extent of this analysis of their standards is debated.

One of the pitfalls in this discussion is that state standards were such a mixed bag and already so low in many cases that Common Core looks head and shoulders above what states had previously. But Common Core in the best light is only as good as standards in some of the top-performing countries. For a country that likes to be number one in everything, the standards discussion will probably take another turn if American students become more globally competitive and the United States wants to outpace other countries.

Focusing on College and Career Readiness

It was only a generation ago that in many rural and urban areas a student who was willing to do manual labor in manufacturing, mining, construction, or a similar field could get a decent job right out of high school (or in some cases drop out of high school and begin working). Academic knowledge and skills were reserved for those who wanted a white-collar job. Students these days face a very different job market. The manual labor jobs of the past have rapidly been replaced by advances in technology, and the new jobs that pay a decent wage in industry increasingly require training before or on the job. As time goes on, the gap between knowledge and skills needed for college and those needed to go into a career field is narrowing at a rapid pace.

For instance, in the area of the state where I live, there is a large manufacturing plant. In order to enter the training and certification program that prepares workers for the jobs in this plant, applicants must have a minimum score of 19 on the ACT. This is the same score required to take credit-bearing courses in the state colleges with no required remedial courses. I remember a former high school student of mine who visited the plant on a field trip and returned a little flustered when he found out this minimum requirement. "I have to make a 19 to work on an assembly line?! I thought anybody could get those jobs." This is not an uncommon realization for students to have, nor is it limited to my little corner of the country. Increasingly, industries across the United States are requiring more from their workers.

The developers of Common Core understood this growing expectation for better-trained and skilled workers, and they also understood that increasingly students who did enter college were being forced to take remedial courses in math and English because their skill level was below the expectations to succeed on college-level work. That is why one of the first steps the developers took was to define what broader skills and knowledge students needed to be college- and career-ready when they graduated high school. These concepts were then supported by the individual standards at each grade level. Because these college- and career-ready standards were the end goal when students graduated and link individual standards together, they are called *anchor standards* in the English and Language Arts (ELA) portion of Common Core.

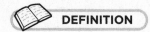

DEFINITION

> **Anchor standards** are the broader concepts in English/language arts that support college and career readiness when students graduate. The basic skills needed to master these concepts are introduced in kindergarten and build on each other each year until graduation.

The beauty of anchor standards is that there is always an end in mind with the skills taught at each grade level. In this case, the end is college and career readiness upon graduation. The anchor standards work in a progression like stairsteps from grade level to grade level. The ELA anchor standards are divided into the categories of Reading, Writing, Speaking and Listening, and Language. If you think of the skills in these areas as a stairstep in each grade level, then the individual standards are the handrail that helps you walk from step to step.

There are no anchor standards in the math portion of Common Core. Instead, the progression from skill to skill is specific enough in math that the college and career expectations are intertwined into the standards. I will discuss the concept of anchor standards in more detail when I talk about the standards themselves.

The Least You Need To Know

- The emphasis on learning standards at each grade level began in states in the early 1980s.

- There have been several movements to create new standards or improve standards based on reactions to events or research studies.

- There have also been movements to create new standards or improve standards based on proactive efforts at the federal and state level to unite for increased student achievement and to find common ground.

- The Common Core standards are fewer in number but higher in expectations for students than previous standards.

- Common Core standards are beneficial to families who move from state to state.

- At each grade level, Common Core contains anchor standards in ELA that prepare students one step at a time to be college- and career-ready when they graduate.

Implementation of the Common Core

The formal unveiling of Common Core standards took place in Suwanee, Georgia on June 2, 2010. It was no coincidence that the event took place far from the shadow of Washington, D.C. in the home state of Governor Sunny Purdue, one of the leaders in the common standards movement. There was a deliberate attempt to show both geographically and symbolically that this was a state-led effort. Although there is now heated political debate about the standards among some groups, there was actually little fanfare or national attention given at the time of the unveiling. The development of the standards was an open process, so there were no surprises.

Once the standards were developed and then adopted, states quietly went about the business of *implementation*. Most states did it in a gradual progression through the grade levels beginning with the elementary grades one year, the middle school grades the next year, and the high school grades the third year. This gradual implementation is a deviation from the way states typically transition to new standards, which is usually a wholesale change in all grades in one year.

In This Chapter

- The first adopters of the Common Core standards

- Why some states have chosen not to adopt the Common Core

- How states can "rebrand" the standards

- Training educators to use the standards in the classroom

In hindsight, some leaders have questioned if the gradual and deliberate implementation created a space for opposition to the standards. As one of my friends who helped oversee implementation for one state put it: "I'm now wondering if we should not have just taken the Band-Aid approach and ripped it off all at once. We tried to move so slowly and thoughtfully that we might have given too much room for the adjustment."

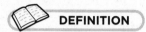 **DEFINITION**

Implementation is the term used to represent the plan for training educators on how to teach the standards, assess the standards, and provide materials to teach the standards.

As of the publication of this book, there are 43 states, 4 territories, the District of Columbia, and Department of Defense Education Activity who have fully adopted Common Core standards. Some states have partially adopted the standards, and other states have adopted the Common Core but then renamed the standards something specific to their state. In this chapter, we will take a look at who has and has not adopted and some of the reasons why.

The First Adopters

The first state to have the distinction of adopting the Common Core standards was Kentucky. In fact, Kentucky's state board of education voted unanimously to adopt the standards in February of 2010, which was four months before the final version of the standards was produced. Other states followed Kentucky's example, and by May of 2010, the states of West Virginia, Hawaii, and Maryland had adopted the standards.

By August 2, 2010, 31 states and the District of Columbia had adopted Common Core. By the end of December 2010, 10 more states adopted the standards. During 2011, five more states adopted, so by the end of 2011, 90 percent of the states in our country had adopted the standards. This was an overwhelming majority, and it was no small feat considering the challenges any attempt at creating a common set of standards for all states had met in the past. Again, there was little or no fanfare about this milestone in American education.

In education circles, there were plenty of discussions taking place about teacher training, resource development, and assessments created to align with the standards, but there was next to no discussion by political leaders or advocacy organizations about the standards. It is often asked why states didn't do a better job of messaging about the standards in the first year of adoption, and the answer is always "because Common Core standards made so much sense, we never imagined having to defend them right after we adopted or one day down the road."

DID YOU KNOW?

Most states undergo changes in standards every few years without much communication to the citizens. Because it is not an unusual occurrence, many people outside of education didn't even realize their state had adopted Common Core standards until it became a political topic two to three years after the fact.

Partial Adoption

The only state to partially adopt Common Core standards was Minnesota. State leaders believed that the current Minnesota math standards were superior to the Common Core math standards. Leaders did leave the door open, promising a more in-depth comparison of Minnesota's math standards and Common Core math standards, with the possibility of modifying the state's standards to align with Common Core. Minnesota did however adopt the ELA standards. They are the only state to date that has partially adopted the Common Core standards, and as of the publication of this book, Minnesota is still just using the ELA standards.

Though Minnesota's partial adoption doesn't win points for solidarity among states, it is a good example of how this is a state-led movement. States have the autonomy to partially adopt, fully adopt, or not adopt at all. States can also stop implementation of the standards if they choose, as we will discuss later. The point is that there is no federal mandate to adopt. It is a state-by-state decision.

DID YOU KNOW?

Each state has a different process for adopting standards, but usually the state board, the state legislators, the state department of education, and the governor's office all have a role in the adoption process at some point. A quick Google search can tell you the process your state undergoes to adopt new standards.

States That Have Not Adopted Common Core

Two states from the beginning have never shown interest in adopting Common Core standards: Texas and Alaska. Leaders in Texas made it clear that they felt it was an attempt at a federal "curriculum," even though it was a state-led standards movement. Another state that decided not to adopt was Virginia. Even though Virginia was one of the states to sign the memorandum of understanding, a newly-elected governor did not support the movement based on Virginia's work in creating their own state standards that state leaders felt were as good as or better than Common Core. Similar to Virginia, Nebraska signed the original memorandum of understanding to help develop the standards, but they never adopted them. It should also be noted that Puerto Rico originally signed on to adopt Common Core in 2010 but currently has not adopted the standards.

 TAKE CARE

Leaders in Texas declared they did not want a national "curriculum." However, it's important to keep in mind that standards and curriculum are not the same thing. Standards outline the expectations (what skills and knowledge students should have at each grade level), while curriculum refers to the actual instructional techniques and materials used to meet those expectations.

Withdrawing from Common Core

During 2013 and 2014, some states saw Common Core become a political football for both sides of the aisle for different reasons. The resulting fallout was one state, Indiana, halting implementation of the standards in early 2014 and several more states withdrawing from the new assessment consortiums created to design tests that would be aligned to Common Core standards. Oklahoma followed Indiana's lead, and in June of 2014, it repealed the Common Core standards and reverted back to the previous standards taught in the state before Common Core was implemented.

The ironic thing about the debates states are having is that there is little or no talk about the standards themselves. The discussion, for the most part, is about the fear of federal control by some conservative organizations in opposition to the standards. This was the worst nightmare come true for the leaders of the movement who took great pains to make it a state-led effort. However, no real argument has been made by these groups against the standards themselves. Their issue is the perception that states are losing their autonomy.

On the left side of the aisle, the issue of teacher accountability associated with new Common Core assessments has raised the hackles of teacher unions and their political advocates. Again, for the most part, the argument against implementation of the standards isn't about the standards themselves but about the associated assessments and accountability tied to those assessments.

The debate surrounding the standards still continues, with supporters on both sides digging in their heels. Several states have held legislative hearings to discuss the standards and give individuals and organizations an opportunity to voice their concern. Many educators balk at the idea of dropping Common Core after investing so much time and resources into implementing the standards, but at the publication of this book, legislation continues to be proposed to pause or repeal implementation of the standards in some states.

 DID YOU KNOW?

> Many states have implemented teacher evaluation models that base part of the teacher's overall evaluation score on the test results of his or her students. This has created some lukewarm support for Common Core among some teachers that worry more challenging standards and challenging assessments that come with them will reflect poorly on teachers during the first years of implementation.

Rebranding the Standards

Some states have renamed and rebranded the standards to give them the feeling of being more state specific. This is perfectly acceptable within the vision and intent of the standards. As William Shakespeare said, "A rose by any other name would smell as sweet." This goes for renaming college- and career-ready standards as well. As long as the standards are not altered or reduced, they can be called just about anything and still get the desired results. For instance, Florida calls the standards the "Next Generation Sunshine State Standards." Iowa calls them the "Iowa Core." Arizona and Alabama cut to the chase and call them "Arizona's College- and Career-Ready Standards" and "Alabama's College- and Career-Ready Standards," and Tennessee simply calls them "Tennessee's State Standards."

Rebranding has been successful on some fronts and less successful on others. Changing the name to something that identifies it with a particular state does create a sense of ownership among educators and other stakeholders. However, on some of the political fronts, this move has only caused more resentment with opposition groups who feel it is just an attempt to pretend the standards are something they are not.

> **KEYS TO THE CORE**
>
> If a state chooses to adopt the Common Core standards and maintain the vision and intent of the standards to prepare students to be college- and career-ready, they cannot alter or remove any of the standards. However, there is a 15 percent rule that allows states to add up to 15 percent of additional standards to the states total number of standards and still maintain the integrity of the Common Core.

Training Educators

Many states that adopted Common Core standards chose to provide training for their teachers as part of the implementation process. Although teachers are used to changing standards, this has not been a typical standards shift for many educators. There is much more emphasis on teaching students skills and application of knowledge rather than just memorizing facts. With this in mind, it's easy to see how implementing these standards not only nudges students out of their comfort zones by challenging them more, but it also requires teachers to facilitate student interactions in critical thinking and problem solving. This is a big leap in some classrooms where memorizing information for multiple-choice tests was the norm and not the exception.

Programs for Teachers

In order to prepare educators for these new expectations, states have spent an unprecedented amount of on teacher training and resources. Some states have allocated hundreds of millions of dollars on the training of teachers, and California alone allocated a little over a billion dollars in funds for the 2014-2015 school year for training teachers and purchasing resources at the district level for the implementation of Common Core.

Tennessee is an example of states taking steps like never before to support the implementation of new standards. Tennessee's Department of Education instituted the largest educator training program in the history of the state. Over 700 practicing classroom teachers were hired and given special training to "coach" other teachers across the state in instructional practices that supported the standards. Over a three-year period, approximately 70,000 teachers were trained across grade levels and subject areas.

Delaware also took meaningful steps to help train teachers and sustain implementation. The state developed an 18-month program that created a network of support among schools to help teachers and administrators make the shift to the standards. States like New York have also created extensive online resources for educators to support the implementation of the standards at www.engageny.com. This site contains an abundance of information on the standards themselves and support resources for teaching the standards.

Programs for Administrators

It's not just teachers who receive training on Common Core standards. Administrators at every level, including superintendents of schools, are participating in trainings and seminars that focus on Common Core. Learning the basics of the standards and the different teaching methodologies and resources that can support the implementation of the standards is especially important for principals.

 DID YOU KNOW?

Higher education is also joining the Common Core training movement. Most teacher preparation programs in states that have adopted Common Core have modified their program to train future teachers how to teach the standards.

The role of the principal has evolved over the past few years from that of primarily a building manager to that of an instructional leader. There is a greater burden on principals to create professional development opportunities for the faculty and to get heavily involved in teacher observations. Where principals used to evaluate teachers an average of one to three times per year, and sometimes less for tenured teachers, many states have adopted evaluation models that require five to ten observations a year. More weight has been given to teacher evaluation, and some states have salary plans, tenure status, and licensure that figure principal evaluations into the equation. Therefore, it is important for principals to be knowledgeable about the standards and the instructional practices that support them.

It is also important for principals, supervisors, and superintendents to understand the standards in order to make informed decisions when purchasing resources and instructional material for schools. As stated earlier, just because something has a "Common Core" sticker on it doesn't mean it necessarily supports instruction of the standards. Without a working knowledge of Common Core, administrators could inadvertently spend money on materials that are not aligned with the standards. The professional development plan to continue to train teachers in Common Core at the district and school level also depends on a working knowledge of the standards by the administration. In the first year of implementation, I saw some schools and districts fail to succeed with Common Core because they treated it like any other standards shift in the past and administrators did not learn about the standards.

Ability to Share Resources

The value in states across the country creating resources and developing training programs for educators is that for the first time these can be shared with alignment to learning expectations in multiple states. In the past, a teacher or administrator might attend a national conference and pick up some good resources or ideas to take back to their school, but these ideas would always have to be tweaked or modified to the standards being taught in their home state. Now educators can share ideas, resources, and best practices across state borders and be on the same page as to what learning expectations are in place for students at each grade level. This aspect of Common Core alone is invaluable to schools across the country that actively seek ways to improve through the sharing of ideas and creating a professional network of support.

 DID YOU KNOW?

Teacher training at the state, district, and school level is nothing new. The idea that teachers get summers off is an outdated myth. Most teachers are required by their districts to attend 3 to 10 days of training during the summer, as well as to participate in grade level or subject area meetings to develop resources for the coming year. The Common Core did not bring professional development and training to the education world, it simply changed the focus.

The Question of Cost

Not everyone is happy with the extensive training teachers are undergoing across the country. There are some who are in opposition to the Common Core that point to the need and cost of training teachers as one of the negatives of transitioning to the standards. They also condemn the money being spent on new instructional materials. However, supporters of the standards applaud the necessity to train teachers and create new resources. They embrace it as a sign that schools are genuinely changing the type of learning that is taking place in classrooms and raising expectations for students and instruction.

Key Dates in Implementation

June 1, 2009	Forty-eight states sign a memorandum of understanding agreeing to help develop common standards.
September 2009	The first draft of the standards is released for review.
March 2010	The second draft of the standards is released for review.
June 2, 2010	The final version of the standards is unveiled at Peachtree Ridge High School in Suwanee, Georgia.
December 31, 2010	Over three-fourths of the states across the country have adopted Common Core standards.
2011	Forty-five states have fully adopted Common Core standards. Implementation begins in earnest in most states.
2013–2014	States that adopted will be fully implemented K-12.
2014–2015	New assessments that are aligned to Common Core standards will be given by most states.

KEYS TO THE CORE

If you have children in school, don't be afraid to visit your child's school and ask about the implementation timeline for the district. It's good to get the big picture on how the standards were implemented and what the plan is for supporting implementation in the future.

The Least You Need To Know

- By the end of 2011, 45 states and the District of Columbia had adopted the Common Core.
- Politics have played a big role in both the success and setbacks of the Common Core.
- Some states have rebranded the standards with names that make them more specific to the state.
- A great deal of time and effort has been invested in training educators on how to implement the standards and in the development of resources.
- By 2014, 43 states were still fully implementing the Common Core.

What Will Be Different About My Child's Work?

It's 6:30 P.M., and you've just gotten ready to help your child with his math homework. You're feeling pretty confident because math was your favorite subject in school, and you still remember many of the shortcuts you memorized for solving fraction problems and long division. You expect your son to pull out a worksheet with a bunch of short equations on it, but instead he pulls out a paper with only two problems. These aren't simple equations; the problems are asking for written explanations, diagrams, and there is even a word problem to solve using the answer from the initial equation. With a sigh, you realize that there might be more than arithmetic shortcuts needed at the kitchen table tonight.

Common Core standards aren't just about giving students a set of new facts and figures to learn. One of the most noticeable differences between the Common Core and previous state standards is the how students are asked to apply information. The role of the teacher has changed from the all-knowing "sage on the stage" to the guide or facilitator of learning. Students' roles have changed, too, from those who just store information to those who are also able to apply it.

In This Chapter

- New approaches to teaching and learning

- Why it's important to understand the process of finding the answer

- The difference between using information and memorizing information

- Understanding text complexity and how it affects your child's reading assignments

- The role of writing and why it's emphasized in the Common Core

A New Approach

If you are like me, you attended a school where the classes at each grade level operated in pretty much the same way. The teacher gave you information through lecture or had you read out of the textbook by yourself or as a class. The class might take notes based on the lecture or information the teacher put on the board, or maybe copy definitions from the textbook.

After the information was covered, you would probably answer questions found in the textbook or on worksheets provided by the teacher. Usually, at the end of the week or end of the chapter, you would have a test on the material. This meant memorizing some facts, formulas, charts, timelines, or definitions—depending on the subject—then spitting back this information on multiple-choice, true/false, or fill-in-the-blank tests. On really crazy days, you might be given short answer questions or an essay to write, where you would again regurgitate information you had been given by the teacher or read in a textbook.

Under this method of education, the student is treated like a vessel of some kind, such as a pitcher. The teacher fills this vessel with enough water (knowledge) over the course of the week to make it full. At test time, the student pours it back out to see how much was retained. If 70 percent or more is retained and poured back, then *presto*, a passing grade is issued.

For a long time, this was a pretty standard process in many schools across the country. There was very little student-created work. It was a repetitive cycle that involved the teacher imparting knowledge, the students attempting to retain the knowledge, and then the students demonstrating how much they learned by completing assessments that relied a great deal on memorization. This process was not only a little boring, it also favored students who were good at memorizing information. And as far as future retention is concerned, how many of you can still give the book definition of a *Gaussian integer*?

Common-Core–based classrooms still incorporate acquiring information; however, there is less information covered throughout the year so that learning can become more in-depth. The teacher has more time to show students how to actually do something with the information rather than just presenting as much information as possible.

Focusing on the *Why* and *How*

Traditionally, our learning has focused on the *what*; however, the Common Core standards also ask students to focus on the *why* and the *how*. This helps the content become more engaging for students. For example, students might have previously been asked, "What was the author's purpose for writing a text?" The answer would be something straightforward like "to entertain." With Common Core standards, students are now being asked, "How can you use the elements of plot to create a story that is meant to entertain? Create your own text."

I like to call the new standards a "thinking" set of standards because they show that it's just as important to acquire skills to understand *how* to use information as it is to retain the information itself. This means there is a great deal of emphasis on the process of learning as well as the application of knowledge.

Real learning has occurred when a student can not only get a correct answer in math but also explain how he or she arrived at that answer. In English class, a student has learned when he can cite evidence from a text that supports an answer or opinion, rather than just recalling facts.

 DID YOU KNOW?

Educators rank levels of learning based on Bloom's Taxonomy, a system developed in the 1950s to classify learning objectives. The lowest level is *Knowledge* and increases to *Evaluation*. The standards previously used by many states were based largely on the *Knowledge* level, whereas Common Core standards lend themselves to the upper levels of thinking and learning.

Knowledge: recall of information

Comprehension: understanding and summarizing information

Application: using and applying knowledge

Analysis: identifying patterns and trends and making predictions

Synthesis: using old concepts to create new ideas

Evaluation: comparing two ideas and making judgments

Using knowledge in a meaningful way is a key skill found in Common Core. You will notice that your children's schoolwork may ask them to justify their answer, not just give an answer. For example, you may see many more questions that require students to write explanations (*why?*) or even draw diagrams (*how?*) to further support the answer they gave. This is where students are being given the opportunity to develop those important critical thinking and problem solving skills.

With this type of learning, you can expect to see much more writing as students learn to produce a product or analyze information. In many cases, the information they use comes from research they have done themselves. This is in stark contrast to the style of learning in which students are given information to memorize and then simply fill in the blanks on a worksheet or write short essays paraphrasing notes from the teacher.

Speaking of worksheets, you will notice a dramatic decline in the use of premade resources like worksheets. As learning becomes more about using information or answers in a meaningful way, the materials students use rely more on teacher-created items, or at the very least worksheets that require more than simple fill-in-the-blank or multiple-choice options. In math, for instance, there might sometimes be additional room for students to draw diagrams and give written explanations about a problem they have solved.

Those who loved the old-fashioned "skill and drill" component of learning should note that memorization is not a bad word or neglected skill. Within the Common Core standards, students are still required to memorize foundational information as we have for decades, such as multiplication facts, definitions of key vocabulary, or the list of common prepositions. The difference in Common Core is that each grade level focuses less on memorizing a wide range of information and spends more time practicing in-depth with the key skills that are foundational to preparing students for the next grade level.

Providing Evidence of Learning

There is a cartoon video on Youtube.com that made the rounds for a while in education circles. It showed a girl interviewing for a job, and the guy interviewing her asks her some basic questions, to which she answers "I choose C" to most of them. Though this was a pretty humorous attempt to highlight how we have created a school culture that does not emphasize critical thinking, it is also unnervingly close to the mark of what our expectations for students have been for many years.

 **TAKE CARE**

If a student is completing a great deal of multiple-choice or fill-in-the-blank questions, then they are probably not deeply engaged in Common Core work.

In the past, students were rarely asked to justify their answers or cite specific evidence to support their answers. The Common Core changes that. In the anchor standards of Common Core for college and career readiness, it is emphasized in several places that students need to be able to give a response or answer and cite evidence that supports their answer. In fact, students aren't just taught to give evidence to support their answers or opinions, they are also taught to evaluate evidence given by other students or found in the material they are studying. This is such an important part of the critical thinking process that it is actually the first anchor standard listed in reading and writing.

Beginning in kindergarten, students learn how to answer key questions about a text they read or that is read to them, but more importantly, they are also taught how to ask key questions themselves. This supports the skill of critical thinking by teaching students how to analyze a text. This skill is continually sharpened as students move from grade level to grade level. By fifth grade, students are taught how to quote from a text to support their answers and use that information to form an opinion. By the time students graduate, they should be able to look at the evidence presented in a text and explain what is left uncertain.

In writing, students in primary grades are taught how to write an argument for or against something by giving specific evidence that supports their opinion. This is a skill that was not typically introduced until middle or high school under previous state standards. By graduation, a student is expected to be able to give both sides of an argument with supporting evidence. In order to do this, research skills must be taught. This is an important component to being able to produce a good argument based on sound information the student gathers.

Even in the anchor standards of speaking and listening, students are expected to be able to listen to information and draw conclusions by middle grades. By graduation, students should be able to give a presentation with evidence that supports their topic. As you can see, all aspects of ELA have a component of using evidence as a very concrete way of making an argument or expressing ideas. This takes students from giving opinions to informed opinions.

What Happened to Worksheets?

Worksheets have been a part of most school curriculums since the days of the old purple ink ditto machines. They have been a staple for many classrooms because the old standards that promoted memorizing facts, figures, and other information lent itself to this type of resource. However, don't be surprised if you see fewer worksheets coming home with Common Core. There is still some room and application for worksheets, but the fact is that the types of questions usually found on worksheets don't push students into those critical thinking zones that are maximized with student-created work.

Because the Common Core standards emphasize writing and evidence-based responses, the products students create don't fit as well into worksheet templates. Even in math, students are exchanging two dozen problems of the same type for five or fewer that ask for the application of the answer, a written explanation, or a diagram. I tell teachers that a good way to gauge their success in implementing the Common Core standards is by comparing the amount of materials they give to the students versus how much the students create and give to them. Classrooms in which teachers rely on worksheets are classrooms where the Common Core standards have not been well implemented.

Are There Common Core Textbooks?

People often incorrectly assume that the Common Core is some sort of organization that produces materials and textbooks for the standards. This is an easy mistake to make since education resource companies put "Common Core" stickers on anything they can. The reality is that there is no Common Core company out there producing materials for sale.

The closest thing to a Common Core organization is the website the developers created that lists the standards and give an explanation of the development process. This can be found at corestandards.org. If you see materials, textbooks, or other resources with a "Common Core" title or theme, it means it is an education resource company that has created materials based on the standards.

 TAKE CARE

> There are many books and software resources that say they are "Common Core aligned" or support the teaching of the standards, but that is not always accurate. If you want to obtain support materials for your child, it's always a good idea to get the opinion of your child's teacher first.

Many publishing companies tried to get ahead of the movement and produced textbooks they claimed were Common Core aligned. I remember my children bringing home a primary grade literature book that had a big, yellow "Common Core" sticker on the front. It only took a few minutes of flipping through to see it was basically the same book I had seen in their school before, but with the addition of the sticker and some tips on Common Core standards scattered throughout the book. In most cases, these early math and literature programs were retrofitted to the standards rather than developed for the Common Core. It is only in the past couple of years that textbooks fully aligned to Common Core have been created.

I offer this information on textbooks in a cautionary way to make you aware that just because something says "Common Core" doesn't mean it is was written completely aligned to the rigor of the standards. In the past few years, more than one negative opinion has been formed about Common Core because a person has reviewed material that claimed to be Common Core compliant but really wasn't. In the spirit of local control, the leaders of the movement and developers of the standards deliberately left the decision on what materials to use to teach the standards up to states, districts, schools, and teachers. It is more important than ever that schools and school districts carefully select the materials they use for their curriculum because the standards are only as effective as the instruction and resources used to teach them.

Diagramming and Modeling

Another change you might see in your child's work is an increase in the number of diagrams, graphs, and models your child will create to accompany the equations they solve. In the past, a student's experience with one of these items was usually only to study one and answer questions about it. With Common Core standards, a student is sometimes asked to create their own visual expression of the calculation they are working.

This moves the student beyond just solving an equation to also being able to analyze the result of the answer or take their answer and apply it in a meaningful way. For example, instead of just solving 9×3, a student might be asked to also explain with a diagram why the answer they provided is correct. In this way, the student goes beyond just memorizing their multiplication facts to also understanding the concept behind multiplication, which is a great way to support critical thinking.

Reading Complex Texts

One of the key components of the ELA standards is the *text complexity* of the materials that students read. Though the standards do not give a required reading list for grade levels, they are clear about the level of difficulty students should be able to read at by the end of the school year to prepare them for the work at the next grade level.

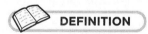 **DEFINITION**

Text complexity is the measure of how challenging reading materials are. There are three aspects teachers consider when determining text complexity:

1. What background knowledge is needed to understand the context of what is being read?

2. How long or complex are the words and sentences? There are software programs that can quickly measure this for teachers.

3. How motivated is the student and what is their interest in the reading material?

Since the mid-1970s, there has been a steady decline in the complexity of texts used in elementary and high school classrooms. However, text complexity at the college level has stayed the same or increased. In the world of industry, text complexity and the need to read more complex texts has increased dramatically in the past decade. Common Core standards attempt to correct the downward course our schools have been on and refocus on the skills needed to not just read complex texts but also comprehend information from those texts.

Rigor Is Key

One of the cornerstones of the Common Core standards in both math and ELA is *rigor*. This idea was at the forefront of the early discussion during development. Put simply, most state standards did not have a high expectation for students. It was clear after studying learning standards from other countries that there were vast differences in the expectations U.S. students compared to students from countries that outperformed the United States on international assessments. By decreasing the number of standards at each grade level and focusing on those that are foundational, teachers are able to improve the rigor of education by covering more complex and challenging concepts.

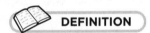 **DEFINITION**

Rigor is a term that typically describes a level of instruction or instructional materials that challenges students to the fullest extent of their learning abilities rather than a middle of the road approach.

Under most previous state standards, teachers were expected to cover a great deal informational type standards throughout the year. This left little time to spend time with individual standards or go in-depth with concepts that are more challenging. Teachers were forced to skim the surface of concepts and move on to the next standard. This type of teaching resulted in middle-of-the-road instruction where it wasn't outpacing lower-level learners and not challenging higher-level learners. When this is combined with standards that didn't have high expectations to begin with, it was a perfect storm of instruction that did not push students to their fullest potential. By increasing the time that can be spent on each standard and the learning expectation, students of all levels of ability are supported in achieving to their fullest potential.

Writing Every Day

Repetition in education is often a great learning tool, especially when it is a skill that can be practiced in multiple subjects like writing. This became even more apparent to me through an accidental find in a closet.

When I was a principal, I found a box of old yearbooks from the 1940s in a closet. I was thumbing through one of them when I came to a section where seniors had submitted short narratives about their time at the high school. The quality and complexity of the writing caught my attention right away. The next thing that caught my attention were the names of the people who wrote them. I knew many of them, but most weren't doctors, lawyers, or in any other white-collar profession. They were miners, railroad workers, builders, stay-at-home moms, and other professions that I knew did not require them to be what I judged as excellent writers.

About a month later, I was at a dinner party with a guy whose narrative in the yearbook I had read. I told him, with more than a little surprise in my voice, about the yearbook and how impressed I was. I then asked him his opinion on what made their writing so good. He never hesitated with his reply: "We were always writing! In our teachers' eyes we never could write too much or too often." This philosophy is supported in Common Core. Writing is a key part to not only ELA but also in math.

Why Written Expression Is Important

Writing is not just a skill that is important for students going to college. It is becoming a more important skill in industry as well. Being able to express oneself in an informative way and explain concepts clearly has become a lost art. We have overemphasized persuasive writing, like essays on why students should be allowed to have cell phones in school, and personal opinion writing. Common Core takes personal opinion to the next level and teaches students how to support their opinions with well-thought-out arguments and supporting facts. Writing of this kind is more in line with real-life situations.

There is also a greater emphasis on informative writing. This not only relates to college level work but also technical jobs and industry jobs. I have a friend who is an auto-mechanics teacher. He teaches his students how to write detailed analyses of problems, solutions, and calculated costs for fixing an automobile. This information is typed into a software program for "customer" review. This is the type of application of writing as a skill that students will be able to use in the changing industry demands.

Writing in Math

I've heard more than a few parents comment on the writing they have seen in their child's math homework. The expectation of going beyond solving the equation is often met by providing a written explanation. These explanations vary from explaining how a student arrived at an answer to explaining what is represented in a diagram or chart. This supports students in making connections and understanding a theory behind a mathematical principle.

I have also heard parents ask the question: "Why do they need to know how an equation works? The answer is the answer, and isn't getting that what's important?" My response is always "yes" because getting the right answer is very important. Being able to explain the theory behind the calculation or explaining the steps to arriving at an answer isn't the goal. The goal is creating and strengthening critical thinking skills by helping students think through processes.

There is still plenty of repetitive problem solving to go around. However, the Common Core standards supplement that with the additional inclusion of explaining a process or visual representation multiple times during the course of study for each grade level.

Targeting Informational Texts

Historically, education in the United States has focused on fiction texts for students to read and study. The problem with this is that colleges give much more attention to nonfiction *informational texts*, and the reading required for a career in industry is entirely informational texts. To address this difference in what students are learning and what the demands of the real world are, the writers of the Common Core standards gave equal attention to fiction texts and informational texts, and more attention to informational texts as students progress into higher grade levels. The skill of being able to read for understanding to learn something new or research a topic to support an argument is critical for career and college readiness.

 **DEFINITION**

An **informational text** is a nonfiction work that is used to inform the reader about a certain topic, process, or idea.

No More Shakespeare?

Some people have taken exception to the decreased focus on fiction literature. People often ask, "What about Shakespeare and Hemingway? What about the classics?" In reality, there is deliberate attention given to fiction literature in the Common Core. For example, there are specific ELA standards that require students to analyze works of Shakespeare. Also, as students get into middle and high school grades, the emphasis on informational texts is shared by other subject areas like history and science. This allows for even more focus on fiction literature in the ELA classes.

Real-World Application of Skills and Information

I remember learning about Stoics in a philosophy of education class I had in college. They were ancient Greek philosophers who were some of the first paid teachers. Part of their role as teachers was to instruct wealthy citizens on how to make logical arguments to avoid potential taxes that might be imposed in their area by the state. Their education was truly one that could be applied in a meaningful way in their life.

One of the benefits of the Common Core standards is that they are also preparing students to apply what they learn in meaningful ways. This is exemplified in critical thinking skills, problem solving, and the ability to process evidence to make an informed argument. From the math standards to the ELA standards, students are supported in the ability to problem solve.

You may wonder why your child needs to know how a math problem works. After all, when we use math in everyday situations, no one is concerned with how we reached the answer. It's important to remember that when students learn to explain processes, it's not just about how a math problem is worked or what connections can be made in reading. It's about training your mind to be able to do that kind of thinking that's necessary when everyday challenges in our lives, academic careers, or jobs confront us.

Sometimes things don't go smoothly and people have to figure out how to fix, build, or make something themselves. Building an educational foundation that has students thinking about the pieces of a problem and how they fit together will better prepare them for these challenges than rote memorization.

 DID YOU KNOW?

Critical thinking and problem solving are two life skills, not just academic skills, which are important for students to learn and continually strengthen throughout their education.

Speaking, Listening, and Using Digital Media

Another key concept found in Common Core is the emphasis on speaking and listening. This might seem like a pretty basic skill, but there is a difference in speaking conversationally with friends and speaking on a topic to give information or to present counterarguments. This is true for listening as well. There is a difference between hearing someone talk and listening carefully to someone as they present information. With the Common Core standards, students are expected to participate in a variety of speaking formats, such as conversation with a partner, a small group, or with the class. Students also learn to present information to a group. Throughout these discussions, the keys to active listening are taught, as well as the ability to listen to information and use it in a meaningful way.

To complement the speaking and listening skills, the Common Core standards integrate the use of technology, such as using digital media used to give a presentation and improve the explanation of information. The Common Core standards also encourage the use of integrated audio and video for learning and for students to present information. I was at a conference recently where a high school ELA teacher presented a music video her students made around one of the themes they were studying. This is just one example of the innovative ways students are encouraged through the standards to utilize technology in presenting information.

The Least You Need To Know

- The Common Core standards support students in going beyond the *what* of a concept and into the *why* and *how* to develop critical thinking skills.

- Students will create more products from their learning and rely less on worksheets and fill-in-the-blank templates.

- Parents and educators must be careful when selecting resources to support students. Just because it has a Common Core label doesn't mean it's completely aligned to the standards.

- The texts that students will learn to read and discuss will be more challenging than in the past.

- Having high expectations for all students to perform at their fullest potential is a cornerstone of Common Core.

- Writing is an important skill that is emphasized repeatedly throughout the standards.

- There is a good balance between fiction and nonfiction in the Common Core ELA standards that prepares students for college-level work and useful industry skills.

The Literacy Standards

This section takes a grade-by-grade look at the English language arts standards. The ELA standards for each grade level are broken down into manageable parts that explain separately the skills taught in reading, writing, and communication and how parents can support the learning of those skills at home. This part also includes an overview of the literacy standards for history, social studies, science, and technical subjects.

The ELA Standards for Grades K-2

The English/language arts standards are crucial to a student's overall academic success because so many other subjects and skills are dependent upon reading, writing, and speaking. The standards for kindergarten through grade 2 are particularly important because they lay the foundation for the subsequent skills that follow in each grade level. It cannot be emphasized enough that one of the main components of Common Core is that skills build on each other from grade level to grade level. That makes it vitally important for students to grasp these foundational concepts in kindergarten, grade 1, and grade 2 in order to find success in middle grades, where the content and skills become increasingly complex.

In This Chapter

- A summary of the Common Core standards for reading literature and informational texts in grades K-2

- The foundational skills for reading in grades K-2

- The Common Core standards for writing in grades K-2

- The communication skills that are important in grades K-2

- How you can support your child in learning the standards

Reading

Reading is a foundational skill for all other subject areas. The Common Core standards take a very deliberate approach in the early grade levels to make sure students can not only perform the skill of reading, but can also comprehend and apply what they read. The type of texts students read are put into two categories: literature (stories, poems, fables, folktales, etc.) and informational texts (reference books, cause-and-effect narratives, speeches, etc.) In the lower grades, the proportion of literature to informational texts is about half and half.

Literature

Kindergartners are expected to master many of their standards with the support from their teacher. If you read the standards, you will see that many of them are similar to the ones found in grade 1, except six of the ten kindergarten standards for literature include the phrase: "with prompting and support" in many places. For example, kindergartners are expected to be able to answer questions about important details from a text with help from the teacher, and they are expected to be able to ask questions themselves about important details. This is also done with the support of the teacher. With prompting from the teacher, students should be able to retell stories that are familiar to them and give important details from the story. There is also the expectation that with prompting students can identify the major characters, events, and settings in a story.

The ability to be able to answer and ask questions about words that are unfamiliar to students is also a key skill. There is also the expectation that students can recognize different types of texts such as poems or storybooks. With support from the teacher, the student should also be able to name who the author and illustrator of a story are and explain how each contributes to the telling of the story.

With support from the teacher, students will also be expected to look at illustrations in a text and be able to explain the relationship between the illustration and what is taking place in the story. There is also an expectation that students will be able to compare and contrast the experiences of characters in stories that are familiar to them with support from the teacher. Being able to participate in group reading activities is also an important skill that will be developed.

COLLEGE AND CAREER READINESS

Students must read texts closely to clearly understand the message and draw conclusions. These conclusions should be supported in writing or speaking through specific examples cited from the text.

Grade 1 students are expected to be able to answer questions about important details from a story with no prompting. First graders should also be able to retell stories with key information and show they understand the main idea, lesson, or message. They should be able to describe the major characters, events, and settings in a story with key information for each.

First graders will be asked to identify words or phrases in stories or poems that describe feelings or the use of the senses. Students are also expected to identify the major differences between texts that tell stories and ones that give information. For example, your child might read or be read a story about characters who visit a dairy farm and an informational text about how a dairy farm is operated. She should be able to distinguish the difference between the two. This is done among a wide range of text types. Students should also be able to identify who is telling the story at different points of the text if there is more than one point of view.

Students will learn how to use illustrations and key details in a story to describe events, settings, and characters. There is also an expectation that students will be able to compare and contrast the experiences of characters in a story. For example, your child might be asked to explain how a player on a winning sports team might feel and react in contrast to the feelings and reaction of a player on the losing team. With support from the teacher, students will also move to reading poetry and prose that is at the appropriate text complexity for this grade level.

Grade 2 students start moving into areas of critical thinking beyond the previous two grade levels. Students will be expected to answer and also ask *who, what, when, why, where,* and *how* questions to show their understanding of important details from a text. Students will also engage in reading fables and folktales from a variety of cultures, and they will be taught how to determine the lesson or moral that is being conveyed. They will also be expected to be able to describe how characters respond to challenges or other events in a story.

KEYS TO THE CORE

There is not a specific reading list of fables or folktales. The teacher has the freedom to choose texts that he or she deems appropriate for the class.

Second graders will be expected to describe words or phrases that supply rhythm and meaning to a song, poem, or story. This is taught through alliteration, rhymes, and repeated lines. Students also learn to explain the structure of a story, such as how the beginning introduces the story and the action that concludes it. Different points of view are also studied, and students are expected to identify different points of view for characters in a story, including using different voices for characters when reading out loud.

Second graders also extend their thinking by using illustrations and words in a print or digital text to not only describe the characters and setting but the plot of the story as well. Students will learn how to compare versions of the same story written by different authors or from the perspective of a different culture. Students might read a version of the Cinderella story from two different cultures and discuss how the stories are the same and how they are different. By the end of Grade 2, students should be able to read and comprehend literature well at the Grade 2 level of text complexity and some of the Grade 3 level texts.

Informational Texts

Some of the standards for literature and informational texts overlap. For example, students are expected to ask and answer questions about both literature and informational texts. This section focuses on the standards that are specific to informational texts.

Kindergartners will be able to identify the main topic of a text and retell the key points of the text with the prompting and support from the teacher. Also with the help of the teacher, students will be able to identify connections between two people, events, or ideas in the text. For example, after hearing a story about a new puppy read aloud, kindergarteners should be able to tell how getting a puppy at the beginning of a story affected a family throughout the rest of the story.

Students in kindergarten will be expected to identify the parts of a book, including the front and back covers and title page, without prompting. They will also learn how to identify the author and illustrator of a text and explain the role of each in presenting the information found in the text.

With help from the teacher, kindergarteners should also be able to explain the relationship between illustrations and the text that they accompany. For example, a book about a tree's life cycle might show a tree at different points in the year. Kindergarten students should be able to explain how the pictures of the tree relate to the words in the book.

Kindergarteners are also expected to identify reasons an author gives support points within the text, with prompting and support from the teacher. They will be asked to identify differences and similarities between two texts that discuss the same topic with additional prompting and support.

Grade 1 students will be asked to retell key details of a text and identify the main topic. They will also be expected to explain the connection between two individuals, ideas, events, or other information in a text. This means they should be able to explain how having a bad day at school affected a boy when he went home, or how making a friend helped a girl feel better about moving to a new town. First graders are also expected to build their vocabularies. Working on their own, they should be able to pose questions or answer questions that help understand the meaning of words or phrases.

Students should also be able to use text features such as the table of contents, glossaries, headings, or icons to find key facts in a text. They will also be able to explain the differences between information found in pictures or other illustrations and information found in the text itself. Students will also be expected to use the illustrations and pictures along with important details to explain the main idea of the text.

 COLLEGE AND CAREER READINESS

Students must determine the main idea of a text and be able to summarize the important details and ideas.

First graders should also be able to recognize the reasons an author gives to support certain points he or she is trying to make, and they should also be able to explain similarities and differences between two texts that have been written on the same topic. This can be done through the illustrations, procedures, or descriptions in a text. With support from the teacher, students in this grade should also be able to read informational texts that have the appropriate text complexity at this grade level.

Grade 2 students will be expected to answer *who, what, where,* and *how* questions related to key details in a text, as well as ask the same type of questions. They should be able to correctly identify the main topic of a text with multiple paragraphs and also be able to identify the focus of an individual paragraph. Students will also be taught how to make connections between a series of events, steps in a technical procedure, and scientific concepts. In second grade, this might mean that students are able to explain how plants need sunlight, water, and the air we breathe out to grow.

Second graders should also be able to figure out the meaning of words and phrases in a grade-appropriate text using context clues. They will be taught to identify and use text features like captions, bold print, subheadings, icons, indexes, and electronic menus in order to find key information in a text quickly. Students will also be expected to correctly identify the main purpose an author has for writing a text, such as what he or she is trying to answer or explain.

In this grade, students will also learn how to use images in a text to explain or clarify information, and they will be able to compare and contrast important information in two texts that discuss the same subject. By the end of second grade, students should be able to read and comprehend informational texts in the subjects of social studies, science, and technical information. The level of complexity for these texts should be at the grade 2 level and extend into the grade 3 level.

Foundational Skills

The elementary grade levels K-5 also have standards for foundational literacy skills that are taught to students in order to build a working base of knowledge around reading fluency. These skills help students understand the mechanics of the written English language and they support the comprehensive literacy program. Among other things, these standards include the skills that are commonly called "phonics" in the classroom.

 **TAKE CARE**

The early elementary years are a critical time in a child's academic development. Parents should make a special effort during these years to support the skills their child is learning.

Kindergartners are taught to follow words in their proper order on a page: left to right, top to bottom, and one page to the next. They should understand that words that are spoken are represented in written language using sequencing of letters and that words are separated by spaces. Students should also be able to name all the letters of the alphabet in upper- and lowercase form.

Students in this grade are also expected to recognize and create rhyming words and be able to pronounce, count, segment, and blend *syllables* in spoken words. They are also expected to be able to add or substitute individual sounds in one-syllable words to make new words. For example, they should be able to replace the short *u* sound in *nut* with the short *e* sound to make *net*.

 **DEFINITION**

Syllables are the units of sound that are the building blocks of words. For example, the word *dog* has one syllable and the word *water* has two syllables. Segmenting syllables means to break a word into its sound parts, such as *wa|ter* and *beau|ti|ful*. Blending syllables means to pull together sound parts to make a word, such as *sur + prise = surprise*.

Kindergartners should also be able to produce the sound of all the individual consonants and correctly identify the common spellings for the long and short sounds of the five major vowels. Students will also be taught how to read by sight common *high-frequency words* such as *the, you,* and *my*. They will also be expected to tell the difference between similarly spelled words by identifying the letters that make different sounds. For example, they should know that the letters *t* and *n* make the words *pat* and *pan* different. The ultimate goal is for students in this grade level to be able to read texts on the emergent-reader level with understanding.

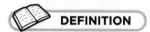 **DEFINITION**

> **High-frequency words** are the words that appear most often in printed materials. For example, the words *I*, *and*, and *the* make up 10 percent of the English words in print.

Grade 1 students should become more familiar with the structure of written language and be able to identify the distinguishing parts of a sentence like the initial capital letter, the first word, and ending punctuation.

The first grade standards build on the phonological and phonemic awareness skills that were developed in kindergarten. Students will be expected to tell the difference between short vowel sounds and long vowel sounds in spoken words, such as the difference between the short *a* in *cap* and the long *a* in *cape*. Students will also be taught how to blend sounds to verbally create single-syllable words.

First graders will learn how to identify the vowel sound in single-syllable spoken words and combine it with the final sound in the word and how to break a single-syllable word into all its individual sounds. For example, students should be able to isolate the sounds in *late* by pronouncing each sound slowly and distinctly, *lll-ayyy-ttt*.

Students will also be expected to *decode* regularly spelled written words that are one syllable and recognize when the final *-e* is making a long vowel sound. First graders will also learn how to determine the number of syllables in a printed word.

 **DEFINITION**

> **Decode** means to translate a printed word into a sound. **Decodable words** are words that follow regular spelling patterns.

The students in this grade level will decode two-syllable words by breaking apart the word into syllables. When students are reading, they will be expected to read words with inflection at the end and read irregularly spelled words from grade-appropriate texts. By the end of first grade, students should be able to read a text on this level with *fluency*, meaning they read with purpose, expression, and understanding. They should also be able to self-correct themselves when reading a word they miss based on the context, word recognition, and rereading as much as needed.

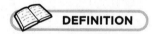 **DEFINITION**

> **Fluency** is the ability to read a grade-appropriate text with purpose, expression, and understanding.

Grade 2 students are expected to recognize long and short vowel sounds when reading one-syllable words. They should also be able decode two-syllable words with long vowels and also decode words with prefixes and suffixes. Students will also be expected to recognize and read irregularly spelled words for this grade level.

By the end of second grade, students should be reading grade-appropriate texts with purpose and understanding, and they should be able to read orally at an appropriate rate, expression, and accuracy on successive readings. They should also be able to self-correct themselves when reading a word they miss based on the context, word recognition, and rereading as much as needed.

Writing

Like the reading standards, the writing standards build on each other year-to-year, so that the level of complexity produced by the student increases at each grade level. The skills range from the basic mechanics of language use and vocabulary to how to organize ideas. Writing is not just taught as a standalone skill. It is also integrated into all the other subject areas as a support and communication tool.

COLLEGE AND CAREER READINESS

Students must be able to write arguments to support an idea using reasoning and evidence.

Kindergartners will be taught to use a combination of writing, dictation, and drawing to create opinion pieces about a book or topic they have read. They will use the same devices to write informative text in which they tell the reader what they are going to talk about and then give information on the topic. Using writing, dictation, and drawing a student will also be able narrate an event or multiple events in the order they happened and give a reaction to the action that took place.

Students will also learn how to respond to questions and suggestions from their peers about their writing and use that information to improve what they have written. This is done with support from the teacher. Support is also given by the teacher in helping students use multiple digital devices to create and publish writing. They will also start learning how to do this in collaboration with their peers.

Kindergartners will also share in projects that involve research and writing, such as giving their opinion on a set of stories or books by the same author. The teacher will also support students in collecting information from sources he or she provides in order for the student to answer questions.

Grade 1 students will be taught how to write an opinion piece on a topic or book. They will give their opinion, reasons for their opinion, and then create a sense of closure at the end of their writing. They will also learn how to write informative texts where they name a topic, then give some facts about the topic, and provide closure at the end. Students will also be expected to write narratives where they recall two or more events, tell what happened in order, and bring closure to their narrative.

First graders will also learn to focus on a topic and incorporate feedback from questions and suggestions from peers to make their writing better. This is done with support and guidance from the teacher. Support is also given by the teacher in helping students use multiple digital devices to create and publish writing. They will also start learning how to do this in collaboration with their peers.

First grade students will share in projects that involve research and writing, such as reading "how-to" books and using them to create a sequence of instructions. The teacher will also support students in collecting information from sources he or she provides in order to answer questions.

Grade 2 students will learn how to write opinion pieces on a book they are reading and give reasons that support their opinion. They will use words like *because* to connect their opinion and the supporting reasons, and then they will be expected to write a concluding statement to the opinion piece. Students will also write informative texts where they use supporting facts and definitions to develop points and create a concluding statement. Students in this grade are expected to be able to write about events in proper sequence, while also using words to describe actions, emotions, and thoughts. The students must create a sense of closure to the events at the end of the writing.

The students will use the support of their teacher and the feedback from peers to improve the quality of their writing through the revising and editing process. Support is given by the teacher in helping students use multiple digital devices to create and publish writing. Students will share in projects that involve research and writing, such as recording science observations or writing a report on a topic that is covered by several different books. Students will ultimately be able to recall information on experiences in order to answer questions in writing.

Speaking and Listening

The speaking and listening standards focus a great deal on collaborating and discussion with classmates through questioning and answering as part of the dialogue.

Kindergartners will learn how to participate in conversations with multiple partners from their peer group and the teacher in large and small group settings to discuss kindergarten topics. This simply means that they will have many opportunities to speak and interact with others both with the whole class and with partners or smaller groups.

Kindergarteners will be expected to follow agreed-upon rules for the discussion, such as giving each person a chance to speak, and they will continue conversations during multiple exchanges. Kindergartners will show their level of understanding of a text that is read aloud or information that is presented through other media by asking and answering questions on the topic that is presented. Students will also be able to ask questions in order to clarify something they did not understand.

With support from the teacher, students will be expected to describe things familiar to them like people, places, and events. They will also be asked to provide drawings or other visuals in order to give more details. They should be able to apply these skills learned for peer conversations and presentations by speaking audibly and expressing ideas clearly.

Grade 1 students will learn how to participate in conversations with multiple partners from their peer group and the teacher in a large and small group setting to discuss grade 1 topics. Students will be expected to follow agreed-upon rules for the discussion, such as giving each person a chance to speak, and they will continue conversations during multiple exchanges.

First grade students are now capable of building the conversation by responding to other students' comments and by asking questions about details that have been read out loud or shown through media devices. They will also ask clarifying question about what a speaker says in order to get information on something that is not understood. Students should be able to describe events, places, things, and people while expressing ideas and emotions clearly. They will be expected to add drawings or other visuals to descriptions in order to clarify ideas or feelings.

COLLEGE AND CAREER READINESS

Students will be able to actively participate in discussions with peers by expressing their ideas clearly and building on the ideas of others.

Grade 2 students will learn how to participate in conversations with multiple partners from their peer group and the teacher in large and small group settings to discuss grade 2 topics. Students will be expected to follow agreed-upon rules for the discussion, such as speaking one at a time. Students will build the conversation by responding to other student's comments and by asking questions about details that have been read out loud or shown through media devices. They will also ask clarifying questions about what a speaker says in order to get information on something that is not understood.

As in first grade, second grade students will be expected to build the conversation by responding to other student's comments and by asking questions about details that have been read out loud or shown through media devices. They will also ask clarifying question about what a speaker says in order to get information on something that is not understood. Students in this grade will be expected to tell a story with important details while speaking audibly and clearly. They will also learn how to create audio recordings of their stories or poems.

Language

The language standards focus on specific grammar skills students need at each level for writing and speaking. The skills build on each other year-to-year and support the overall literacy program.

Kindergartners will be expected to print almost all upper- and lowercase letters. They will also learn frequently used nouns and verbs and how to form plural nouns by adding *s* or *es*. Students will be expected to learn the use of questioning words like *who, what, where, why, when,* and *how*. Kindergartners will also learn how to capitalize the first word in a sentence and the pronoun *I*. They will be taught to name end punctuation for sentences and also spell simple words phonetically.

Students will learn how to identify new meaning to words that are familiar to them and apply them in the right context. For example, *duck* can mean a bird (noun), but it can also mean *to duck* (verb). They will be expected to use affixes, such as *pre-, -ed, -ful, un-,* and *re-,* to help identify meanings of unknown words. Kindergartners will be taught how to sort objects into categories, such as shapes, color, or food, to understand the concepts represented by the categories. Students will be expected to demonstrate an understanding of frequently used verbs and adjectives by relating them to their opposites, or antonyms, and they will also be asked to make real-life connections between words and their use, such as noting places at school that are *loud*. They learn to distinguish variations in meaning among similar action verbs such as *walk, strut, march,* and *skip*.

Grade 1 students must be able to print all upper- and lowercase letters, and use common, proper, and possessive nouns correctly. They will be expected to use singular and plural nouns to match correctly with action verbs, and students to use verbs to give a sense of past, present, and future. First grade students will also be expected to use frequently used adjectives and frequently used conjunctions, such as *and, but, or, so,* and *because.* First graders will learn how to use prepositions, and they will also create various types of sentences in response to prompts.

Students will learn how to capitalize dates and names of people, and they will also learn to use end punctuation and some uses for the comma. There will be an expectation that students can use phonics to spell words with common spelling patterns, including untaught words. Students will be taught to use sentence-level meaning as a clue to the meaning of the word, and they will be taught to use affixes as a clue to the meaning of a word. Students will be expected to identify root words and their different forms, such as *looks, looked,* and *looking.*

Grade 1 students will learn how to sort words into different categories like colors or clothing to understand the concepts the categories represent. They will also be able to define words by categories by one or more unique attribute. Students will be expected to recognize and identify real-life connections between a word and its use like identifying a room in the house that is *cozy.* There is also the expectation that students can distinguish differences in meaning among similar verbs, such as *look, peek, glance, stare, glare,* and *scowl,* and they should also be able to distinguish the difference between similar adjectives like *large* and *gigantic.*

 COLLEGE AND CAREER READINESS

Students must be able to use the foundational elements of standard English grammar when speaking or writing.

Grade 2 students learn how to use collective nouns, like *group,* correctly. They will also be expected to form and use irregular plural nouns, such as *teeth, mice,* and *children.* Grade 2 students will learn to use adjectives and adverbs and also rearrange or create compound sentences. Students will also learn to capitalize geographic names, holidays, and product names, as well as how to use commas in greetings and closings when writing a note or letter. They will also learn how to use apostrophes with contractions with possessive nouns, and consult reference materials, like dictionaries, to check spelling.

Grade 2 students must be able to compare formal and informal uses of English and use sentence-level context as a clue to the meaning of words or phrases in a sentence. They are also expected to determine the new meaning of a word when a prefix is added to it. This type of word analysis is also applied to root words where a student must use the root of an unknown word to help identify its meaning. Students are also taught to use the meaning of an individual word to help understand the meaning of a compound word like *birdhouse* or *bookshelf.*

Using glossaries and beginning dictionaries, students will learn to clarify the meaning of words, and they will learn to identify real-life connections between words and the use of those words. Students will be expected to distinguish between the meanings of similar verbs, such as *toss*, *throw*, and *hurl*, as well as distinguishing between similar adjectives, such as *thin*, *slender*, *skinny*, and *scrawny*.

Text Complexity

As mentioned in the previous chapter, text complexity is the measure of how challenging reading materials are. There has been a decline in the complexity of texts used in schools during the past few decades, even though the level of text complexity at the college level has stayed the same or increased. Many sectors of industry have also increased the level of text complexity in operation manuals, technical guides, and manufacturing process guides.

In order for the reading and language standards to be effective, it is important for teachers to select texts that sufficiently challenge students and continue to build their skill set of not only reading complex texts but comprehending them as well.

For more information on text complexity as well as examples of appropriately complex texts at each grade level, see Appendix C of this book. Take some time to review the examples and use them as a guideline for what to expect from your child's school work and what to select for reading at home.

 DID YOU KNOW?

On average, newspapers in the United States are written at an eighth-grade reading level.

How to Support Your Child

The early elementary years are a critical time for your child in developing literacy skills. These skills will be the building blocks for more complex tasks and expectations as your child moves into middle grades. It is important that the foundation is strong and that your child masters the required skills at each grade level in order to be prepared for the next grade. Since the standards are like stairsteps from grade to grade, it is difficult for students to be successful in their current grade if they did not master the standards from the year before.

There are many ways that you can support your child's academic success from home. Keeping a dedicated time each night to read to and read with your child is one of the most important things you can do. As you read together, periodically ask your child questions about the text. Questioning is one of the best ways to expand your child's learning. Try to ask questions that promote critical thinking and require your child to make connections between ideas. Have your child describe pictures or graphics from a book and tell how they relate to the story.

After you read together, encourage your child to respond to what you read by offering an opinion or idea about the book. It is also a great idea to share your opinion and ideas about what you read together to give your child examples on how to explain, question, and discuss events or characters in a story.

There are many free websites that give recommendations on grade-appropriate books, but your child's teacher can also recommend books or possibly let you borrow books from the class library. This time together not only reinforces the learning going on at school, but it is a great bonding time without all the distractions that tend to consume our lives.

Give your child multiple opportunities to practice writing. Get them in the habit by having them write explanations or titles for drawings they create. Having them write short notes or cards to friends and family members is another simple and easy way to give them practice. Consider starting a family journal and take turns writing entries and responding to each other. This is a great way to practice writing skills and a good way to encourage family communication.

Talk to your child's teacher to see if there are things they would like for you to do or practice to support the literacy activities that are going on in the class. Teachers love it when parents want to support what is going on at school with activities at home, and they will have lots of ideas to keep your child on pace to acquire the skills they need to learn.

You can also ask the teacher to return specific examples of your child's work with explanations on how it could be better or if it was satisfactory, what was an important part to replicate in the future. Also, practicing the rules of participating in the discussion would also be very helpful for your child. They need to learn how to wait their turn, make comments that relate specifically to the topic being discussed, and ask questions that relate specifically to the topic being discussed or a comment made by someone in the group. It's helpful to ask your child each day about what they discussed in class and even more helpful to ask your child the questions they asked in class that day.

As your child progresses into first grade, you should start seeing them read with more confidence, fluency, and understanding with texts on their grade level. Help them to identify information from texts they read or listen to and be able to explain it back to you. Don't be afraid to give them texts to read that challenge them at times. Help them sound out the words they have difficulty with, or read it to them the first time through, while they follow along. It is also a good practice to have a "word of the day" that can be a new vocabulary word. You can focus on spelling, in addition to the definition of the word.

By second grade, your child should begin to expand the type of texts they read to include subjects like history, social studies, and science. There are many children's magazines out there for this age level that cover these subjects, and your local library can help you with finding books as well. The point is to diversify your child's reading to include informational texts along with fictional stories.

In the end, there is no magic formula or specific activity that will be more beneficial than that of giving your time. Taking 20 to 30 minutes each night to read with or to your children not only gives them practice, but it also shows you are making what they do at school a priority at home.

The Least You Need To Know

- The Common Core reading standards focus on informational texts as well as fictional stories.

- Foundational skills in reading build on each other from year to year, so it is important to master those skills at each grade level.

- The Common Core includes specific writing standards, but writing skills are also promoted in other subject areas.

- Speaking and listening are important skills that are taught so that students can interact productively with their teacher and peers.

- In order for students to be college- and career-ready, they must be reading appropriately challenging texts at each grade level.

- Parents can support the learning that takes place in their child's classroom by spending time each night reading to and reading with their child.

The ELA Standards for Grades 3-5

The ELA standards for grades 3–5 push students to the next level, requiring them to apply the foundational skills they learned in the earlier grades to reading, writing, and speaking. Students learn to explore and explain more complex concepts through literacy. The role of the student evolves into one that is not just learner, but collaborator as well. Students do more independent work, and they are given multiple opportunities to make arguments to support their opinion or ideas.

In This Chapter

- A summary of the Common Core standards for reading literature and informational texts in grades 3-5

- The foundational skills for reading in grades 3-5

- The Common Core standards for writing in grades 3-5

- The communication skills that are important in grades 3-5

- How you can support your child in learning the standards

Reading

In the later elementary grades, the purpose for reading moves from learning basic skills to collecting information. Students use the information they collect for research, to answer questions, and to support their arguments. The type of texts students read becomes more diverse, as students are exposed to more texts related to social studies, history, science, and technical subjects.

Literature

Grade 3 students will be expected to ask and answer questions about a text and give evidence from the text to support their answers. They will be able to retell folktales, myths, and fables from various cultures and explain the lesson or moral of the story using details from the text. Students should also be able to describe the characters in a story, their emotions, and how the character's actions contributed to events in the story.

 COLLEGE AND CAREER READINESS

Students must analyze how and why characters, events, and ideas progress and interact throughout a text.

Third graders will be expected to determine the meaning of words or phrases in a story and be able to tell the difference between literal and nonliteral meanings. Students learn how to reference parts of a story, poem, or play by citing the chapter, scene, or stanza in both written and oral work. They will be expected to explain how certain parts build on previous sections, and they will have to tell the difference between their point of view and that of the characters and narrator of the text.

Third grade students must explain how pictures or illustrations in a text help tell the story, and they will be expected to compare and contrast the themes and plots of different stories written by the same author (such as books in a series). By the end of third grade, students will be expected to read and comprehend literature from the grade 2 and grade 3 levels of text complexity proficiently and on their own.

Grade 4 students will be expected to cite specific details from text when giving answers to questions about the text and drawing conclusions. They must be able to determine what the theme of a text is using details from the text, and they must be able to summarize it. Students must be able to describe with great detail the characters, setting, or events from a story.

Fourth graders must determine the meaning of words and phrases based on the way they are used in the text such as those found in mythology. For example, understanding what "Herculean task" means. They should be able to explain the major differences in a poem, a play, or prose by citing examples from the elements of each. Students will also learn how to compare and contrast different points of view in telling a story, such as first- and third-person narration.

 KEYS TO THE CORE

Parents can support classroom learning by taking their children to plays or poetry readings. Discuss what you see and ask specific questions about the dialogue or have children identify their favorite parts. This helps children think critically about a body of work and formulate opinions.

Students in this grade should be able to make connections between the written version of a story and an oral or visual presentation of the story. They will learn how to compare and contrast similar themes and ideas across literature from different cultures. Students will also be expected to read proficiently and comprehend texts at the level of text complexity for grades 4 and 5, with support at the grade 5 level as needed.

Grade 5 students will learn how to quote a text accurately to explain something within the text. They will be able to identify the theme of a story, poem, or play from details in the text, and they will be expected to summarize the text. Students will be expected to compare and contrast characters, settings, or events from the text and give specific details as evidence.

Fifth graders will determine the meaning of words or phrases in a text, and they must also determine the meaning of similes and metaphors. Students must explain how multiple chapters, stanzas, or scenes fit together, and they will be expected to explain how the narrator's perspective influences the description of events.

In fifth grade, students must analyze visual and multimedia elements and explain how they enhance the text, for example, by reading and discussing a graphic novel. They will learn how to compare and contrast stories in the same genre and identify how they approach similar themes. By the end of the year, students should be able to read and comprehend proficiently literature in the grade 4 and 5 levels of text complexity.

Informational Texts

Some of the standards for literature and informational texts overlap. This section focuses on the standards that are specific to informational texts for grades 3–5.

Grade 3 students will be expected to ask and answer questions about a text and give evidence from the text to support their answers. Students must determine the main idea of a text by giving important details and explaining how those details support the main idea. They will explain relationships between events, scientific ideas, or steps in a technical process. Students will be expected to determine the meaning of topic-specific words or phrases in a text that are relevant to grade 3 subjects.

Third graders will learn to use text features, such as sidebars, key words, or hyperlinks, to more quickly locate information on the topic they are studying. They will be required to distinguish the differences between their point of view and the point of view of the author. Students must use information found in illustrations to prove they understand the text. Students must also describe connections between specific sentences and paragraphs, such as cause and effect or sequencing of actions, and they will be expected to compare and contrast the most important ideas in two texts on the same topic. By the end of third grade, students will be proficiently reading and comprehending informational texts from history, science, and technical subjects at the grade 2 and 3 text complexity level.

 COLLEGE AND CAREER READINESS

Students must interpret how figurative words and phrases are used in a text to shape the meaning and tone.

Grade 4 students will be expected to cite specific details from a text when giving answers to questions about the text and drawing conclusions. Students must determine the main idea of a text by giving key details from the text, and they must be able to summarize the text with important details. Students will be expected to explain events, procedures, ideas, or concepts in a historical, scientific, or technical text by telling what happened using specific information from the text as evidence.

Fourth graders are expected to determine the meaning of topic-specific words or phrases that are relevant to grade 4 subjects. They must be able to describe the structure of events, ideas, or information in a text, such as chronology, cause and effect, or problems and solutions. Students will also be expected to compare and contrast a firsthand and secondhand account of the same event or topic, and they must be able to explain the differences. For example, students might read a journal entry from a pioneer and compare it to a nonfiction book about westward expansion.

Fourth grade students must be able to interpret visual information that accompanies a text, such as charts, graphs, diagrams, time lines, or interactive elements on a webpage, to explain how it supports the understanding of the text. They must also explain how an author of a text uses evidence to support specific points in a text. Students will be expected to combine information from two texts on the same topic in order to more knowledgably speak or write about a subject. By the end of the year, students will be expected to read and comprehend historical, scientific, and technical texts at the grade 4 and 5 text complexity level, with support given as needed with the grade 5 texts.

Grade 5 students will learn how to quote from a text accurately to explain something within the text. Students must identify two or more main ideas in a text and explain how key points in the text support these ideas, and they must also be able to summarize the text. Students will be expected to explain the relationships between two or more individuals, events, or ideas in a historical, scientific, or technical text using precise details from the text.

Students in this grade will determine the meaning of topic-specific words or phrases in a text that are relevant to grade 5 subjects. Students in this grade will learn to compare and contrast the structure of events, ideas, or information in two or more texts, and they will also be expected to study multiple accounts of the same event or topic and explain similarities and differences in each point of view.

Fifth graders will use information from multiple print and digital sources to quickly locate answers to questions or solve problems. They must explain how authors use evidence to support their points in a text, and students must be able to identify which evidence supports which point. Students will learn how to combine information from several texts on the same topic to write or speak about the topic knowledgably. By the end of fifth grade, students should be proficiently reading and comprehending historical, scientific, and technical texts at the high end of the text complexity level for grades 4 and 5.

Foundational Skills

Grade 3 students must know the meaning of most prefixes and suffixes, the word parts that carry meaning and are added to the beginning and end of words, such as *un-* and *-ful*. They must also learn to decode words with common Latin suffixes, such as *-logy*. Students will learn to decode multi-syllable words and read irregularly spelled words. Third grade students must read with accuracy and fluency to support comprehension. This also means reading grade 3 texts with understanding and expression on successive readings.

Grade 4 students will be expected to read accurately unfamiliar words with multi-syllables. They must read these in context and out of context using skills they have learned about syllables, root words, and affixes. Students will also read grade-level texts with emotion and understanding. They will use context clues to confirm or self-correct for word recognition and understanding and rereading text as necessary.

Grade 5 expectations are identical to the grade 4 expectations, except texts are on the grade 5 complexity level.

Writing Expectations

The writing standards build on each other from year to year, so that the level of complexity produced by the student increases each grade level. The skills range from the basic mechanics of language use and vocabulary to how to organize ideas. Writing is not just taught as a standalone skill. It is also integrated into all the other subject areas as a support and communication tool. As students progress through grades 3–5, the complexity of writing skills increases, as does its use in analyzing and discussing texts.

Grade 3 students must be able to introduce a topic they are writing about and state their opinion about it. They must use specific reasons from the text to support their ideas. They must also use linking words and phrases, such as *because, since, therefore*, and *for example*, to connect their opinion to the reasons they list. Students must be able to form a concluding statement or section to their opinion piece.

Third graders will be expected to write explanatory texts about a topic and group related information together. They must include drawings or illustrations to aid the reader in understanding the ideas presented. Students must use definitions, facts, and details to develop their topic, and they must use linking words and phrases, such as *also, more, but*, and *another*, to connect ideas within categories of information. Students must then be able to provide a concluding statement or section to their explanatory writing piece.

Students will learn to create situations with characters and/or a narrator and organize events in a natural sequence. They must use dialogue, describe the actions taking place, and show the response of characters to situations. Students must use chronological words to describe event order, and they must create a sense of closure to their writing.

Third graders will be expected to plan, revise, and edit their writing with the help of teachers and peers. Also with help from their teacher, students should be able to use technology to produce and publish writing and collaborate with others. This includes using keyboarding skills in the production process.

COLLEGE AND CAREER READINESS

Students must be able to write a narrative with real or imagined experiences with specific details and event sequences.

Students will be taught how to conduct short research projects and how to build knowledge about a topic. They will be expected to recall information from their own experiences and gather information from different print and digital sources, and they will learn how to take brief notes in order to provide evidence for their research. Third graders will write consistently and for both long and short timeframes on a range of topics and subject areas.

Grade 4 students will be expected to introduce a topic clearly and state an opinion on the topic. They must provide reasons for their opinion that are supported by evidence. Students must be able to link their opinions to reasons using words and phrases, such as *for instance*, *in order to*, and *in addition*, and they must provide a concluding statement or section related to the opinion that was given.

Students in this grade will be expected to introduce a topic clearly and group information in paragraphs. They will include headings, illustrations, and multimedia as appropriate to help the reader understand the topic. The students should develop topics with facts, definitions, quotes, and other examples related to the topic, and they should connect ideas within categories of information using words or phrases like *another*, *for example*, *also*, and *because*. Students will be expected to use precise language and topic-specific vocabulary to explain the topic more clearly, and they must provide a concluding statement or sections related to the topic being discussed.

Fourth graders will learn to create situations with characters and/or a narrator and sequence events in a natural order. They must use dialogue, describe the actions taking place, and show the response of characters to situations. Students must use a variety of transitional words to explain the order of events, and they must use concrete phrases and sensory details to describe events precisely. Students will be expected to write a conclusion to the narrated events.

Students will be expected to plan, revise, and edit their writing with the help of teachers and peers. Also with help from their teacher, students should be able to use technology, including the internet, to produce and publish writing and collaborate with others. This includes using keyboarding skills in the production process to type a minimum of one page in a single sitting.

Fourth grade students will be taught how to conduct short research projects and how to build knowledge about a topic through investigation. They will be expected to recall information from their own experiences and gather information from different print and digital sources, and they will learn how to take brief notes in order to provide evidence for their research and provide a list of sources.

Students must apply grade 4 reading standards in literature to describe characters, settings, and events in stories. They must also apply grade 4 reading standards for informational texts to explain how an author used reasons and evidence to support an idea or point. Fourth graders will write consistently for both long and short time periods on a range of topics and subject areas.

Grade 5 students will be expected to introduce a topic clearly and state an opinion on the topic. They must provide reasons for their opinion that are supported by evidence. Students must be able to link their opinions to reasons using words, phrases, and clauses such as *consequently* or *specifically*, and they must provide a concluding statement or section related to the opinion that was given.

COLLEGE AND CAREER READINESS

Students must be able to write clearly and coherently with organization, style, and development appropriate to the audience or task.

Students in this grade will be expected to introduce a topic clearly, group information in paragraphs, and include headings, illustrations, and multimedia when appropriate to help the reader understand the topic. Students should develop topics with facts, definitions, quotes, and other examples related to the topic, and they should connect ideas within categories of information using words, phrases, and clauses like *in contrast* and *especially*. Students will be expected to use precise language and topic-specific vocabulary to explain the topic more clearly, and they must provide a concluding statement or section related to the topic being discussed.

Fifth graders will learn to create situations with characters and/or a narrator and sequence events in a natural order. They must use dialogue, describe the actions taking place, and show the response of characters to situations. Students must use a variety of transitional words to explain the order of events, and they must use concrete phrases and sensory details to explain events precisely. Students will be expected to write a conclusion to the narrated events.

Students will be expected to plan, revise, and edit their writing with the help of teachers and peers. Also with help from their teacher, students should be able to use technology, including the internet, to produce and publish writing and collaborate with others. This includes using keyboarding skills in the production process to type a minimum of one page in a single sitting.

Fifth graders will be taught how to conduct short research projects and how to build knowledge about a topic through investigation of several sources. They will be expected to recall information from their own experiences and gather information from different print and digital sources. They will learn how to summarize and paraphrase this information when taking notes and in the finished work. Students will use this information to provide evidence for their research and provide a list of sources.

Students must apply grade 5 reading standards in literature to compare and contrast two or more characters, settings, and events in stories. They must also apply grade 5 reading standards for informational texts to explain how an author used reasons and evidence to support an idea or point. Grade 5 students will write consistently for both short and long time periods on a range of topics and subject areas.

TAKE CARE

It is important to cultivate good typing skills early, before bad habits develop. Parents who have computers or tablets at home should consider downloading one of the many free or low-cost programs available for practicing keyboarding skills.

Speaking and Listening

The speaking and listening standards focus a great deal on collaboration and discussion with classmates through questioning and answering as part of the dialogue.

COLLEGE AND CAREER READINESS

Students must be able to integrate and evaluate information presented in multiple media formats.

Grade 3 students will learn to engage in a variety of discussion formats, such as one-to-one, group, and teacher-led, building on other students' thoughts and expressing their own ideas clearly. They will be expected to come to discussions prepared by reading required texts beforehand, and to follow agreed-upon rules for the discussion. Third grade students will learn to ask questions to check for their own understanding, to stay on topic, and to link their comments to the comments of others. They will determine the main ideas of a text that is read aloud or of information that is presented through other media formats. Students will also be expected to ask and answer questions about the information presented by a speaker by giving appropriate elaboration and detail.

Students will be expected to report on a topic or tell a story, providing important facts and relevant details while speaking clearly at an appropriate pace. Third graders will learn how to create audio recordings of stories or poems that demonstrate reading at an understandable pace and provide visual displays when appropriate to enhance points or details. Students must speak in complete sentences in order to provide detail or clarification.

Grade 4 students will learn to engage in a variety of discussion formats, such as one-to-one, group, and teacher-led, building on other students' thoughts and expressing their own ideas clearly. They will be expected to come to discussions prepared by reading required texts beforehand, and to follow agreed-upon rules for the discussion. Fourth grade students will learn to ask questions and respond to questions in order to check for their own understanding, to stay on topic, and to link their comments to the comments of others. They will paraphrase the main ideas of a text that is read aloud or of information that is presented through other media formats. Students will also be expected to identify reasons and evidence used by a speaker to make particular points.

Students will be expected to report on a topic or tell a story, giving important facts and relevant details in an organized manner, and speaking clearly at an appropriate pace. Fourth graders will learn how to create audio recordings of stories or poems and provide visual displays when appropriate to enhance main points or details. Students must be able to differentiate between contexts that should use formal English, such as giving a speech, and situations where informal English can be used, such as talking with a friend.

Grade 5 students will learn to engage in a variety of discussion formats, such as one-to-one, group, and teacher-led, and to build on other students' thoughts and express their own thoughts clearly. They will be expected to come to discussions prepared by reading required texts beforehand, and to follow agreed-upon rules for the discussion. Fifth grade students will learn to ask questions and respond to questions in order to check for their own understanding, to stay on topic, and to link their comments to the comments of others. They will summarize the main ideas of a text that is read aloud or of information that is presented through other media formats.

Students will also be expected to summarize the points a speaker makes and provide reasons and evidence used by a speaker to make particular points.

Students will be expected to report on a topic or tell a story, giving important facts and relevant details in an organized manner while speaking clearly at an appropriate pace. Fifth graders will learn how to create multimedia components to enhance presentations. Students must be able to differentiate between contexts that should use formal English, such as giving a presentation, and situations where informal English can be used, such as speaking to a friend.

Language

The language standards for grades 3–5 focus on the specific grammar skills students need at each grade level for writing and speaking. The skills build on each other from year to year and support the overall literacy program.

COLLEGE AND CAREER READINESS

Students must be able to correctly use standard English capitalization, punctuation, and spelling in their writing.

Grade 3 students will be expected to explain the use of nouns, pronouns, verbs, adjectives, and adverbs in general and specifically their role in sentences. Students should be able to create regular and irregular plural nouns, and use abstract nouns, such as *childhood*. They must also create regular and irregular verbs, and they must learn to make and use simple verb tenses like *I walked*; *I walk*; *I will walk*. Students will be expected to understand subject-verb and pronoun-antecedent agreement, and they must use comparative and superlative adjectives and adverbs. Students must also use coordinating and subordinating conjunctions and be able to produce simple, compound, and complex sentences.

Third graders will be expected to use capitalization correctly in titles. They must correctly use commas in addresses and use commas and quotation marks in a dialogue. Students must be able to create and use possessives and use conventional spelling for high-frequency words and other studied words in third grade. They must also be able to add suffixes to base words, such as *sitting*, *smiled*, *cries*, and *happiness*. Students in this grade will also learn how to use reference materials, like dictionaries, to check spelling. Students must also recognize the differences between spoken and written standard English.

Students will learn to use sentence-level context of words to understand the meaning, and they will learn to determine the meaning of a new word when an affix is added to it. Third grade students will be expected to use a known root word as a clue to determine the meaning of an unknown word with the same root, such as using the word *agree* to determine the meaning of *disagreement*. Students will learn to use glossaries and beginning dictionaries to clarify or find the meaning of a word.

Students in this grade will learn to distinguish the literal and nonliteral meanings of words and phrases depending on the context, and they will be expected to identify real-life connections between words and how they are used. Students must distinguish between degrees of meaning among words that describe states of mind or levels of certainty, such as *knew*, *believed*, and *suspected*. They must also accurately use grade 3 conversational, subject-specific, and academic words and phrases.

Grade 4 students should be able to use relative pronouns, such as *who*, *whose*, *whom*, and *which*, and relative adverbs, such as *where*, *when*, and *why*. They should create and use progressive verb tenses like *I was walking*; *I am walking*; and *I will be walking*. Students will be expected to order adjectives within sentences in the correct pattern, such as *small red bag* rather than *red small bag*. They must create and use prepositional phrases to make complete sentences and recognize sentence fragments and run-on sentences. Students will also learn to correctly use homophones like *to, too,* and *two* and *there, they're,* and *their*.

Students in fourth grade must also use correct capitalization, and they must use commas and quotation marks to identify direct speech and quotes from a text. Students will learn to use commas before coordinating conjunctions in a compound sentence, and to spell grade 4 words correctly by consulting references as needed.

Students will be expected to explain the meaning of simple similes and metaphors and explain the meaning of common idioms (such as "take the cake"), adages ("don't burn your bridges"), and proverbs ("a bird in the hand is worth two in the bush"). They must show an understanding of words by relating then to synonyms and antonyms. Students must also accurately use grade 4 conversational, subject-specific, and academic words and phrases.

Grade 5 students must explain the use of conjunctions, propositions, and interjections in general and their specific role in sentences. They must create and use perfect verb tenses, such as *I had walked; I have walked,* and *I will have walked*, and they will be expected to use verb tense to convey time and conditions. Students must also correct inappropriate shifts in verb tense and be able to use correlative conjunctions like *either/or* and *neither/nor*.

Students in fifth grade must use punctuation to separate items in a series, and they must correctly use a comma to separate an introductory word or phrase from the rest of the sentence. Students must further correctly use a comma to set off the words *yes* and *no*, and to set off a question from the rest of the sentence, such as, *It's true, isn't it?* They should also use commas to indicate direct address, such as, *Is that you, Steve?* Students will be expected to use underlining, quotations marks, or italics to indicate the title of a work, and they must also spell grade 5 words correctly, using a reference as needed.

Fifth graders will learn to expand, combine, and reduce sentences to make them more appealing to the reader. They will learn to compare and contrast different dialects used in English stories, dramas, and poems. Students will be expected to use context clues to figure out the meaning of words or phrases, and they must use Latin and Greek affixes and roots as clues to the meaning of a word, such as *biosphere*. Students will learn how to consult reference materials, like dictionaries in print and digital form, to find the pronunciation and meaning of a word.

Students in this grade will be expected to explain figurative language, like similes and metaphors, and they must explain the meaning of common idioms, adages, and proverbs. They must use the relationship between words, such as synonyms and antonyms, to better understand the meaning of both words. They will also be expected to use subject-specific words in fifth grade to explain contrast and other relationships, such as *although, similarly,* and *in addition*.

Text Complexity

As mentioned in Chapter 5, text complexity is the measure of how challenging reading materials are. It is important for teachers to select texts that sufficiently challenge students and continue to build their skill set of not only reading complex texts but comprehending them as well. Appendix C of this book provides more information about text complexity, as well as examples of appropriately complex texts at each grade level. Take some time to review the examples and use them as a guideline for what to expect from your child's school work and what to select for reading at home.

 DID YOU KNOW?

Twenty-one percent of adults in the United States read below a fifth grade reading level.

How to Support Your Child

In the later elementary years, children begin flexing their academic muscles a little with the foundational skills they learned in K–2. Students will be discussing and writing about topics in greater detail and with more depth. Students will also be broadening the subject areas from which they read, including social studies, history, science, and technical texts. Students in grades 3–5 will be expected to justify their opinions or viewpoints with evidence from research and to make logical arguments.

There are many ways that you can support your child's academic success from home. You still need to keep a dedicated time each night to read to and read with your child. For some reason, many parents think reading with their child is only an activity you do when children are younger than 10 years old, but a dedicated time for reading has no age limit and is one of the most important things you can do. As you are reading together, periodically ask your child questions about the text. Questioning continues to be one of the best ways to expand your child's learning. There are many free websites that give recommendations on grade-appropriate books, but your child's teacher can also recommend books or possibly let you borrow books from the class library.

Encourage your child to make logical arguments about everyday situations, such as getting to stay up late to watch a special program. Your child is learning skills to defend and justify their answers, opinions, and ideas, so the more you can model this at home the better you will support what they are learning in class.

Give your child multiple opportunities to practice writing. Continue having them write short notes or cards to friends and family members as a simple and easy way to give them practice. Also, have them read their writing to one or more family members. Ask questions about their style, ideas, and reasons for choosing certain words or phrases. This supports the peer discussion skills they are learning at school.

 KEYS TO THE CORE

The National PTA (pta.org) has some great resources on their website to help parents support Common Core standards at each grade level.

Talk to your child's teacher to get an understanding of the different types of texts that will be studied in class, so that you can support this with similar texts at home. Students in grades 3–5 start reading more poems and articles, so it's a good idea to get an understanding of what is appropriate for each grade level. Starting in third grade, make sure that reading is a part of your child's everyday routine and not something that is done for punishment or only occasionally. It is also a good practice in third grade to have your child cut out pictures from a magazine or newspaper, stick it on a page, and write their own story about it, or you could select a picture for them. You can also continue having your child learn a new vocabulary word every day but put a twist on it by having them use the word correctly in a sentence for a small treat or extra playtime.

As your child is entering fourth grade, they will be doing more short research projects. This is a great way to work with your child and help them create supporting materials like posters or dioramas for their research. This is also a great time to have your child make logical arguments. For example, if your child wants a later bedtime, have them create a logical argument that explains why he or she should be able to stay up later and defend their position. You can also listen to the nightly news and pick a story or pick a story from the newspaper to discuss and have them give their opinion on the story.

In fifth grade, you can help your child by exploring resources on the internet for their research or to further study news topics you may be discussing together. There is rarely a day that goes by that one of my fifth-grade twins isn't Googling something on my phone. When they ask me a question, I often just hand them my phone and say: "You tell me." You can also help your child by having them read their essays or other writings out loud and ask questions about their particular word choice or phrasing. This helps them analyze their own work and be able to justify their ideas. This is also a great age to attend plays or musicals, and it's also good to go see the movie versions of stories after reading the book to do a compare and contrast of the differences.

As mentioned earlier, the most valuable thing you can do at this age to support their academics is the giving of your time for discussion, research, or feedback on their writing. You don't have to have all the answers, but it shows your child the priority you give to their education by the commitment of a certain amount of your time each day to supporting what they are doing in class.

The Least You Need To Know

- The Common Core reading standards for grades 3-5 focus on both informational texts and fictional stories. In these grades, students will begin to have increased exposure to topics related to social studies, history, science, and technical texts.

- Foundational skills such as decoding words and reading with fluency continue to build on each other from year to year, so it is important to master those skills at each grade level.

- Students will start to use writing as a way to put forth their research, explore new ideas, and provide answers to questions.

- Students in grades 3-5 continue to build speaking and listening skills in order to interact productively in the classroom, and begin to differentiate between formal and informal spoken English.

- Reading appropriately challenging texts at each grade level prepares students to be college- and career-ready.

- Reading together at home continues to be an important way for parents to support literacy, even once students are reading confidently on their own.

The ELA Standards for Grades 6-8

The ELA standards for grades 6–8 move students beyond learning foundational skills and ask them to begin applying the skills they have learned. There is more emphasis on students being able to find information, articulate responses, and form opinions through discussion and writing.

In This Chapter

- A summary of the Common Core standards for reading literature and informational texts in grades 6-8

- The Common Core standards for writing in grades 6-8

- The communication skills that are important in grades 6-8

- Examples of the text complexity required for grades 6-8

- How you can support your child in learning the standards

Reading

In the middle school grades, reading begins to incorporate a wider variety of texts, and the level of rigor is increased. Students use their reading skills to complement their argumentative writing skills and their discussion skills. The text complexity increases to the point that some historical documents can be included as texts for students to read and study.

Literature

Grade 6 students learn to cite evidence from the text to support their analysis of what is said explicitly in the text as well as what can be inferred from the text. They must be able to identify a theme or main idea of a text and the way it is conveyed to the reader through specific details, and they must be able to provide an unbiased summary of the text. Students should also be able to describe how a story's plot unfolds, as well as how characters react as the plot moves to its conclusion.

COLLEGE AND CAREER READINESS

Students must be able to analyze texts and explain how specific sentences, paragraphs, and larger sections relate to each other and the text as a whole.

Students in sixth grade should be able to determine the meaning of words and phrases as they are presented in the text, and they must be able to analyze word choice as it affects the meaning or tone of the text. Students are expected to be able to analyze a sentence, chapter, scene, or stanza and determine how it fits into the overall text and how it contributes to the theme of the text. Students must also explain how an author develops the perspective of a narrator or speaker.

Sixth grade students will be expected to compare and contrast the experiences of reading a story, drama, or poem to listening to an audio, video, or live version of the same text. They must compare and contrast how texts in different genres approach the same or similar topics. By the end of the year, students must proficiently read and comprehend literature, such as poems, plays, and stories, at a grade 6–8 text complexity level, with support given as needed at the high end of complexity.

Grade 7 students will be expected to cite several pieces of evidence from text to support their analysis of what the text explicitly says, as well as drawing inferences from the text. They must identify a theme or main idea of a text and how it develops over the course of the text, and students must provide an objective summary of the text. Students in this grade must be able to analyze how certain elements of a story interact, such as how the story's setting shapes the characters.

Students will be expected to determine the meaning of words and phrases as they are presented in the text, and they must be able to analyze how rhymes and other repetitions of sounds affect a verse or stanza in a poem. They must analyze how a play or poem's structure supports its meaning, and students must also analyze how an author develops different perspectives of characters in a text.

Seventh graders will learn to compare and contrast a written story, poem, or play to the audio, film, or stage version. Students will be expected to compare and contrast a fictional version of a time, place, or character and a historical account of the same time period. The student will use this information to see how the authors of fiction sometimes alter history. By the end of seventh grade, students must proficiently read and comprehend literature, such as poems, plays, and stories, at a grade 6–8 text complexity level, with support given as needed at the high end of complexity.

Grade 8 students will be expected to cite several pieces of evidence from text to support their analysis of what the text specifically says, as well as drawing inferences from the text. They must identify a theme or main idea of a text and how it develops over the course of the text, including its impact on characters, setting, and plot, and students must provide an objective summary of the text. Students will learn how to analyze how specific lines of a dialogue or events in a story propel the action and reveal traits of the characters.

Students must determine the meaning of words and phrases as they are presented in the text and analyze how word choice can impact meaning and tone, including analogies. Students in this grade will compare and contrast the structure of two or more texts and analyze how the different structure of each affects its meaning and style. They must also analyze how the differing perspectives of the characters, audience, and reader create effects like humor and suspense.

COLLEGE AND CAREER READINESS

Students must be able to evaluate and use content presented in various media formats ranging from visual to oral.

Eighth graders must analyze a filmed or live production of a story or play to see how faithful it is to the text by evaluating the choices made by the director and actors. They will learn to analyze how a modern work of fiction draws on themes and character types found in myths, traditional stories, and religious works like the Bible, including how it is changed from the original version. By the end of grade 8, students must proficiently read and comprehend literature, such as poems, plays, and stories, at a grade 6–8 text complexity level, with support given as needed at the high end of complexity.

Informational Texts

Grade 6 students learn to cite evidence from the text to support their analysis of what is said specifically in the text, as well as what can be inferred from the text. They must be able to identify a theme or main idea of a text, and explain how it is conveyed to the reader using specific details. They must also be able to provide an unbiased summary of the text. Students will be expected to analyze in detail how important individuals, events, or ideas are introduced, illustrated, and expanded upon in a text. This is done through examples or anecdotes.

Students in sixth grade must determine the meaning of words and phrases as they are used in a text, including technical and figurative meanings. Students will learn to analyze how a particular sentence, paragraph, or chapter fits into the overall text and supports the development of ideas in the text.

Sixth graders must integrate information that is presented in different formats or media to create an understanding of a topic or issue. They must evaluate arguments made in a text and distinguish claims that are supported by reason and ones that are not. Student will also be expected to compare and contrast one author's perspective of events with that of another author. By the end of sixth grade, students should proficiently read and comprehend nonfiction texts at the grade 6–8 complexity level, with support given as needed at the high end of complexity.

Grade 7 students will be expected to cite several pieces of evidence from text to support their analysis of what the text specifically says, as well as drawing inferences from the text. They must identify a theme or main idea of a text and be able to explain how it develops over the course of the text. Students must also be able to provide an objective summary of the text, and they must analyze the interactions between individuals, events, and ideas in a text, such as how individuals influence ideas or events.

Students in this grade will be expected to identify the meaning of words and phrases as they are used in the text, including figurative and technical meanings. They must analyze the structure an author uses to organize a text, such as how major sections contribute to the whole. Students must also determine the author's point of view or purpose in a text and how their position differs from others.

Seventh grade students will be expected to compare and contrast a text to the corresponding audio, video, or multimedia version of the text. They must evaluate arguments in a text and determine whether the reasoning is sound and can support the claims made by the author. Students must also analyze how two or more authors writing on the same topic shape their arguments by emphasizing different evidence. By the end of the year, students should proficiently read and comprehend nonfiction texts at the grade 6–8 complexity level, with support given as needed at the high end of complexity.

DID YOU KNOW?

Because the Common Core emphasizes reading complex texts, students in middle school are prepared to read historical texts, including those related to the founding of the United States.

Grade 8 students will be expected to cite several pieces of evidence from the text to support their analysis of what the text specifically says, as well as draw inferences from the text. They must identify a theme or main idea of a text and explain how it develops over the course of the text, and students must provide an objective summary of the text. They will also analyze how a text makes connections between individuals, ideas, and events.

Students will identify the meaning of words and phrases as they are presented in a text, including figurative and technical meanings, and they will analyze how specific word choice can impact meaning and tone in a text, like using an analogy. Students in this grade will learn to analyze in detail how the structure of a specific paragraph contributes to the overall structure of the text, and they will determine an author's perspective or purpose in a text and discuss how the author responds to conflicting evidence.

Eighth graders will evaluate the advantages and disadvantages of using different methods for presenting information on a topic, such as print, digital text, or video. They must evaluate the arguments made for a specific claim in a text and assess whether the reasoning is sound and if there is enough evidence to support the point. Students must also analyze a case in which two or more texts present conflicting information on the same topic and determine where the texts disagree on matters of fact or opinion. By the end of eighth grade, students should proficiently and independently read and comprehend nonfiction texts at the grade 6–8 complexity level.

Writing

Grade 6 students will be expected to introduce claims and support those claims clearly with evidence using credible sources. They must use words and phrases to clarify the relationships among the claims and reasons given, and they must maintain a formal style of writing through-out their text. Students must also provide a concluding statement or section for the argument that is presented.

Students will learn to introduce a topic and organize ideas using strategies such as compare/contrast or cause/effect, and they will learn how to include graphics and media when appropriate in aiding in comprehension. Students in grade 6 must be able to develop a topic with important facts, definitions, quotations, or other examples to support the topic. They must use appropriate transitions to clarify relationships among ideas and use precise language or subject-specific vocabulary to explain the topic. Students will also be expected to provide a concluding statement or section for the information that is presented.

COLLEGE AND CAREER READINESS

Students must develop and improve writing through planning, revising, editing, rewriting, or trying a new approach.

Sixth grade students will be expected to write narratives to develop real or imagined experiences. Students must orient the reader by establishing context and organizing events so they unfold naturally. They will learn to use techniques such as dialogue to develop events, experiences, and characters. Student will be expected to use a variety of transition words and phrases to convey sequence of events, and they must use precise words to give descriptive details. Students must also provide a conclusion from the experience or event.

Students in sixth grade will learn to produce clear and coherent writing that is appropriate to the task at hand and audience. They will also edit and revise their writing with support and input from peers and the teacher. Students will also learn to use technology to produce and publish writing, as well as working and collaborating with others. Students must have sufficient keyboarding skills to type three pages in one sitting.

Students will be expected to draw evidence from literary or informational texts to support analysis of the text or for research. For example, students will compare and contrast texts in different genres in how they approach similar themes. They will also be expected to evaluate arguments found in a text.

Sixth graders should use multiple print and digital sources to conduct short research projects to answer a question, and they must quote or paraphrase sources while avoiding plagiarism and providing basic bibliographic information. By the end of the year, students should be able to write regularly over short and long time periods for specific tasks, audiences, and purposes.

KEYS TO THE CORE

As students are increasingly being asked to provide evidence to validate their points in speaking and writing, it is important to emphasize the need to do proper citations and give credit where credit is due without plagiarizing.

Grade 7 students will be expected to introduce claims and support those claims clearly using logical reasoning and credible sources, and they must introduce alternate claims. They must use words and phrases to clarify the relationships among the claims and reasons given, and they must maintain a formal style of writing throughout their text. Students must also provide a concluding statement or section for the argument that is presented.

Students will learn to introduce a topic and organize ideas by previewing what is to come and using strategies such as compare/contrast or cause/effect, and they will learn how to include graphics and media when appropriate in aiding in comprehension. Students in seventh grade must be able to develop a topic with important facts, definitions, quotations, or other examples to support the topic. They must use appropriate transitions to clarify relationships among ideas and use precise language or subject-specific vocabulary to explain the topic. Students will also be expected to provide a concluding statement or section for the information that is presented.

Seventh graders will be expected to write narratives to develop real or imagined experiences. Students must orient the reader by establishing context and organizing events so they unfold naturally. They will learn to use techniques such as dialogue to develop events, experiences, and characters. Students will be expected to use a variety of transition words and phrases to convey the sequence of events, and they must use precise words to give descriptive details. Students must also provide a conclusion from the experience or event.

Students in this grade will learn to produce clear and coherent writing that is appropriate to the task at hand and audience. They will also edit and revise their writing with support and input from peers and the teacher. Students will also learn to use technology to produce and publish writing and link to and cite sources, as well as working and collaborating with others.

Students will be expected to use evidence from literary or informational texts to support analysis or research. For example, they may be asked to compare and contrast a fictional portrayal of a particular time period and a historical account from the same time. They should also be able to evaluate the arguments made in a text and assess whether the points made are sound.

Seventh graders should be able to use multiple print and digital sources to conduct short research projects to answer a question, and they must quote or paraphrase sources while avoiding plagiarism and providing basic bibliographic information. Students should also propose questions for future research on the topic. By the end of grade 7, students should be able to write regularly over long and short time periods for specific tasks, audiences, and purposes.

 COLLEGE AND CAREER READINESS

Students must be able to use technology platforms, such as the internet, to publish writing and collaborate with other students.

Grade 8 students will be expected to introduce claims and support those claims clearly with logical reasoning using credible sources, and they must acknowledge and distinguish opposing claims. They must use words and phrases to clarify the relationships among the claims and reasons given, and they must maintain a formal style of writing throughout their text. Students must also provide a concluding statement or section for the argument that is presented.

Students will learn to introduce a topic and organize ideas by previewing what is to come, and they will use formatting strategies like headings and include graphics and media when appropriate in aiding in comprehension. Students in eighth grade must be able to develop a topic with important facts, definitions, quotations, or other examples to support the topic. They must use appropriate transition to clarify relationships among ideas and use precise language or subject-specific vocabulary to explain the topic. Students will also be expected to provide a concluding statement or section for the information that is presented.

Eighth graders will be expected to write narratives to develop real or imagined experiences. Students must orient the reader by establishing context and organizing events so they unfold naturally. They will learn to use techniques such as dialogue to develop events, experiences, and characters. Student will be expected to use a variety of transition words and phrases to convey a sequence of events, and they must use precise words to give descriptive details. Students must also provide a conclusion from the experience or event.

Students in this grade will learn to produce clear and coherent writing that is appropriate to the task at hand and audience. They will also edit and revise their writing with support and input from peers and the teacher. Students will also learn to use technology to produce and publish writing and present relationships between ideas, as well as working and collaborating with others.

Students will be expected to use evidence from literary and informational texts to support analysis and research. For example, they might be asked to analyze how a modern work of fiction mirrors themes or character types from myths or traditional stories and describe how they are made new. They must also evaluate arguments and claims in a text by assessing whether the reasoning is sound and recognize when evidence is introduced that is irrelevant.

Eighth graders should use multiple print and digital sources to conduct short research projects to answer a question, and they must quote or paraphrase sources while avoiding plagiarism and providing basic bibliographic information. Students should also propose questions for future research on the topic. By the end of grade 8, students should be able to write regularly over long and short time periods for specific tasks, audiences, and purposes.

Speaking and Listening

Grade 6 students will be expected to engage in a variety of collaborative discussion formats, including one-on-one, group, and teacher-led. Students must come to discussions prepared by studying required materials and use that preparation to give evidence supporting their thoughts in the discussion. They must follow predetermined rules for peer discussions and define individual roles as necessary. Students must pose and answer specific questions with details in their responses, and they must review the main ideas expressed and demonstrate an understanding of the multiple perspectives given through reflection and paraphrasing.

Students will be expected to interpret information that is presented in various media and formats and explain how it supports the topic being studied and discussed. They must explain the difference between a speaker's arguments that are supported by claims and those that are not supported by claims.

Sixth graders will present findings by sequencing ideas logically and using key facts and details to support the main idea or theme. Students will be expected to use adequate volume and clear pronunciation. Student will learn how to include multimedia components in presentations, and they will also be expected to adapt their speech to a variety of contexts, demonstrating the use of formal English when appropriate.

 COLLEGE AND CAREER READINESS

Students must be able to evaluate a speaker's perspective, ideas, reasoning, and use of evidence to support their points.

Grade 7 students will be expected to engage in a variety of collaborative discussion formats, including one-on-one, group, and teacher-led. Students must come to discussions prepared by studying the required materials, and they must use that preparation to give evidence supporting their thoughts in the discussion. They must follow predetermined rules for peer discussions and define individual roles as necessary. Students must pose and answer specific questions with details in their responses, and students must redirect the conversation back to the topic as needed. They must also acknowledge when new information is given by others and modify their own view when needed.

Students will be expected to analyze main ideas that are presented in various media and formats and explain how they support the topic being studied and discussed. They must explain the difference between a speaker's arguments that are supported by claims and those that are not supported by claims.

Seventh graders will present findings by sequencing ideas logically and using key facts and details to support the main idea or theme. Students will be expected to use adequate volume and clear pronunciation. Student will learn how to include multimedia components into presentations to emphasize important points, and they will also be expected to adapt their speech to a variety of contexts, demonstrating the use of formal English when appropriate.

Grade 8 students will be expected to engage in a variety of collaborative discussion formats, including one-on-one, group, and teacher-led. Students must come to discussions prepared by studying the required materials, and they must use that preparation to give evidence supporting their thoughts in the discussion. They must follow predetermined rules for peer discussions, define individual roles as necessary, and set deadlines as needed. Students must pose and answer specific questions with details in their responses, and students must connect the views of several speakers. They must also acknowledge new information that is given by others and justify or qualify their own views when warranted.

Students will be expected to analyze main ideas that are presented in various media and formats, explain how they support the topic being studied and discussed, and evaluate the motives behind the work (for example, social, commercial, or political). They must explain the difference in a speaker's arguments that are supported by claims and those that are not supported by claims and determine when irrelevant evidence is introduced.

Eighth graders will present findings by sequencing ideas logically and using key facts and details to support the main idea or theme. Students will be expected to use adequate volume and clear pronunciation. Student will learn how to include multimedia components into presentations to increase interest, and they will also be expected to adapt their speech to a variety of contexts, demonstrating the use of formal English when appropriate.

Language

Grade 6 students must ensure that pronouns are in their proper case, and they must use intensive pronouns, such as *myself* and *ourselves*. Students must correct inappropriate shifts in pronoun number or person, and they must also correct when vague pronouns are used. Students must be able to recognize when their own writing and speaking and the writing and speaking of others differs from standard English. They must also use strategies to improve expression in their conventional language.

COLLEGE AND CAREER READINESS

Students must be able to apply their knowledge of language to grasp how language functions in different contexts in order to make effective choices meaning or style. This also supports students in comprehending more fully when reading or listening.

Students in sixth grade should demonstrate command of standard English capitalization, punctuation, and spelling when writing. They should use punctuation to set off elements in a sentence, such as commas, parentheses, or dashes, and students should spell all words correctly. Sixth graders will be expected to use knowledge of language when writing, speaking, reading, or listening to varying sentence patterns for meaning and reader interest. Students should maintain consistency in style.

Students must clarify the meaning of unknown and multiple-meaning words and phrases based on grade 6 content. This means using context as a clue for word or phrase meaning. Students will be expected to use Latin or Greek affixes and roots as clues to the meaning of a word. They will also learn to consult reference materials, such as dictionaries and thesauruses, to find the pronunciation of a word or clarify its meaning or its part of speech.

Sixth grade students must demonstrate an understanding of figurative language and nuances in word meanings. This means interpreting figures of speech in the context presented and using relationships between words to better understand both words. Students must be able to distinguish between words with similar meanings, such as *stingy, scrimping, economical,* and *thrifty.* Students will also be expected to use grade-appropriate and subject-specific words and phrases.

Grade 7 students must explain the function of phrases and clauses in specific sentences, and they must use simple, complex, and compound sentences to signal different connections between ideas. Students will be expected to place phrases and clauses appropriately in sentences and to correct misplaced and dangling modifiers.

Students in seventh grade should demonstrate command of standard English capitalization, punctuation, and spelling when writing. They should use commas to separate coordinate adjectives, and they are expected to spell all words correctly. Students will learn to choose language that expresses ideas precisely and eliminates wordiness.

Students must clarify the meaning of unknown and multiple-meaning words and phrases based on grade 7 content. This means using context as a clue for word or phrase meaning. Students will be expected to use Latin or Greek affixes and roots as clues to the meaning of a word. They will also learn to consult reference materials, such as dictionaries and thesauruses, to find the pronunciation of a word or clarify its meaning or its part of speech.

Seventh graders must demonstrate an understanding of figurative language and nuances in word meanings. This means interpreting figures of speech in the context presented and using relationships between words to better understand both words. Students must be able to distinguish between words with similar meanings, such as *refined, polite,* and *diplomatic.* Students will also be expected to use grade-appropriate and subject-specific words and phrases.

Grade 8 students must explain the function of verbs and how they are used in specific sentences, and they must form and use verbs in active and passive voice. Students should also correct inappropriate shifts in verb voice. Students in eighth grade should demonstrate command of standard English capitalization, punctuation, and spelling when writing. They should use commas, ellipses, and dashes to indicate a pause and ellipses to indicate an omission. They are also expected to spell all words correctly. Students will learn to use verbs in the active and passive voice to achieve certain effects, such as emphasizing the action.

Students must clarify the meaning of unknown and multiple-meaning words and phrases based on grade 8 content. This means using context as a clue for word or phrase meaning. Students will be expected to use Latin or Greek affixes and roots as clues to the meaning of a word. They will also learn to consult reference materials, such as dictionaries and thesauruses, to find the pronunciation of a word or clarify its meaning or its part of speech.

Eighth graders must demonstrate an understanding of figurative language and nuances in word meanings. This means interpreting figures of speech in the context presented and using relationships between words to better understand both words. Students must be able to distinguish between words with similar meanings, such as *willful, firm,* and *resolute.* Students will also be expected to use grade-appropriate and subject-specific words and phrases.

Text Complexity

Text complexity continues to be of great importance in the middle school grades. If students are not reading and comprehending texts that sufficiently challenge them, they will not be able to build the necessary skills they need for college and technical careers.

Appendix C of this book provides more information about text complexity, as well as examples of appropriately complex texts at each grade level. Take some time to review the examples and use them as a guideline for what to expect from your child's school work and what to select for reading at home.

DID YOU KNOW?

Kids who don't read proficiently by grade 4 are four times more likely to drop out of school than those who meet grade-level expectations.

How to Support Your Child

Your child will be spending a good deal of class time supporting or creating arguments in his or her speaking, reading, and writing, and they will be doing short research projects to collect evidence to support a certain perspective. Your child will also be learning how to cite sources and to support their ideas and opinions. Encourage your child to give logical reasons for their opinions on news-related issues or issues within your community. It's not too early to ask their opinion on things like a proposed landfill or increasing local taxes to support schools. Starting early in supporting your child in making rational arguments will continue to benefit them throughout out their academic career, even if it is adult concepts or issues they may not completely understand.

What Can I Do at Home?

Have your child listen to a public figure like a news anchor or policymaker speak on a topic and then ask questions about the main points the speaker made. Encourage them to think critically by coming up with alternative viewpoints or counterarguments and by sharing their own opinion. It is also very valuable to discuss books your child is currently reading. Ask them specific questions that really make them think about what they have read. To give your child context and perspective, visit museums and discuss items of historical and cultural importance. It's also not too early to visit a college campus or the site of an industrial training program. Planting the seed early about life after high school is a valuable perspective as students sometimes wonder, "Why am I doing this?"

As your child enters sixth grade, they will be expected to be able to evaluate arguments to see if the logic and evidence supports the argument a person is trying to make. Watch a news program and ask your child questions about the arguments each side is making and have them choose the best points that are made. You can also read an opinion piece or op-ed in a newspaper and discuss the rationale the author is giving to make their point. Students in middle grades will increasing be asked to perform *close reading*.

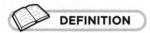 **DEFINITION**

Close reading is the practice of reading and rereading a text that is at the appropriate grade level complexity to gain deeper meaning and comprehension by analyzing key words, phrases, and how ideas unfold.

This means in class your child will read the same text multiple times in an effort to analyze it in a meaningful way that uncovers more information and understanding each time they read it. You can support this at home by encouraging your child to read short articles or parts of a text and discussing new insight they get after each read. The main thing is to emphasize that re-reading a text is not a waste of time.

You can also support your child by having them do historical research about a specific time period because history and social studies texts will be increasingly used as texts for their ELA classes. Help them research the changes your local city or community has undergone in the past hundred years, or have them select a time period and geographic region in which they are interested.

As your child enters seventh grade, they will be doing more research and citing more evidence to support their claims. It is important to help them understand the difference in citing another author or source and plagiarism. This means helping them rephrase content in their own words, while still giving credit to the author for their ideas or direct quoting an author. Direct quoting should be used sparingly, however, since they should be learning how to take information and present it as part of their own argument.

Your child probably has a favorite author or authors by now. Have an ongoing conversation with them about why they like the author and what their favorite books are. It would also be great if you could read some of their favorite books to be able to discuss it with them, and it shows that you are taking an interest in what they like.

When your child is in eighth grade, he or she will be analyzing a lot of material by authors who disagree or have different perspectives on a topic. Having conversations with your child about both sides of an argument helps them better understand the complexities and evidence that can be found. It's a good idea at times to have them take the opposite view that they may have to argue a point. This helps them see both sides and can also help them understand where their evidence for their true beliefs has weaknesses. If you have children close in age, have them debate a topic. You can make this a fun activity by having them give evidence and rationales why the other sibling should be the one to take out the trash that night or another chore.

One of the most powerful things you can do for your child at this age is to show an interest in their interests, like reading one of their favorite books. This shows you are not only giving value to what they value, but it also gives you street cred with them when you want to discuss topics to strengthen their reasoning abilities or when you have an article you want them to read for discussion. If you show them it's a two-way street, you get a lot less resistance when you are supporting their academics at home.

The Least You Need To Know

- The Common Core reading standards focus on informational texts as well as fictional stories. In grades 6-8, students will begin to read more texts related to social studies, history, and science, as well as technical texts.

- Foundational skills in reading build on each other from year to year, so it is important to master those skills at each grade level.

- In grades 6-8, students will start to use writing as a way to put forth their research, explore new ideas, and answer questions, while giving specific supporting evidence.

- Speaking and listening are important skills that are taught so that students can interact productively with their teacher and peers. Strong speaking and listening skills can improve students' understanding of texts and as well as their writing.

- In order for students to be college- and career-ready, they must be reading appropriately challenging texts at each grade level.

- Parents can support the learning that is taking place in their child's class by spending time discussing evidence-based opinions and arguments.

The ELA Standards for Grades 9-12

The ELA standards for grades 9–12 challenge students to dive deeply into texts in order to find evidence to support logical arguments for research projects and opinion pieces. There is an emphasis on working together to improve individual and group work, both in group discussions and online collaboration. Students engage with texts on multiple levels and through multiple presentation mediums. The goal is to immerse students in reading, writing, speaking, and listening in order to provide a complete picture of the content being studied.

In This Chapter

- The Common Core standards for reading literature and informational texts in grades 9-12

- The Common Core standards for writing in grades 9-12

- The communication skills that are important in grades 9-12

- How you can support your child in learning the standards

Reading

In high school, the reading expectations for students become even more rigorous. The levels of text complexity in literary and informational texts are the final building blocks for preparing students to successfully engage in work or studies that require proficient literacy skills. Writing becomes a constant for students as they build out ideas and create evidence-based arguments to support ideas or answers to specific questions.

COLLEGE AND CAREER READINESS

Students must be able to assess how individual perspective or purpose influences the content and style of a text.

Literature

Grades 9-10 students are expected to cite evidence from text to support their analysis of what the text specifically says and to draw inferences from the text. Students must identify the theme or central idea and analyze its development over the course of the text, including how it emerges and is refined by precise details. Students will provide an unbiased summary of a text, and they must also analyze how complex characters develop throughout the text in their interaction with other characters and the development of the plot.

Freshmen and sophomores will determine the meaning of words and phrases based on how they are used in a text. They will be able to identify and explain the impact of word choice on the meaning and tone of the text. They must analyze an author's choices in creating the structure of the text, ordering events, manipulating time, and creating effects like tension or surprise. Students must also analyze a particular point of view or cultural experience that is reflected in a text from outside the United States in an effort to expose students to world literature.

Students must analyze the representation of a topic or key event in two different artistic mediums, identifying qualities such as what is emphasized or what is absent in each work. For example, students might be shown a painting of a battle scene and a journal entry written by a soldier in the same battle and asked to compare and contrast what is shown and described. Students will be expected to analyze how an author transforms source material in a specific work, for example how Shakespeare uses a topic from Ovid or the Bible, or how other authors draw from one of Shakespeare's works.

By the end of ninth grade, students must read and comprehend literature at the grades 9-10 level of text complexity with support at the high end of complexity. By the end of tenth grade, students should be reading and comprehending literature at the grades 9-10 complexity band with no support.

Grades 11-12 students are expected to cite evidence from text to support their analysis of what the text specifically says and to draw inferences from the text, as well as where the text leaves things uncertain. Students must be able to identify two or more themes or central ideas and analyze their development over the course of the text, including how they build on one another. Students will provide an unbiased summary of a text, and they must also analyze the choices an author makes regarding the development of a story or drama, such as where the story is set, how the action is ordered, and how characters are introduced.

Juniors and seniors will determine the meaning of words and phrases based on how they are used in a text. They will also identify how word choice can impact the meaning and the tone of the text, especially language that is engaging and beautiful. They must analyze an author's choices in creating the structure of the text and how it contributes to the overall meaning and aesthetics. Students must also analyze a case in which understanding a certain perspective requires distinguishing what is directly stated from what is actually meant, such as sarcasm, satire, or irony.

Students in eleventh and twelfth grades must analyze multiple interpretations of a poem, story, or play and evaluate how each version interprets the common source text. (Teachers must include at least one play from Shakespeare and one play from an American dramatist in the curriculum.) Students will be expected to demonstrate knowledge of eighteenth-, nineteenth-, and early-twentieth-century foundational works of American literature. This includes explaining how two or more texts from the same time period treat themes or ideas that are similar.

By the end of their junior year, students must read and comprehend literature at the grade 11 level of text complexity with support at the high end of complexity. By the end of their senior year, students should be reading and comprehending literature at the high end of grade 11 complexity with no support.

Informational Texts

Grades 9-10 students will be expected to cite strong evidence from the text to support an analysis of what the text is explicitly saying, as well as what can be inferred. Students should be able to determine a central idea of a text and analyze its development throughout the text, including how it is shaped by specific details. They should also be able to provide an unbiased summary of the text. Students must analyze how the author presents a series of events or ideas and the connections that are drawn between them.

COLLEGE AND CAREER READINESS

Student must be able to evaluate the merits of an argument in a text and validate whether there is sufficient evidence to support the claims or ideas.

Students in these grades must determine the meaning of words and phrases as they are used in the text, including figurative and technical meanings, and they must identify the impact of word choice on the tone of the text. Students will be expected to analyze how an author's ideas or claims are refined by specific sentences, paragraphs, or large sections of a text. They must also determine an author's perspective or purpose in a text and explain how the author uses rhetoric to support the perspective or purpose.

Freshmen and sophomores will be expected to analyze multiple accounts of a subject told through different mediums and identify which details are emphasized in each account. For example, they might look at the famous painting that depicts Washington crossing the Delaware, read a poem about the crossing, and read an account of the event from the time.

Students must be able to evaluate the argument and specific claims in a text by assessing whether the reasons given are valid and the evidence sufficient. They must also identify false statements and misleading reasoning. Students will analyze seminal documents of historical and literary significance in the United States, such as the Gettysburg Address and Roosevelt's Four Freedoms speech, and discuss how they address similar concepts and ideas.

COLLEGE AND CAREER READINESS

Students must be able to proficiently read and comprehend complex literary texts and informational texts on their own without support.

By the end of their freshman year, students must proficiently read and comprehend literary nonfiction at the grades 9-10 level of text complexity, with support as needed at the high end of complexity. By the end of their sophomore year, students should proficiently read and comprehend literary nonfiction at the high end of the grades 9-10 level of text complexity with no support.

Grades 11-12 students will be expected to cite strong evidence from the text to support an analysis of what the text is explicitly saying as well as what can be inferred, and they must be able to determine where the text leaves matters uncertain. Students should be able to identify two or more central ideas of a text and analyze their development throughout the text, including how they are shaped by specific details and how they build on each other. They should also be able to provide an unbiased summary of the text. Students must analyze how the author presents a series of events or ideas and the connections that are drawn between them.

Students in these grades must determine the meaning of words and phrases as they are used in the text, including figurative and technical meanings. Students will be expected to analyze how an author's structure makes points clear and engaging. They must also determine an author's perspective or purpose in a text and explain how the author uses rhetoric to support the perspective or purpose.

High school juniors and seniors will be expected to analyze multiple accounts of a subject told through different mediums in order to address a question or solve a problem. Students must evaluate the reasoning in seminal texts from U.S. history, including the application of constitutional principles and the premises and arguments made in public advocacy works, such as presidential addresses.

 COLLEGE AND CAREER READINESS

Students must be able to analyze two or more texts that discuss similar topics and compare the approaches the authors take.

By the end of eleventh grade, students must proficiently read and comprehend literary nonfiction at the grade 11 level of text complexity, with support as needed at the high end of complexity. By the end of twelfth grade, students should proficiently read and comprehend literary nonfiction at the high end of the grade 11 level of text complexity with no support.

Writing

Grades 9-10 students will be expected to write arguments to support claims in an analysis of substantive topics, and they must use valid reasoning and sufficient evidence to support their ideas. Students must be able to introduce a specific claim, distinguish that claim from opposing claims, and create a clear relationship between the claims, evidence, and counterclaims. They must be able to develop claims and counterclaims fairly by supplying evidence for both sides, while pointing out strengths and weaknesses of each.

Students must use words and phrases to link major sections of text to create cohesion and clarify relationships between claims, evidence, and counterclaims. Students should maintain a formal style in their writing and unbiased tone, and they must provide a concluding statement or sections that support the argument that has been presented.

COLLEGE AND CAREER READINESS

Students must conduct short and sustained research to answer specific questions posed to them and demonstrate an understanding of the topic being researched.

Students will be expected to write informative texts to examine and convey complex ideas clearly and accurately through the analysis of content. They must introduce a topic and organize complex ideas and information to make important connections. Students should include formatting, graphics, and multimedia when useful in supporting comprehension.

Students will be expected to develop the topic with sufficient facts, definitions, concrete details, and quotes. They should use varied transitions to link major sections of the text and clarify the relationships among complex ideas. Students must use precise language and subject-specific vocabulary to manage the complexity of the topic being discussed. Students should maintain a formal style and objective tone in their writing, and they will be expected to provide a concluding statement or section that supports the explanation that has been presented.

COLLEGE AND CAREER READINESS

Students must be able to collect information on a topic from multiple print and digital sources. Students should be able to determine the credibility of the sources and integrate the information into their work while avoiding plagiarism.

High school freshmen and sophomores will be expected to write narratives to develop real or imagined experiences. They will engage the reader by putting forth a problem, establishing multiple points of view, and introducing a narrator and/or characters. Students will use narrative techniques, such as dialogue, reflection, and multiple plot lines, to develop events and characters. They must also provide a conclusion that reflects what is experienced over the course of the narrative.

Students will be expected to produce clear writing in which the development and style are appropriate to the task and audience, and they must develop and strengthen writing through revising, editing, and rewriting. Students will be expected to use technology to produce, publish, and update individual or group writing projects.

Students must conduct short- and long-term research projects to answer a question or solve a problem, and they should incorporate multiple sources on the subject. Students should gather relevant information from multiple sources in print and digital formats, including using *advanced searches* in an effective manner. They are expected to integrate information into the text selectively to maintain the flow of ideas and avoid plagiarism. Students will draw from evidence from literary or informational texts to support analysis and research, such as analyzing how an author draws on source material in a specific work. For example, they may examine how Shakespeare addresses a theme from the Bible. They should also assess whether the reasoning given by authors is valid and if there is enough evidence to support ideas.

 **DEFINITION**

Advanced searches use digital libraries and search engines on the internet to conduct searches in scholarly journals beyond a basic Google search. These digital libraries often require a fee the school pays each year in order to access information in journals specific to subjects like science or history.

Students in grades ninth and tenth grades should write regularly over extended time frames and shorter time frames for a wide range of tasks and audiences.

Grades 11-12 students will be expected to write arguments to support claims in an analysis of substantive topics, and they must use valid reasoning and sufficient evidence to support their ideas. Students must be able to introduce a specific claim, distinguish that claim from opposing claims, and create a clear relationship that logically sequences the claims, evidence, and counterclaims. They must be able to develop claims and counterclaims fairly by supplying evidence for both sides, while pointing out strengths and weaknesses of both and accounting for audience values. Students must use words and phrases to link major sections of text to create cohesion and clarify relationships between claims, evidence, and counterclaims. Students should maintain a formal style in their writing and unbiased tone, and they must provide a concluding statement or sections that support the argument that has been presented.

Students will be expected to write informative texts to examine and convey complex ideas clearly and accurately through the analysis of content. They must introduce a topic and organize complex ideas and information to make important connections. Students should include formatting, graphics, and multimedia when useful in supporting comprehension.

Students will be expected to develop the topic by selecting the most important facts, definitions, concrete details, and quotes. They should use varied transitions to link major sections of the text and clarify the relationships among complex ideas. Students must use precise language and subject-specific vocabulary to manage the complexity of the topic being discussed. Students should maintain a formal style and objective tone in their writing, and they will be expected to provide a concluding statement or section that support the explanation that has been presented.

COLLEGE AND CAREER READINESS

Students must be able to collect evidence from literary and informational texts to support their own analysis, ideas, and research.

High school juniors and seniors will be expected to write narratives to develop real or imagined experiences. They will engage the reader by putting forth a problem, establishing multiple points of view, and introducing a narrator and/or characters. Students will use narrative techniques, such as dialogue, reflection, and multiple plot lines, to develop events and characters that lead to a particular outcome. They must also provide a conclusion that reflects what is experienced over the course of the narrative.

Students will be expected to produce clear writing in which the development and style are appropriate to the task and audience, and they must develop and strengthen writing through revising, editing, and rewriting. Students will be expected to use technology to produce and publish individual or group writing projects and update them in response to ongoing feedback or to include new information.

Students must conduct short- and long-term research projects to answer a question or solve a problem, and they should incorporate multiple sources on the subject. Students should gather relevant information from multiple sources in print and digital formats, including using advanced searches in an effective manner. They are expected to integrate information into the text in a selective manner to maintain the flow of ideas and avoid plagiarism. Students will draw from evidence from literary or information texts to support analysis and research.

Students will be expected to demonstrate knowledge of eighteenth-, nineteenth-, and early-twentieth-century foundational works of American literature. This includes explaining how two or more texts from the same time period treat themes or ideas that are similar. Students must evaluate the reasoning in seminal texts from U.S. history, including the application of constitutional principles and the premises and arguments made in public advocacy works, such as presidential addresses.

High school juniors and seniors should also write regularly over extended time frames and shorter time frames for a wide range of tasks and audiences.

COLLEGE AND CAREER READINESS

Students must consistently write over sustained longer periods while engaging in things like research and shorter times when in engaging in specific tasks in class.

Speaking and Listening

Grade 9-10 students will be expected to initiate and participate in a range of discussion formats, including one-on-one, group, and teacher-led. Students will converse with diverse partners, building on others' ideas and conveying their own ideas clearly and persuasively. Students must come to discussions prepared by reading all materials being studied and explicitly draw on that preparation by referring to evidence and ideas from texts and other research on the issue being discussed.

Students must work with peers to make rules for discussion and to set clear goals, deadlines, and individual roles as needed. They should propel conversation by posing and answering questions that relate the discussion to broader ideas, and actively incorporate others into the discussion by clarifying, verifying, or challenging ideas. Students must also respond thoughtfully to diverse points of view and be able to summarize points of agreement and disagreement.

COLLEGE AND CAREER READINESS

Students must present information and supporting evidence so that listeners can follow a clear line of reasoning that is appropriate to the audience.

Students should integrate multiple sources of information from diverse media or formats, and they should evaluate a speaker's perspective, reasoning, and use of evidence by identifying any false reasoning or exaggerated claims.

Students will be expected to present information, findings, and evidence in a clear and concise manner that listeners can follow and is appropriate to the audience and task. They must make strategic use of digital media in presentations to enhance understanding and add interest. Students will also be expected to adapt speech to a variety of contexts and tasks and demonstrating command of formal English when appropriate.

COLLEGE AND CAREER READINESS

Students must make use of digital media and visual displays of data to express ideas and support the understanding of a presentation.

Grade 11-12 students will be expected to initiate and participate in a range of discussion formats, including one-on-one, group, and teacher-led. Students will converse with diverse partners, building on others' ideas and conveying their own ideas clearly and persuasively. Students must come to discussions prepared by reading all materials being studied, and explicitly draw on that preparation by referring to evidence and ideas from texts and other research on the issue being discussed.

Students must work with peers to set rules for civil discussion and to set clear goals, deadlines, and individual roles as needed. They should propel conversation by posing and answering questions that relate the discussion to broader ideas, and they should actively incorporate others into the discussion by clarifying, verifying, or challenging ideas. Students must also respond thoughtfully to diverse points of view and be able to summarize points of agreement and disagreement and identify areas where research is required to complete a task or deepen the investigation.

Students should integrate multiple sources of information from diverse media or formats in order to make informed decisions, and they should evaluate a speaker's perspective, reasoning, and use of evidence by assessing stance, word choice, premises, and tone used.

COLLEGE AND CAREER READINESS

Students must be able to adapt their speech to different contexts and tasks by showing command of formal English when appropriate.

Students will be expected to present information, findings, and evidence in a clear and concise manner that listeners can follow and is appropriate to the audience and task. They must make strategic use of digital media in presentations to enhance understanding and add interest. Students will also be expected to adapt speech to a variety of contexts and tasks and demonstrate command of formal English when appropriate.

Language

Grades 9-10 students will be expected to use parallel structure and various types of phrases and clauses to convey specific meaning and add interest to writing or presentations. Students must demonstrate a command of standard English capitalization, punctuation, and spelling when writing. They must use a semicolon to link two or more independent clauses, use a colon to introduce a list of quotations, and spell all words correctly.

COLLEGE AND CAREER READINESS

Students must be able to use context clues, references, and analyze word parts to determine the meaning of an unknown words or multiple-meaning words.

Students must use their understanding of language to understand how language functions in different contexts in order to make effective choices for meaning and style. They will be expected to write and edit a work that conforms to the guidelines in a style manual appropriate for the subject and writing type.

High school freshmen and sophomores will be expected to clarify the meaning of unknown or multi-meaning words and phrases by choosing flexibly from a range of strategies. They will use context as a clue to meaning and identify patterns of word changes that indicate different meanings or parts of speech. Students should consult reference materials, such as dictionaries and thesauruses, in print and digital form to determine or clarify the precise meaning of words.

COLLEGE AND CAREER READINESS

Students must show they can identify and differentiate figurative language, relationships between words, and minor differences in the meanings of words.

Students must demonstrate an understanding of figurative language, word relationships, and small nuances in word meanings. They will be expected to interpret euphemisms in context and analyze their role in a text, and students also must acquire and accurately use subject-specific words sufficient for reading, writing, speaking, and listening at the college and career readiness level.

Grades 11-12 students will be expected to use parallel structure and various types of phrases and clauses to convey specific meaning and add interest to writing or presentations. Students must demonstrate a command of standard English capitalization, punctuation, and spelling when writing. They must also use a semicolon to link two or more independent clauses, use a colon to introduce a list of quotations, and spell all words correctly.

Students must use their understanding of how language functions in different contexts to make effective choices for meaning and style. They will be expected to write and edit a work that conforms to the guidelines in a style manual appropriate for the subject and writing type.

High school juniors and seniors will be expected to clarify the meaning of unknown or multi-meaning words and phrases by choosing flexibly from a range of strategies. They will use context as a clue to meaning and identify patterns of word changes that indicate different meanings or parts of speech. Students should consult reference materials, such as dictionaries, glossaries, and thesauruses, in print and digital form, to determine or clarify the precise meaning of words.

 COLLEGE AND CAREER READINESS

Students must acquire and correctly use a range of academic and subject-specific words and phrases at a college and career readiness level for each grade. Students should also be able to gather vocabulary knowledge when they encounter an unknown word that directly relates to comprehension or expression.

Students must demonstrate an understanding of figurative language, word relationships, and small nuances in word meanings. They will be expected to interpret hyperbole and paradox in context and analyze their role in a text, and students also must acquire and accurately use subject-specific words sufficient for reading, writing, speaking, and listening at the college and career readiness level.

Text Complexity

Text complexity continues to be a key component in academic success. By the end of high school, students should be able to read and comprehend texts at the level they will be expected to meet when they enter college or a career. In order to reach this point, using appropriately challenging texts throughout their high school career is critical.

As previously discussed, determining text complexity is not an exact science. Appendix C of this book provides more information as well as some examples of appropriately complex texts for grades 9–12. Review these examples and use them as a benchmark for the level of reading material your student should be using in class and at home.

 DID YOU KNOW?

It is estimated that more than $2 billion is spent each year on the students who repeat a grade because they have reading problems.

How to Support Your Child

Your child will be reading a greater variety of texts when they enter high school. There will be a focus on more informational texts than in previous grades, and historical accounts and authentic documents like the U.S. Constitution and Declaration of Independence will be utilized more as a learning medium. They will use writing much more as a way to articulate their arguments, and writing will be emphasized in other subjects besides their English/language arts classes. It will be even more important for them to be able to cite material and make logical arguments based on evidence they have collected from multiple sources.

In high school, your child will be reading and analyzing many historical documents. This is a great discussion point for you both as you probably studied some of these same documents in school or are aware of them through cultural context. Talk about how some of these documents or speeches influenced our country and help your child make historical connections related to a document or speech from the past to the present. Your child will be analyzing and writing about events, ideas, and theories like never before, so the more you can have discussions that challenge your child to exercise some of these skills, the better aligned you will be at home to what your child is learning in the classroom.

It is a good idea to meet with your child's guidance counselor during their freshman year to discuss the goals your child might have after high school. This gives a clearer picture of what they need to do the next four years to prepare for those goals. They don't have to lock in to a specific career, but if they can at least discuss their interests, it will help formulate a plan for preparing them. There are career inventories that guidance counselors can assist you with that help students narrow down what fields they may be interested in based on their skills and interests.

It's also important for them to be involved in extracurricular activities beyond sports that help support their academic progress as well, such as drama club, the debate team, or a book club. Ultimately, a big part of high school is having at least a loosely-developed plan for what your child wants to do after graduation in order to maximize their time in high school.

The Least You Need To Know

- The Common Core reading standards focus on informational texts as well as just fictional stories. In grades 9-12, students will increase their use and study of historical documents, scientific texts, and technical texts.

- Students will start to use writing as a way to put forth their research, new ideas, and answers to questions, while giving specific supporting evidence.

- Speaking and listening are important skills that are taught so that students can interact productively with their teacher and peers on projects to improve their understanding of texts and improve their writing.

- Each grade has an appropriate measure of text complexity that challenges students to read at a level that prepares them to be college- and career-ready.

- Parents can support the learning that is taking place in the classroom by discussing topics and encouraging their child to make connections between ideas, evidence, and theories.

Common Core Literacy Across Other Subjects

In addition to the main ELA standards, beginning in grade 6, the Common Core includes separate literacy standards that support more in-depth learning in other subjects outside of English and language arts. They focus on three key areas of study: history and social studies, science, and career and technical subjects. These literacy standards promote and support reading for deeper understanding in the content area. They also promote and support writing to explain or argue ideas or opinions in that subject based on evidence. These standards act as a guide on how students can engage the content in ways beyond just memorizing facts but also learning how to analyze and apply information in meaningful ways.

In This Chapter

- How other disciplines are supported by the Common Core literacy standards

- The role of the arts in the Common Core standards

- Using the Common Core writing standards in other content areas

It's important to recognize that these are literacy standards that support other disciplines; not standards for the disciplines themselves. The developers included these additional ELA standards because reading and writing are critical to success in nearly every field, and learning how to apply literacy skills effectively for discipline-specific purposes is important in preparing students to enter college and careers.

Literacy Standards for Science and Technical Subjects

Science and technical subjects are enhanced by the emphasis given to evidence-based arguments and research, as well as by the expectation that students produce technical and process-based writing. The use of technology to research information and create presentations that explain concepts and processes is also useful for scientific and technical subjects.

Grades 6–8

In their science and technical classes, middle school students will be expected to cite specific evidence to support an analysis of a technical or scientific text. They must determine the main ideas or conclusions of a text and present an accurate summary of the text that is unique from prior opinions. Students must also be able to carry out an experiment by following precisely a multistep procedure, taking measurements, and other technical tasks.

 DID YOU KNOW?

There have been movements the past two decades to "read across the curriculum" or "write across the curriculum," but in many cases this simply meant reading or writing more in other subjects, with little attention given to the specific literacy skills needed for other subjects or application of those skills. The Common Core is very deliberate in developing the specific literacy skills students need to more deeply engage subjects other than English.

Students will learn to determine the key terms, symbols, and other subject-specific words and phrases as they are used in writing and discussion for grade-appropriate topics. They must be able to analyze the structure authors use to organize texts, such explaining how major parts contribute to the whole and help the reader understand the topic being discussed. Students will also be expected to analyze the author's purpose in providing explanations, descriptions of procedures, or discussions of an experiment in the text. For example, an author's purpose in some texts might be to entertain or retell an event, whereas in scientific texts, the author's purpose is usually to support, defend, or explain a scientific theory or process. When a student analyzes the purpose, they must determine what the author is trying to accomplish and if his or her arguments are sound.

Middle school students will be expected to integrate quantitative or technical information that is expressed in word form in the text and make a visual representation of that same information, like a flowchart, graph, diagram, or table. Students must explain the difference among facts, judgments based on research, and speculation in a text. They must be able to compare and contrast information that is learned from experiments, simulations, videos, or other multimedia sources and what they read in a text that is on the same topic. By the end of eighth grade, students must be able to proficiently and independently read and comprehend science and technical texts in the grade 6-8 text complexity level.

Grades 9–10

High school freshman and sophomores will be expected to cite specific evidence from text to support an analysis of science and technical texts, while attending to specific details of descriptions or explanations. They must be able to determine the central ideas or conclusions of a text, follow the explanation of a complex process, and provide an accurate summary of the text. Students will also be expected to precisely follow complex procedures with multiple steps when performing an experiment, taking measurements, or performing a technical task, while also addressing *special exceptions* defined in the text.

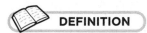 **DEFINITION**

> A **special exception** is when a process or substance doesn't act in a typical way. For example, when dry ice is continually heated, it doesn't melt into a liquid and then turn into a gas as regular ice does. Instead, it sublimates, or turns directly from a solid into a gas when heated.

Students will learn to determine the key terms, symbols, and other subject-specific words and phrases as they are used in writing and discussion. They must be able to analyze the structure authors use to form relationships among key terms, such as *force, friction, reaction force,* and *energy*. Students will also be expected to analyze the author's purpose for providing explanations, descriptions of procedures, or discussions of an experiment in the text. They must also be able to define the question the author is seeking to answer.

Ninth and tenth graders must be able to translate quantitative or technical information that is expressed in words in a text into visual forms, like a table or chart, and in turn, they must be able to take information expressed visually or mathematically and express it in words.

They will learn to assess the extent to which an author's claim or recommendation for solving a problem is supported by reasoning and evidence. They must also be able to compare and contrast findings presented in a text to findings from other sources, including their own experiments, and they must note when findings support or contradict previous explanations. By the end of tenth grade, students must be able to proficiently and independently read and comprehend science and technical texts at the grade 9-10 text complexity level.

 **TAKE CARE**

Remember, text complexity is not limited to fiction works, poems, or other literature. Text complexity is an important factor in every subject at every grade level in order to support the literacy goals for students each year.

Grades 11–12

High school juniors and seniors will be expected to cite specific evidence to support an analysis of science and technical texts, while identifying any gaps or inconsistencies in the account. They must be able to determine the central ideas or conclusions of a text, follow the explanation of a complex process, and paraphrase the process in a simpler way. Students will also be expected to precisely follow complex procedures with multiple steps when performing an experiment, taking measurements, or performing a technical task, while also addressing special exceptions defined in the text.

Students will learn to determine the meaning of key terms, symbols, and other subject-specific words and phrases as they are used in context. They must be able to analyze the structure authors use to put information into categories or hierarchies and demonstrate an understanding of this structure. For example, an author might put different high-energy foods into categories of healthy sugars and unhealthy sugars. Students would be asked to explain what the difference is between healthy and unhealthy sugars, put foods into one of the two categories, or explain the process the body used to absorb and use both kinds of sugars.

Students will also be expected to analyze the author's purpose for providing explanations, descriptions of procedures, or discussion of an experiment in the text and identify issues that remain unresolved.

Juniors and seniors must integrate and evaluate information from multiple sources and formats in order to address a question or solve a problem. They will learn to evaluate a hypothesis, data, and conclusions in a scientific or technical text, while verifying the data and supporting or challenging the conclusions that were drawn using other sources of information. Students will also be expected to synthesize information from many sources, such as experiments or texts, into a clear understanding of a process or phenomenon in order to resolve conflicting information. By the end of grade 12, students must be able to proficiently and independently read and comprehend science and technical texts in the grade 11 text complexity level.

 DID YOU KNOW?

Being able to read, comprehend, and reproduce steps in an experiment is one of the skills that many college students struggle with when they enroll in lab science classes. Common Core standards put a great deal of emphasis in teaching students to understand process thinking and create their own processes as well.

Literacy Standards for History and Social Studies

The ELA standards support history and social studies by incorporating primary and secondary source materials as subject references. These sources also provide great material for gathering evidence to compare differing ideas and perspectives on historical events. By applying the Common Core standards in their reading and writing, students are utilizing skills in critical thinking, analysis, and the presentation of ideas at a much deeper level than just memorizing important dates and events.

Grades 6–8

In their history and social studies classes, middle school students must be able to analyze *primary and secondary sources* and cite specific evidence to support their analysis. They must also be able to determine the main ideas of primary and secondary sources and provide a summary of the source that is distinct from prior opinions. For example, students might read a textbook chapter about Nazi occupation in Europe and then read an account of the experience written by a Jewish person living in Poland. The student would analyze both texts and discuss the things in common, as well as the ways the two accounts differ from each other.

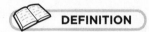
DEFINITION

> A **primary source** is a document that was written during the time being studied. Examples of primary sources include important historical documents such as the Declaration of Independence and United States Constitution, as well as documents that provide a firsthand account of a particular time or event such as letters, journals, or newspaper articles.
>
> A **secondary source** is a document that is written after an event occurs that provides a secondhand account, perspective, or analysis. A biography or history book would be a secondary source.

Students will also learn to identify key steps in a text's description of a process related to history or social studies, such as how a bill becomes a law or how interest rates are raised and lowered.

Students in grades 6–8 will be expected to determine the meaning of words and phrases as used in texts, including vocabulary that is specific to topics relating to history or social studies. They must describe how a text presents information, such as sequentially, comparatively, or causally. They will also learn how to identify aspects of a text that explain an author's perspective or purposes, like the avoidance of certain facts or loaded language.

Middle school students will be required to integrate visual information, such as graphs, charts, photographs, maps, and videos, with other information that is in print or digital text. They must learn to distinguish between facts, opinions, and reasoned judgments that are found in a text, and they must also analyze the relationship between a primary source and a secondary source that are written on the same topic. By the end of eighth grade, students must proficiently and independently read and comprehend texts on topics related to history or social studies at the grades 6–8 level of text complexity.

Grades 9–10

During their freshman and sophomore years, students will continue to be expected to cite specific evidence to support their analysis of primary and secondary sources, while making sure to attend to such features as the date and origin of the information they collect. They must identify the main ideas or information of a primary or secondary source and provide an accurate summary of how key events develop over the course of the text. Students must also be able to analyze in detail a series of events that are described in a text and determine if earlier events caused later events. For example, students could study the international events that resulted in the conflicts leading to World War I, and then research to see if similar events led to the conflicts that resulted in World War II.

Students will learn to determine the meaning of words and phrases in the context they are used in texts, including vocabulary that relates to political, social, or economic dynamics in history or social studies. They must analyze how a text uses structure to highlight key ideas or support and explanation. Students will be expected to compare the perspective of two or more authors in how they treat the same topics, such as which details they include in their respective versions of the events.

Students in these grades must integrate quantitative or technical analysis, like charts, with a qualitative analysis in a print or digital text. They must assess the extent to which evidence given in texts supports the claims the author makes, and they must compare and contrast the explanations of the same topic in multiple primary and secondary sources. By the end of tenth grade, students must proficiently and independently read and comprehend texts on topics related to at the grades 9-10 level of text complexity.

Grades 11–12

By their junior and senior years of high school, students will be expected to cite specific evidence to support an analysis of primary and secondary sources and to connect the smaller details that contribute to the text as a whole. For example, students might be asked to analyze the memoirs of Theodor Roosevelt from his time with the Rough Riders and compare that account with historical narratives. Students would discuss discrepancies or embellishments and see if multiple secondary sources support each other's account or Roosevelt's account and give specific evidence as to why.

Students must identify the central idea of a primary or secondary source and provide an accurate summary that makes clear the connections between key details and ideas. Students will learn to evaluate different explanations for actions or events in order to determine which explanation best aligns with the evidence from the text and to acknowledge where things are left uncertain. An assignment that would support these standards would be to take information from multiple sources on a topic like drilling for oil in the arctic and summarize what the student considers the best evidence for or against the idea. The student would also identify areas he or she felt there was not enough evidence to support a claim and needed more research to fill a gap in the literature.

 KEYS TO THE CORE

Speeches are great primary sources for students to read. They offer candid perspectives from political figures or leaders who were intimate with the actions of the time.

Students will learn how to determine the meaning of words and phrases based on how they are used in a text, including how the author refines the meaning of a particular word or phrase throughout the text. They must analyze how a complex primary source is structured, including how larger portions of the text contribute to the whole. Students must also evaluate the different perspectives of two or more authors on the same historical event or issue by assessing the claims, reasoning, and evidence of each.

Students in these grades must integrate and evaluate information from multiple sources and formats in order to address a question or solve a problem. They must evaluate an author's claims by supporting or challenging them with other information. Students will also be expected to integrate information from diverse primary and secondary sources coherently and note discrepancies among sources. For example, a student might be asked to research what battle that took place on American soil had the most impact on our history and compare it to a battle that a historian felt was the most important. The student would also compare their ideas and evidence to other students in the class and defend their position.

By the end of their senior year, students must proficiently and independently read and comprehend texts on topics related to history and social studies at the grade 11 level of text complexity.

The Arts

In general, the arts are considered classes in music, drama, and visual arts like painting. Although there are no specific Common Core standards for the arts, educators in these subjects have embraced the standards and integrated them into their instructional practices. The following are brief overviews of some of the ways that Common Core standards are used with the three main domains of the arts.

Drama

Reading and analyzing a drama is referenced or suggested in each grade level of the literacy standards. Analyzing a text version of a drama or a performance plays an important role in developing critical thinking skills. Students are asked to explain how specific lines or stanzas contribute to the meaning of the action, and they are also asked to analyze the different perspectives and motivations of characters.

Drama can also be used in supporting the speaking and listening standards as students act out plays or create their own original work based on the topic being learned. Dramas can also be used as a way to convey information as a type of presentation. Students would hone the skill of writing and speaking and listening through this type of activity.

KEYS TO THE CORE

A great way for students to support critical thinking skills is to read a story or play and then do a comparison of a dramatized version or movie. It offers students the chance to compare and contrast main events and the consistency of the roles of characters.

Art

Analyzing and interpreting visual art helps support students in developing their critical thinking and evaluation skills. There are seventeen places the literacy standards ask students to analyze and explain the relationships between a text and images or illustrations in the text. Students are also required to explain the different roles of an author and an illustrator of a story and how each of them helps convey the ideas within a story. Students must understand the role of images or graphics and their relationship to actions, events, characters, or the main ideas of a text. Students are also required to occasionally incorporate images into their writing or presentations when it better supports the argument or ideas being conveyed.

Music

The only specific standard referencing a task with music is a grade 2 standard that requires students to describe how words affect rhythm and meaning in a song. The literacy standards all deal specifically with analyzing text, so music can be a great medium to study for interpreting emotions and the intent of the composer. Music can also be used as part of the media integration in presentations, especially supporting the speaking and listening standards.

Writing for Specific Disciplines

The writing standards for discipline-specific content areas differ from the ELA standards, which cover more generic skills and content related to reading and writing. Discipline-specific writing acknowledges that teachers in different subjects gather, share, and analyze information in distinct ways, so the way students write in those subjects must also be nuanced to those distinctions as well. For example, students in history or social studies spend a great deal of time analyzing and discussing primary and secondary sources, and in science classes, students spend a great deal of time analyzing and discussing processes and theoretical ideas. Each class requires a different kind of writing to discuss and explain the student's ideas and answers to questions.

Grades 6–8

Students in grades 6–8 will be expected to write arguments focused on subject-specific content. They must introduce claims about a topic, acknowledge the opposing claims, and give evidence that logically supports their position. They must support claims with using accurate data and credible sources. Students will use words and phrases to create relationships among claims and counterclaims, while maintaining a formal style in their writing. Students must also provide a concluding statement or section that supports the argument that has been presented. For example, a science class might discuss and study the process of fracking to extract natural gas. Students could be asked to write arguments for or against the process based on evidence found in printed and online texts.

Students must write informative texts, such as a narration of a historical event, an explanation of a scientific procedure, or a description of a technical process. They will learn to introduce a topic clearly by previewing what is to follow. They must organize ideas and information into broader categories and include headings, graphics, and multimedia when it is useful in supporting comprehension. Students must develop the topic with relevant facts, definitions, details, quotations, and examples. They must use appropriate transitions to create and clarify relationships among ideas, and they must use precise language and subject-specific vocabulary to explain the topic. Students must also establish and maintain a formal style and unbiased tone, and they must provide a concluding statement or section that supports the information being presented. An example of an assignment that would put these skills into practice might be found in a technical class that requires students to write a narrative to accompany a presentation that explains the easiest way to build a simple website for a community club.

Students will learn to produce clear and coherent writing using a style and organizational structure appropriate to the task and audience. With support from the teacher and peers, students will develop their writing as needed through planning, revising, editing, and trying new approaches. Using technology, students will produce and publish writing and present their ideas on the relationships between information in an efficient way.

Middle school students will conduct short research projects to answer questions posed by the teacher or generated themselves. They will draw on several sources to come up with additional questions that support multiple avenues of exploration. Students will gather relevant information from several print and digital sources by using search terms effectively. They will assess the accuracy of each source and quote or paraphrase the conclusions of others, avoiding plagiarism. Students will also draw evidence from informational texts to support analysis and their research. Students in grades 6–8 will be expected to write consistently over short and long periods of time for several different subject-specific tasks and audiences.

Grades 9–10

High school freshmen and sophomores will also be expected to write arguments focused on subject-specific content. They must introduce claims about a topic, acknowledge opposing arguments, and give evidence that logically supports their position. They must develop claims and counterclaims fairly, using accurate data and credible sources. Students will use words and phrases to create relationships among claims and counterclaims, while maintaining a formal style in their writing. Students must also provide a concluding statement or section that supports the argument that has been presented. For example, students might be asked to take an opposing or supporting position for the practice of clear-cutting areas of forest. Students would have to support their arguments with evidence from multiple sources and present them in a way that attempts to convince the reader that their position makes the most sense.

 DID YOU KNOW?

Argumentative writing, which requires students to present an opinion supported by evidence, is one of the best ways to determine the level of knowledge a student has gained on a topic. It also provides a good exercise in critical thinking and application of skills needed for comparing and contrasting ideas.

Building on the skills they developed in earlier grades, freshmen and sophomores must write informative texts, such as a narration of a historical event, an explanation of a scientific procedure, or a description of a technical process. They will learn to introduce a topic clearly by previewing what is to follow. They must organize ideas and information into broader categories and include headings, graphics, and multimedia when it is useful in supporting comprehension.

Students must develop the topic with relevant facts, definitions, details, quotations, and examples that are appropriate to the audience's knowledge of the topic. They must use appropriate transitions to create and clarify relationships among ideas, and they must use precise language and subject-specific vocabulary to explain the topic based on the expertise of the readers. Students must also establish and maintain a formal style and unbiased tone, and they must provide a concluding statement or section that supports the information being presented, while also articulating the significance of the topic.

An assignment that incorporates these skills might be to research and write on how a historical event like the Louisiana Purchase impacted the North American continent and contributed to the rise of the United States as a powerful nation. Students would have to analyze the infrastructure and economic situation of bordering countries and territories at that time, the diplomatic situation between nations and territories in North America, and the opportunities this afforded the United States. As you can see, students would have to research multiple sources and factor in different perspectives and variables when presenting their ideas and supporting evidence.

Students will learn to produce clear and coherent writing using a style and organizational approach appropriate to the task and audience. Students will develop their writing as needed through planning, revising, editing, and trying new approaches. Using technology, students will produce and publish writing and present their ideas on the relationships between information in an efficient way. They will update individual or shared writing, such as collaborative blogs, as new information becomes available.

Ninth and tenth graders will conduct short research projects to answer specific questions. They will draw on several sources to generate additional questions that support multiple avenues of exploration and show an understanding of the subject being investigated. Students will gather relevant information from several print and digital sources by using search terms effectively. They will assess the accuracy of each source and quote or paraphrase the conclusions of others, while avoiding plagiarism. Students will also draw evidence from information texts to support analysis and their research. Students in grades 9 and 10 will be expected to write consistently over short and long periods of times for a variety of subject-specific tasks. An example of a project utilizing these standards might be to ask students to research the life expectancy for someone living in California in 1914 compared to someone in 2014 and list and analyze the reasons for any differences.

Grades 11–12

High school juniors and seniors will be expected to write arguments focused on subject-specific content using more complex and sophisticated strategies than they have in previous years. They must introduce claims about a topic, acknowledge opposing arguments, and give evidence that logically supports and sequences their claims. They must develop claims and counterclaims fairly using reasoning based on accurate data and credible sources, while taking into account their audience's biases, knowledge level, and values. Students will use words and phrases to create relationships among claims and counterclaims, while maintaining a formal style in their writing. Students must also provide a concluding statement or section that supports the argument that has been presented.

An example of a project like this that students might be required to undertake would be to study the impact on the fish population in a region since the construction of a dam on the major tributary. Students would analyze and discuss the economic, environmental, and community impact that followed the construction of the dam.

As they have in other years, students must write informative texts, such as a narration of a historical event, an explanation of a scientific procedure, or a description of a technical process. They will learn to introduce a topic clearly by previewing what is to follow. They must organize ideas and information into broader categories and include headings, graphics, and multimedia when it is useful in supporting comprehension. Students must develop the topic with relevant facts, definitions, details, quotations, and examples that are appropriate to the audience's knowledge of the topic. They must use appropriate transitions to create and clarify relationships among ideas, and they must use precise language and subject-specific vocabulary to explain the topic. This includes using metaphors, analogies, and similes in response to the expertise level of the readers.

For example, if the student knows the reader is very knowledgeable in science, they could use a more complex metaphor that relates specifically to that subject. For example, "The results for the two experiments were as different as a proton and electron," or "We feel our results are as solid as matter at zero degrees Kelvin."

Students will learn to produce clear and coherent writing using a style and organizational approach that are appropriate to the task and audience. Students will develop their writing as needed through planning, revising, editing, and trying new approaches. Using technology, students will produce and publish writing and present their ideas in a shared format to continually update their text in response to ongoing feedback that includes new arguments or information.

Juniors and seniors will conduct short research projects to answer a specific question from the teacher or a question they generate themselves. They will draw on several sources to generate additional questions that support multiple avenues of exploration and show an understanding of the subject being investigated. Students will gather relevant information from several print and digital sources by using search terms effectively. They will assess the accuracy of each source and quote or paraphrase the conclusions of others, avoiding plagiarism and overreliance on one source. Students will also draw evidence from information texts to support analysis and their research.

The Least You Need To Know

- The Common Core includes literacy standards in history and social studies, science, and technical subjects for grades 6–12.

- Subject-specific literacy standards address the skills students need to read, understand, and explain informational texts in different disciplines.

- Subject-specific writing standards take into account the different ways information is gathered, analyzed, and explained in different disciplines.

- The Common Core standards can be integrated into arts education, such as drama, music, and visual arts.

The Math Standards

This section explains the math standards for each grade. The explanations are written in a way that is not too technical and highlights major concepts that support the necessary skills students need to progress successfully to the next grade. Since math is an intimidating subject for many people, helpful advice is presented that you can use to support your child as they progress through the math standards each year.

The Math Standards for Grades K–2

The Common Core standards for mathematics are built on a desire to create math standards that are both coherent and focused. The designers of the standards have taken to heart extensive research on mathematics education in high-performing countries, and want to challenge the current "mile wide and an inch deep" curriculum that they believe is holding back mathematics achievement in the United States. To that end, the standards are designed to do more than teach students mnemonic devices for formulas and instead build students' competency in understanding, applying, and justifying mathematical skills.

This chapter will introduce some of the foundational skills that underpin the mathematics standards and summarize the Common Core standards for mathematics in grades K–2. It will also provide some helpful guidance for supporting your child's developing math skills at home.

In This Chapter

- The foundational skills supported by the standards

- The counting skills that are important for kindergarten

- The operations and early algebra skills that are important in grades K–2

- The measuring, time-telling, and money skills that are important in grades K–2

- The geometry skills that are important in grades K–2

- How you can support your child in learning the standards

Foundational Skills Supported by the Common Core

The Common Core mathematics standards consider both the understanding of mathematical concepts and the procedural skill needed to apply and solve math problems as equally important. They emphasize word problems, reflecting the Common Core standards for reading and writing and the focus on informational texts. They also emphasize numbering and computation, algebraic and geometric concepts, and other math skills needed in the real world, whether in a career or post-secondary school study..

Additionally, the standards hope to encourage students to "persevere," a word that's found in the recommended practices at every level. Math can be daunting when new concepts are introduced, and frustrating at every level. Thinking like a mathematician is not easy to grasp for many young people. Students will need to learn to keep at it.

Another word that pops up frequently is "precision." Getting close to the right answer may seem good enough, especially for young children, but the demand for precision grows as the student matures. Encouraging careful measuring, describing, and other work at a young age will help students prepare to be precise in their later years of school and beyond.

Finally, the standards emphasize "structure." As with all of the Common Core standards, the math guidelines encourage skill-building amongst students by careful scaffolding within the standards. Math can be an odd, chaotic subject for schools that aren't sure how to schedule and build a curriculum. The standards' suggestions hope to help to ease some of that chaos and allow a natural progression in learning.

 KEYS TO THE CORE

As with the reading and writing standards, the math standards do not dictate curriculum or teaching methods. Teachers have the discretion to teach topics in math in the order they best see fit for each class.

Counting

Kindergarten is the only grade level in which this category, or domain, appears with suggested standards. That's because counting skills are the basis for all math, and students must have a good grasp of them before more complex mathematical problem solving is possible. Kindergarteners are taught and asked to use a great deal of math-related vocabulary, including numbers themselves ("1, 2, 3…"), mathematical concepts ("If I take away two, how many are left?"), and geometric figures (e.g., *square, cube,* and *circle*).

By the end of kindergarten, students should be able to count to 100 by ones and by tens. They should also be able to count to 100 from any given number; for example, if a kindergartener is given the number of "56," they should be able to count forward from there, and not need to return to 1 to begin. Kindergarten students should also be able to write the numbers from 0 to 20.

Kindergarteners who are ready to progress on to grade 1 should be able to tell the number of objects they are shown (up to 20), and be able to compare numbers. For example, students might be shown a pile of blocks and asked to determine how many are in the pile, or to look at two bowls with candies in them to determine which bowl holds more candies.

Operations and Early Algebra Skills

Operations is the term the Common Core standards use for what most people think of as plain old math: adding, subtracting, and, eventually, dividing and multiplying numbers. These skills are emphasized in the early elementary grades in order to form a good foundation for higher-level math. While it may seem strange to think of simple calculations as "early algebra," doing so does help us remember that these skills are building blocks for what's to come. Also included under this section are the Common Core standards for working with place value. Learning to work with larger numbers (including decimals and fractions) necessitates understanding place value.

Kindergarten

In kindergarten, students should be able to understand addition as (according to the Common Core's language) "putting together and adding to" and subtraction as "taking apart and taking from." Kindergarten students are encouraged to talk through problems aloud, using vocabulary that is comfortable to them.

Students are expected to develop the ability to compute both numeric and word problems within 10, and to understand that there's more than one way to reach a set numerical goal. In other words, students should be able to understand that 5+1 and 4+2 will both equal 6. Notice that 10 is the highest number students are expected to use for computing, even though they should be able to count up to 20. This shows the expectation that students can begin to work with and understand numbers higher than they can actually compute.

These standards suggest that kindergarteners should be able to "work with" numbers from 11-19. This is not a contradiction, but rather means that they should understand 11-19 as being able to be broken down into ones and "further ones." For example, 12 is "10 ones" (or, "one, two, three, four, five, six, seven, eight, nine, ten ones") and "one, two ones." Again, this provides a foundation for much more complex operations with tens and ones in higher grades. Parents who are not familiar with this way of thinking about numbers may want to ask the child's teacher for clarification and help, as it can be confusing. You should strive to use the same methods for speaking about numbers with your child as they are learning in school.

DID YOU KNOW?

Children are often asked by the adults who care for them to "count to ten." Expanding on this skill by presenting a further challenge, such as "Count how many dogs you see. Are there more cats than dogs?" is an easy way to reinforce the standards.

Grade 1

As with the standards for ELA, the Common Core standards for math are designed to build on what students have already mastered. Thus, the standards for grade 1 assume that students have mastered the kindergarten standards and are ready to move on.

Now students are asked to work within 20 in adding and subtracting, and several strategies are suggested for teachers to choose from in order to help students. Make sure you understand which strategy your child's teacher chooses, so that you can use similar language at home.

Word problems are emphasized, using language that builds on what they learned in kindergarten. Students are also encouraged to understand the underlying properties of operations and the relationships between numbers. For example, a teacher might ask students to find the number "that makes 9 when added to 3" (6). This introduces the concept of an unknown into mathematical reasoning, which will be very important in higher grades. As you may recall, algebra is essentially solving for unknowns. Math equations are also introduced, so the formal language of math is now part of a student's vocabulary. First graders know the meaning of the equal sign (=) and are expected to use it.

Just as kindergarteners counted beyond 10 in order to develop an awareness and beginning facility with higher numbers, students in grade 1 should be able to count up to 120 just to get familiar with larger numbers. (Of course, some students will be able to work with numbers higher than 120 and that's great. Just because standards don't ask for more than the stated skill during this year doesn't mean children can't learn past them.)

The standards also suggest that first graders comprehend that the two digits in a two-digit number represents the amount of tens and ones. Thus, the number 60 is "six tens." This is a step up in complexity from understanding all numbers as variations of "ones" in kindergarten. Also, grade 1 students should be able to use the greater than (>) and less than (<) symbols as well as the equal sign to compare numbers. Finally, students should be able to add and subtract two-digit numbers, understanding that they should add the tens to the tens and the ones to the ones, and that it might be necessary to compose a ten when doing so.

This last concept might seem particularly difficult to grasp for parents or guardians who learned math in another way, but it's easy once you understand. For example, a grade 1 student might need to add 48 and 50. They will need to think of adding 4 tens and 5 tens (90) and eight ones and zero ones (8) to arrive at the final answer of 98. If the problem was 48 plus 52, they will need to think of 4 tens and 5 tens (90) and eight ones and two ones (10), adding up to 100, or 10 tens.

 KEYS TO THE CORE

It can be tricky to remember which symbol means "greater than" and which means "less than." Children are often advised that the "mouth" wants to eat the larger number. Take a look:

   5 > 4 (5 is greater than 4).

   4 < 5 (4 is less than 5).

These examples are obvious, but the symbols are used in much more complex math in the future.

Grade 2

Second graders are expected to be able to "fluently" subtract and add within 100, and to be able to solve word problems that have more than one step. They should also learn to "fluently" add and subtract within 20 "using mental strategies." These aren't supposed to be code words: "Fluently" indicates that a student can do it without a struggle, while "using mental strategies" means that they don't need to count aloud or calculate using ones and tens on paper or on their fingers to do this kind of problem.

The concept of odd and even numbers appears for the first time in grade 2. The standards suggest that that students learn to count by twos or "by pairing up" objects. Students will also see grids more frequently, and be asked to calculate how many objects are in that grid. For example, a student might be shown a checkerboard with five columns of white checkers that are five rows high. They could be asked to "write an equation to express the total as a sum of equal addends."

Having mastered tens and ones, second graders are ready for hundreds, which introduces another way of talking about numbers. They will learn that 100 is ten tens. For example, the number 151 is made up of 1 hundred, 50 tens and 1 one. Students in grade 2 should also be able to count to 1,000, and—a new idea—be able to "skip count" by fives, tens, and hundreds. (Skip counting to 50 by tens would mean 10, 20, 30, 40, 50.) Many teachers will call this "counting by fives" (or tens or twenties).

Additionally, second grade students learn to write numbers up to 1,000 in a variety of ways, as well as compare them using >, <, and = symbols. This means that students learn to write out numbers ("nine hundred and fifty-one") as well as use numerals ("951") and ones, tens and hundreds ("9 hundreds, 50 tens, and 1 one"). In some schools, they may learn to write in computer code, as well.

Second graders are expected to be fluent in adding and subtracting within 100, and to be able to implement strategies they've learned that involve place value. This is another way of saying that they should be able to understand how hundreds, tens, and ones work in mathematics. They'll also begin adding and subtracting numbers within 1,000, using a variety of methods as taught to them this year. While they are expected to add and subtract within 1,000 while employing writing, there is an additional expectation that a second grader can *mentally* add or subtract 10 or 100 to a number between 100-900. Notice that the complexity is limited by only using 10 or 100 in this grade. Later grades will introduce less user-friendly numbers.

Students also should be able to explain why different math strategies yield the correct answer. This refers back to the expectation that the Common Core standards for mathematics will help students understand why the math works instead of simply announcing the right number.

Measuring, Time-telling, and Money Skills

Within these standards, students are tasked with describing the "measurable attributes" of objects. In grade 1, they also begin to understand and tell time. And, in grade 2, they are introduced to mathematical properties of money.

Kindergarten

To develop beginning measuring skills, children in this grade might be asked to state whether something is taller than it is wide. Students are also asked to compare objects with a measurable attribute in common. They might be asked to line up by height, for instance, which allows the children to make comparisons between each other. Notice how this standard emphasizes observation instead of numerical measurement at this stage. Students are taught to refine and trust their observational skills.

> **KEYS TO THE CORE**
>
> Notice how the standards for the lower grades anticipate what students will need to know in higher grades. The ability to estimate length, for example, will be helpful in higher geometry.

Grade 1

First graders are moving into using measuring and data collection that builds on the language-based work they did as kindergarteners. Instead of just describing the qualities of what they see generally, they begin to use simple mathematical measuring concepts.

They now should be able to compare three objects by length and be able to articulate which object is the longest, and which is the shortest. They will also be able to use a smaller object to measure the length of a larger object. A student might be given a piece of wood the length of an index card and be asked to measure is the length of a table in card-lengths. Or, they could be asked to measure something by hand-width.

Telling and writing time are introduced in this grade; note that students should be able to interpret both digital and analog clocks. Many teachers will emphasize being aware of time as part of a well-functioning grade 1 classroom, but time will also be considered as a numeric concept.

Grade 2

Second graders use the measuring skills they developed in kindergarten and grade 1 but also learn to use standard measurement tools, including rulers and measuring tapes. They learn to measure the same object by different length units, too; for example, they might measure a desk in both feet and inches, and discuss how the two are related. They also learn to estimate lengths and to employ their subtraction and addition skills in word problems that involve length. For example, a teacher might ask his students to calculate the length of two pieces of string laid end to end.

Geometry

As with the other mathematical standards, here students are beginning their foundational grasp of geometric principles. Don't worry; your young children are not going to be asked to figure out the area of a triangle or anything as complicated as that. But, once again, the emphasis here is on precision and perseverance, so that when it is time for theories and formulas, they will have the foundational skills down.

Kindergarten

Graduating kindergarteners should be able to identify and describe shapes (the standard specifies "squares, circles, triangles, rectangles, hexagons, cubes, cones, cylinders, and spheres") as well as their positions in relation to each other, as in "The cube is *behind* the sphere." It is especially important for young children to understand that just because they cannot see a shape doesn't mean that it isn't there (or measurable). Understanding that some objects are two-dimensional, or flat, and others are three-dimensional, or solid, is necessary as well.

Kindergarteners are also asked to work with shapes as well as identify them. They might be asked to describe ("analyze") them, compare them, make models of them or compose larger shapes out of smaller shapes (for example, using two squares to make a rectangle).

Grade 1

In their understanding of shapes, first graders should be able to describe distinguishing features of shapes as well as non-defining attributes. A student can be shown a variety of shapes and be able to point out that all the triangles have three sides, but that a number of shapes, both triangles and other forms, can be "large" or "blue." Sorting is an important part of geometry practice at this age.

Building shapes from smaller pieces (both in two and three dimensions) is still part of the standards, with some complexity expected, and, finally, the concept of portions is introduced, asking students to divide two-dimensional shapes into two and four equal shares, and using words like "halves" and "quarters." Also, phrases such as "half of" and "fourth of" are introduced. These concepts create a foundation for later, more complex ideas in geometry.

KEYS TO THE CORE

Notice that the standards at this level emphasize the use of vocabulary that is used in everyday life. Teachers are not encouraged to have students use specific math jargon (such as "right rectangular prism") but instead learn words such as "interpret" and "reason" which will be used in many classes and careers. Similar vocabulary is used in other Common Core standards.

Grade 2

Second grade geometry is when line diagrams are introduced. These become more important in higher math, but at this level they are simply a way to show integers equally spaced on a line. This helps children understand how space can reflect numerical value, and introduces them to graphing, which is important in later geometry.

Second graders are also expected to improve their ability to tell time, being able to write down the time from either an analog or digital clock to the nearest five minutes. They should also understand and use the abbreviations A.M. and P.M.

Money joins time as a practical use of math that students learn about. They are expected to solve word problems involving dollar bills, quarters, dimes, nickels, and pennies, as well as use dollar sign ($) and cents symbol (¢) correctly. Parents and guardians should note that money appears somewhat abruptly in the grade 2 standards, and making sure your child is familiar with the different coins before second grade is a helpful way to prepare them for this part of the suggested curriculum.

The ability to present data is also an important part of the grade 2 math standards. Students are expected to be able to take down data (perhaps by measuring a series of similar objects) and then plot that data on either a picture graph or a bar graph. They should also be able to interpret and come to conclusions from data presented in the same way. For example, a student might be asked to measure the rainfall in a jar outside a classroom over the course of several weeks. They would then use that collected data to make a bar graph that shows how many inches of rain fell.

Finally, second graders are asked to both identify and be able to draw shapes with a specific attributes, such as a given number of angles or faces. A teacher might ask a student to draw a shape with three angles (a triangle) or six square faces (a cube). Being able to evenly divide a rectangle into equal-sized squares builds on grade 1 skills, while students are also expected to be able to divide circles and rectangles into equal shares. Vocabulary such as "halves, thirds, half of, a third of" and so on is also expected. Additionally—and importantly—the idea that equal shares may not have the same shape is introduced.

How to Support Your Child

Students' math skills progress significantly from kindergarten to grade 2. The foundational skills of kindergarten are the building blocks for the far more complex tasks and skills of grades 1 and 2, which are, in turn, necessary for the higher grades. Mastering each grade's skills is necessary for success in higher grades; after all, how can a student learn to compare and graph measurements in second grade if they do not learn how to measure correctly in kindergarten and first grade?

The good news is that there are many ways to support your child's academic development in math skills. There's no need to enforce a nightly diet of dull worksheets; math skills are needed in regular life, and finding ways to help your child use them is not only key, but much more fun.

The ability to count to 10 or 20 is often prized as a great way to show off by parents and guardians, but encouraging your child to do more is simple. During preschool and kindergarten, ask your child to count objects in your home or when out and about. If you ask your child to count seven apples, take one away and challenge them to figure out how many are left. As the child gets older, construct math problems using what's around you. If you are cleaning up toys, for example, ask your child to count the number of toys, then take away a few and count them again. This supports early addition and subtraction skills. First- and second-graders should be encouraged to do math in their heads, so give your child a few problems to calculate while out and about, or ask them to help you figure out if you can go into the "12 items or less" lane at the supermarket if you add in three more items.

Measuring is another key skill for students at this age. If you have to measure something, such as a piece of fabric or the back of the sofa, show your child what you're doing. Show younger children how they can measure using their hand lengths. Make sure you give them the chance to use the information gathered, such as by measuring a picture in hand lengths and then checking to see if it will fit on the wall. As your child gets older, help them measure on their own. Challenge your child to figure out how many inches long the hallway is, or to use a height chart to calculate how much they've grown. Classifying and sorting objects is important, too, so your child might like to try sorting their toys or books into categories by color or approximate weight.

You can greatly help your child by making them familiar with telling time and using money. For younger children, this can be as simple as pointing out the time on a clock (remember to use both digital clocks and clocks that have hands), or counting your pocket change. As children get older, they can be encouraged to keep track of time ("Let me know when five minutes are up") and to make change, perhaps at a store with a patient cashier.

KEYS TO THE CORE

If your home is almost entirely digitalized in telling time, buying an inexpensive wall analog clock for your child's room can help him learn how to read one.

Geometry skills must also be developed at this age. Many young children have toys that are clearly cubes, spheres, or pyramids. Help your younger child describe and sort these. As your child gets older, challenge them to find shapes in and out of the home, and help him articulate the qualities of these shapes. ("Triangles have three sides and make three points," for example.) It's helpful to have your child learn to sort shapes by qualities such as color or size as well as by strict definition.

Emphasize to your child that using math skills is a necessary part of life. It's easy for even very young children to start to believe that math is difficult (an idea adults may reinforce by saying words to that effect). You can help your child feel mastery over their math skills by making sure it's clear how needed they are. Talk to your child's teacher about what your child needs to work on, and don't be shy about asking any questions you may have about newer ways of doing math.

Finally, pay attention to the skills that will be taught in the coming year over the summer. You can help your child practice and prepare for the coming school year if you casually introduce some of the coming year's curriculum before school begins. Even practicing computation over the summer and using the math vocabulary your child learned can be very helpful.

The Least You Need to Know

- The Common Core math standards at K-2 emphasize developing early skills in algebra and geometry as well as standard math.

- There is an emphasis on word problems throughout the math standards.

- Each grade's standards expect a significant step forward in developing both theoretical and practical math skills.

- As students progress from kindergarten to grade 2, it is expected that students will move from competency in ones and tens to hundreds and then to thousands.

- Standards are set up so that students demonstrate ability, then fluency in math skills, followed by the ability to calculate problems mentally.

- Students in grades K-2 must learn to tell time, use money, and work with geometric shapes.

The Math Standards for Grades 3–5

Mathematics concepts and skills in the later elementary years begin to develop abstract thinking, but there is also an emphasis on memorizing things like multiplication tables. Students will be exposed to more complex word problems, and they will also learn about fractions and decimals. These grade levels also teach students about weights and measures and how to use these concepts in real life situations. Students will also get a rudimentary understanding of graphing and creating or finding points on a graph. As you will see, students are challenged to apply knowledge and skills in meaningful ways that apply to their lives.

In This Chapter

- The operations and early algebra skills that are important for grades 3-5

- The skills in working with fractions that are key for grades 3-5

- The measuring skills that are important for grades 3-5

- The geometry skills that are crucial for grades 3-5

- How you can support your child in learning the standards

Operations and Early Algebra Skills

In prior grades, "operations" in math referred to adding and subtracting. Now, multiplication and division will be taught as well. You can expect to see the problems becoming more complex, both in the size of the numbers involved as well as in the properties of the actions students will learn to take. By grade 5, students will be forming equations that reflect significant complexity in operations performed.

Grade 3

Grade 3 teachers are encouraged by the Common Core standards to build on the sorting principles children were taught in earlier grades. As students begin to understand multiplication and division, the standards suggest that they "interpret products *of whole numbers*"—that is to say an equation such as 6 × 3—as the total number of objects in six groups of three objects each. Similar logic is used in division, when, for example, 90 divided by 3 is presented as 90 partitioned equally into 3 shares for 30. Thinking this way about multiplication and division allows students to build on concepts they learned earlier in their schooling, instead of making these operations seem troublingly new and complex.

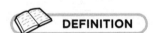 **DEFINITION**

> **Whole numbers** are positive integers of any denomination: 0, 1, 2, 3 ....
> Whole numbers cannot be negative or fractional. Whole numbers do not
> use a decimal.

Third graders should also be able to use multiplication and division within 100 to solve word problems using the same sort of thinking. And third graders should be able to solve for an unknown whole number in an equation. For example, a third grader could determine which number might solve 8 × _____ = 24 or ___ ÷4 = 5. Learning to think this way is helpful for later grades when students will be asked to "solve for *x*" and similar operations.

Rounding whole numbers is a new skill for third graders. A student might be asked to round 6, 13, and 78 to the nearest 10, for example. (Answers: 10, 10, and 80). Remember that rounding to the nearest 10 may mean going down in numbers.

Third graders continue to work with place value (as a reminder, those are the ones, tens and hundreds) and are expected to be fluid in adding and subtracting using this style of operation. As part of this, students should be able to multiple any one-digit number by any multiple of 10 (up to 90), understanding how to do so through place value. Thus, a student asked to multiply 9 × 30 would find the answer to be 24 tens and 0 ones = 240, or 2 hundreds, 4 tens, and 0 ones.

KEYS TO THE CORE

Remember that when a standard suggests students work "within 100," it means that their competency by the end of the year should include being able to solve any problem within that 1 to 100. It doesn't mean students won't work with higher numbers.

Grade 4

By this year in school, students are expected to be able to use all four operations (addition, subtraction, multiplication, and division) with whole numbers. They should be able to decipher a word problem in order to know whether to solve for an unknown number with multiplication or addition.

In other words, fourth graders should be able to decide on the best way to move forward with the problem, and not be dependent on addition if multiplication is more efficient. Students in grade 4 will also be presented with multi-step word problems, requiring more than one operation (e.g. they might have to add, then divide). They are expected to figure out which operation to perform first, and then to use the resulting solution in the next needed operation.

Factors are introduced in grade 4, a very important part of mathematical skill. *Factors* are the numbers you can multiply to get another given number. Students should be able to find all *factor pairs* for whole numbers between 1 and 100.

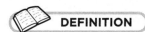

DEFINITION

A **factor pair** is the term used for two numbers that, when multiplied, result in another given number. For example, the factor pairs of 24 are: 1 and 24, 2 and 12, 3 and 8, and 4 and 6.

Fourth graders also learn to determine whether a given whole number from 1-100 is *prime* or *composite*.

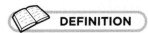

DEFINITION

A **prime number** is a whole number greater than 1 that cannot be divided by any number except itself and 1. 2 and 3 are prime numbers.
A **composite number** is a whole number that can be divided by at least one other number besides itself and 1. 4 is the first composite number.

Fourth graders are encouraged to generate and analyze patterns in numbers, and to formulate hypotheses about the continuing pattern. A student might be asked to "add 3" to the starting number 1, and look at the sequence that results: 4, 7, 10, 13, 16. The student might predict that the sequence will continue switching between odd and even numbers, and give their reasoning why this will happen. Notice that the pattern identification and prediction by itself isn't enough; in keeping with the standards' usual interests, students must also explain *why* they think the pattern will continue. They must understand the principles behind how numbers work in order to do so.

In addition, fourth grade students learn about place value in multi-digit whole numbers. In other words, a student understands that a digit in one place represents ten times what it represents in the place to its right. In 777, the first 7 is ten times the second 7, which is ten times the last 7. Students use this knowledge to help them round multi-digit whole numbers to any place. Being able to do such rounding is helpful when asked to find the characteristics of the answer (e.g. "larger than 500"), but not necessarily the precise answer in a problem.

Finally, in multiplication, students can multiply up to a four-digit number (that is, a number in the thousands, such as 5,682) by a one-digit number (5,682 × 4), and two two-digit numbers together (e.g., 65 × 89). They should also be able to divide to find quotients and remainders with up to four-digit dividends and one-digit divisors.

This is the first time in the Common Core standards that these words appear, so here's a quick review: a *quotient* is the whole-number result of division (in other words: the answer). A *remainder* is the amount left over. The *dividend* is the original number to be divided, and the *divisor* is the number with which one is dividing. In the problem 88 divided by 8, 88 is the dividend and 8 is the divisor. The quotient is 11, and there is no remainder in this problem. In other words, fourth graders should be able to divide numbers as large as 9,999 by numbers as large as 9, and understand that in some problems they will get an uneven result.

Grade 5

For many people, "algebra" means writing equations, and in grade 5, this skill is finally taught. Fifth graders learn to use parentheses (also called "brackets" or "braces") in numerical equations, as well as how to calculate the numbers within them. Students are expected to be able to write such calculations as well, translating words into an equation. For example, a student might be given the phrase "add 5 and 6, then multiply by 3" and be able to write "3 × (5 + 6)."

The ability to estimate recurs in this grade, too. By the end of the year, students in fifth grade should understand that 4 × (5,000 + 941) is four times larger than 5,000 + 941 without actually calculating the problem. Students should also be able to compare two patterns in strings of numbers and notice aspects of those patterns.

Students should understand the place value system, building upon what they learned in prior grades. They're expected to be able to articulate how digits in larger numbers reflect the power of 10. More importantly, students at this level are now working with decimals. They learn to read and write them to the thousandths, such as in 5.001.

Working with Fractions

You most likely know that a fraction is a part of a whole. In math, a fraction is thought of as a part of a whole number. Fractions are written with one number over the other, as in $\frac{1}{2}$. In that fraction, the 1 is the top number, called the *numerator*, which shows how many you have. 2, the bottom number, is the *denominator*, which shows how many parts the whole has been divided into. In other words, you have one of the two halves. Students in grades 3–5 spend much of their math class learning about fractions, if the administration is using the Common Core standards at their school.

Grade 3

Students are introduced to fractions this year, and begin to learn about their properties. They also learn to mark fractions on a number line; for $\frac{1}{2}$, they learn to make a mark exactly halfway between 0 and 1. Students also learn that fractions with different numerators and denominators can be equal, so that $\frac{1}{2} = \frac{2}{4}$, and $\frac{4}{6} = \frac{2}{3}$. Again, they learn to plot this on a number line as well as to write it out. And they learn that whole numbers can be expressed as fractions ($3 = \frac{3}{1}$, for instance), an important concept for when they begin to calculate with fractions.

Finally, they learn to compare fractions, beginning to understand that comparisons can only be correct when the fractions refer to the same whole. Note that graders are expected to master only fractions that have 2, 3, 4, 6 or 8 as their denominator, although, as always, they may work with larger denominators.

Grade 4

By the time they finish fourth grade, students have learned to break a fraction down into the equivalent equation. They'll know that $\frac{a}{b}$ is equal to $\frac{n \times a}{n \times b}$, for example. They will also understand how to compare two fractions with different numerators or denominators by creating a common denominator or numerator. For example, you can compare $\frac{1}{3}$ and $\frac{5}{6}$ by multiplying the first fraction by 2, so that the denominators match: $\frac{2}{6}$ and $\frac{5}{6}$. Students in this grade are only asked to work with fractions that have the denominator 2, 3, 4, 5, 6, 8, 10, 12 or 100.

Fourth graders also learn to add and subtract fractions, which will also involve creating a common denominator. Another new skill is multiplying a fraction by a whole number. This might mean a problem such as $6 \times \frac{1}{4} = \frac{6}{4}$, or $3 \times \frac{2}{5} = 6 \times \frac{1}{5} = \frac{6}{5}$. Students continue to work with word problems as well, particularly those involving fractions. The Common Core standards give the following example: "If each person at a party will eat $\frac{3}{8}$ of a pound of roast beef, and there will be 5 people at the party, how many pounds of beef will be needed?"

Lastly, fourth graders understand that decimal notation can be used for fractions. They learn to use decimal notation for fractions with denominators 10 or 100, so that .57 is rewritten to be $\frac{57}{100}$. A common task would be to ask students to translate a series of fractions into decimals. They also continue to use the number line to plot solutions, as a precursor to graphing.

Grade 5

By the end of fifth grade, students should be adept at adding and subtracting fractions. Being able to add or subtract fractions with unlike denominators should not be a difficult challenge. (This means that your child will know that to add $\frac{2}{3}$ and $\frac{5}{4}$, and they'll convert the fractions to a common denominator of 12. Thus, $\frac{8}{12} + \frac{15}{12} = \frac{23}{12}$.) Word problems continue to present mathematical challenges in grade 5, most often using decimals and fractions (or both) and asking students to move from one to the other.

Also, students can multiply and divide fractions. They understand that a fraction specifies the division of the numerator by the denominator so that $\frac{4}{5}$ means 4 divided by 5 ($\frac{a}{b} = a$ divided by b). They can also multiply and divide fractions by whole numbers.

Multiplying fractions by resizing them is part of the Common Core standards. Students learn that they can use fractions to complete comparisons about size and do not need to compute the actual equation. All of these operations are often presented in word problems, asking students to set up the equation, not just solve for it. A typical example from the standards reads: "If 9 people want to share a 50-pound sack of rice equally by weight, how many pounds of rice should each person get?" This grade is the first time the word "real-world" appears in the math standards, showing a new emphasis on math skills that are needed in life outside the classroom.

DID YOU KNOW?

Many math teachers will take pains to emphasize to students how the ability to calculate with fractions and decimals is a necessary skill in careers ranging from fashion design to teaching to nursing to mechanical work of all kinds.

Measuring Skills

By third grade, students are expected to have competency in telling time and using money, as well as in measuring and comparing lengths of objects with standard tools. Now, the standards in measurement grow more complex, involving more than just length, while students fine-tune basic time skills (money skills are not mentioned in the standards for these grades). This is all part of preparing students for being able to participate fully in geometry as well as chemistry and other advanced science classes.

Grade 3

Students are expected to tell time to the nearest minute and measure time intervals in minutes. They'll also learn to calculate amounts of time using addition and subtraction to the nearest minute.

In other measuring skills, third graders begin to use liquid volume and mass measurements, including grams, kilograms, and liters. They're asked to calculate one-step work problems with these measurements, such as looking at a beaker filled with liquid and calculating how much has evaporated over the course of a week. In measuring lengths, students continue to use the ruler, but now are asked to measure objects to the nearest half- or quarter-inch.

 KEYS TO THE CORE

Notice that the Common Core standards emphasize metric system measurements in liquids. Cooking with your child is a great way to review measuring skills; try to use the metric measuring cups and spoons if you can.

Also in measurement, third graders continue to develop their skills at representing and interpreting data, principally through drawing graphs. They're asked to complete more sophisticated graphing in this grade. For example, they might be assigned to "draw a bar graph showing how many cookies your classmates would like to eat in which each square in the graph represents two cookies."

Perhaps the most challenging aspect of measuring skills for third graders is in learning to understand the concept of area. For the first time, students are asked to use the "unit square" (a square with side length 1 unit—such as one inch or one foot—that can be used to measure a larger area). Instead of thinking about "flat" objects, students now think of "plane figures" (meaning figures which lay on the flat plane), which have a measurable area. They're then asked to measure plane figures by counting unit squares; this means that they measure the size of a plane figure by counting how many unit squares they can fit within it.

Following logically after this new knowledge, multiplication and addition are related to calculating area. For example, students are might be asked to find the area of a rectangle (with whole-number side lengths) by tiling the square unit around it. Then, they should be able to show that they could also find the area by multiplying the side lengths. This is the first building block in understanding the formula for area.

Third graders work with perimeters too. Remember that *area* means the entire expanse of a shape, while *perimeter* is the border (or sides) of the shape. Students should be able to measure the perimeter of polygons, and should be able to calculate an unknown side length based on knowing the two of the other sides' length (in polygons, which include rectangles and squares, two opposite sides are of equal length and the other two are of equal length).

Grade 4

In this grade, measuring skills form a large portion of the math curriculum. Students are expected to learn the units of measurement (including how measuring systems progress from smaller to larger), such as kilometers (km), meters (m), and centimeters (cm); kilograms (kg) and grams (g); pounds (lb) and ounces (oz); liters (l) and milliliters (ml); and, as before, hours, minutes, and seconds. Students can convert a measurement in a larger unit to smaller units. For example, they know that 12 inches make up a foot, and 1,000 meters make up a kilometer.

It's not a surprise to learn that fourth graders are also asked to perform mathematical operations with units of measurement. In particular, students should be able to work with simple fractions and decimals within measurement units, such as calculating how many liters are in a tank, which might result in a decimal or fraction.

Students in fourth grade begin to learn about *angles*, defined as the amount of turn between two straight lines that have a common end point (called the *vertex*). This includes learning how to measure angles with a protractor. You may recall that in a triangle, all the angles added together will equal 180 degrees. Students use this formula as well as the formula for figuring out area, which is that area = length × width ($a = l \times w$). They will particularly use this formula in calculating the area of rectangles (instead of less standardized shapes during this school year). All of this is introductory; students are generally not expected to be fluent in calculating such answers yet.

Grade 5

By grade 5, students' measurement skills should move toward fluency. Whereas in fourth grade they were asked to convert large units to smaller units, in fifth grade, they should be able to convert smaller to larger as well. For example, they should understand that 5 centimeters (cm) = .05 meters (m). The standard again suggests "multi-step, real world" problems.

KEYS TO THE CORE

The Common Core standards in measuring often refer to metric measurements, although the examples given are sometimes in inches, feet, and other more common American measurements. Your child's teacher may emphasize one over the other as well.

In measuring volume, students use cubic measurements: cubic cm, cubic inches (in), and cubic feet (ft). They will also learn the formula for measuring *volume*; that is, $V = l \times w \times h$, or volume = length × width × height. They will also learn to use this formula to solve for the volume of solid figures.

Geometry

The standards for geometry often go hand-in-hand with the standards for measurement at these grade levels, as will be clear from the following. For grades 3 and 4, the standards are comparatively short, but when considered with the prior standards, form a complexity in thinking demanded. In grade 5, more manipulation of geometric principles is requested.

Grade 3

Third graders are introduced to categorizing shapes by larger type; for example, they learn that *rhombuses*, rectangles, and squares are all quadrilaterals, but that not all quadrilaterals are rhombuses, rectangles, or squares. Understanding which rules apply to which categories and sub-categories is important. Third graders also continue to work with partitioning shapes, such as into halves, and then expressing the pieces as fractions: ½.

DEFINITION

A **rhombus** is a four-sided shape in which all sides have the same length. All opposite angles in a rhombus are equal. We often think of a rhombus as diamond-shaped, although a right-angle square is technically also a rhombus.

Grade 4

Perhaps because so much geometric measuring is covered in the grade 3 standards, the grade 4 standards for geometry are relatively light. However, students are asked to learn a key concept this year: angles. In two-dimensional drawings, students should be able to illustrate *right, acute,* and *obtuse* angles.

DEFINITION

Right angles are 90-degree angles of any orientation. An **acute angle** is any angle of less than 90 degrees, whereas an **obtuse angle** is more than 90 degrees but less than 180 degrees.

Fourth graders also learn or recall terms such as points, lines, *line segments, rays,* and *parallel* and *perpendicular lines.*

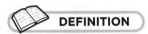

DEFINITION

Parallel lines are always the same distance apart and never meet. Parallel lines do not have to be straight, by the way, so long as they are always the same distance apart. **Perpendicular lines** cross at a 90-degree angle. A **line segment** is part of a line connecting two points, whereas a **ray** is a line with a starting point but no end point.

Students at this level are expected to be able to identify all of the above in drawings, and to be able to locate right triangles, which are triangles that possess a right angle. Finally, fourth graders should be introduced to the concept of symmetry, which is when one side of a shape is just like the other if it is flipped, turned or slid. They'll look at two-dimensional figures and be able to draw a line through the figure to show how the halves would be symmetrical.

Grade 5

Building on their grades 3 and 4 learning about plane figures, fifth graders begin to work with graphing points on a coordinate plane. The Common Core standards suggest that they use this skill to solve real-world as well as mathematical problems. Graphing in this way involves learning to use a pair of perpendicular number lines, which we call axes. The intersection of those lines is given the coordinate of 0 on both lines. From there, a unit of measurement is established (generally whole numbers), which proceed equally up or across each line.

Students are then given (or asked to solve for) a pair of coordinates (numbers). If given the numbers (3, 5), the student would learn that the first number, the 3, is the *x*-coordinate and would be found on the first axis (called the *x*-axis) and the second number, the 5, would be called the *y*-coordinate and found on the second axis (called the *y*-axis). Real world mathematical problems might want students to compute a problem that asks them to plot several pairs of coordinates that represent how far and how fast a car was traveling on a given day.

Fifth graders should also be able to understand that if a category of two-dimensional figures has a characteristic, all sub-categories of those figures also have that characteristic. For example, they would understand that all rectangles have four right angles, and squares are rectangles, so all squares have four right angles.

How to Support Your Child

Teachers for grades 3–5 will most likely provide guidance for you to follow in helping your child develop math skills at home. It's important to keep in touch with your child's teacher, especially if you think your child is struggling to understand a mathematical concept, or if you are not clear on the skill that is being taught. It is ultimately unhelpful to your child if you try to teach them a method of calculating an answer that does not follow the steps they are learning in the classroom. Resist the urge to help them "get the answer right" at the expense of understanding how to get to the answer.

There is a large variety of math workbooks on the market that may prove helpful to your child. Instead of forcing your child to complete a worksheet on top of their homework, you might make a workbook available for downtime, such as waiting at the doctor's office, or at a sibling's soccer game. Try not to emphasize the speed at which your child completes such workbooks, but allow them to work slowly and carefully.

Computer, phone, and tablet games are also all available to help with math skills. These are especially helpful for children who are still mastering basic math (addition, subtraction, division, and multiplication) while their class is moving on to more complex ideas. Your child's teacher should be able to provide information on helpful games and may even be able to advise you which are in use in the classroom.

Provide rulers, tape measures, and liquid measuring cups for your child's use. Once your child knows how to use a protractor and a compass, make sure they have such tools at home, too. Working with these tools, whether at a water or sand table, or at an art station with paper, will support their learning to work with measuring. Children at this age may also be very interested in cooking or baking with you, which allows for thoughtful use of measuring devices as well.

Cooking may also provide opportunities to discuss halves and quarters. Additionally, tying these ideas, as well as those of fractions, to a favorite hobby for your child is also worthwhile. Kids who play football or soccer might be interested to think of the lines on the field as dividing it into fractions. Children who dance might want to calculate how many of the minutes of a class they spend warming up. Even video games can provide opportunities for math, as you can ask your child to form a fraction for how often a character dies before they succeed in getting to the next level.

Younger children will enjoy looking for shapes with you, and classifying them into categories. Both indoor and outdoor environments should provide opportunities to do so. As children get older, they can look more specifically for—and then classify—angles.

You can also help your child with graphing. Pay attention to the type of word problems they are being asked to graph in school, and find similar material to work with at home. All you need are two quantifiable elements for each axis. You could ask them to graph the amount of time it takes to cook dinner vs. the cost of the ingredients, for example. Or make it something less "real world" and ask them to graph the number of times a superhero saves the day in a given set of comic books.

The Least You Need to Know

- Students in grades 3–5 learn to work with numbers that are up to four digits long.

- Fractions are introduced in grade 3. By the end of grade 5, students should know how to add and subtract fractions and will begin working with decimals.

- Students learn a wide variety of two-dimensional and three-dimensional shapes and their properties, as well as how to calculate area and volume.

- Three types of angles—right, obtuse and acute—are taught. Students learn to measure and calculate angles.

- It's important that students learn to collect and work with data, not just arrive at the correct answer.

- Graphing data is an important part of math in the later elementary school years.

The Math Standards for Grades 6-8

The categories of the Common Core standards for mathematics change almost completely between grade 5 and grade 6. The emphasis moves away from mathematical calculations, as students are ready to begin the formal study of algebra, as well as learning about statistics. Students also learn about ratios, beginning in grade 6, as well as advanced calculations with fractions and similarly more complex numbers. And middle schoolers also advance in their study of geometry. For many American middle school students, their math classes may now be titled "Geometry" or "Algebra I."

In This Chapter

- The skills in working with ratios and within the number system that are important for grades 6-8

- The standards for working with expressions and equations for grades 6-8

- The skills in geometry that are important for grades 6-8

- The skills in statistics and probability that are key for grades 6-8

- Ways you can support your child in learning the standards

Ratios, Proportional Relationships, and the Number System

Grade 6

Ratios, a comparison of the relative sizes of two or more values, appear for the first time in the Common Core standards in grade 6. As is typical, fluency is not expected, but the ability to "understand" ratios and use "ratio reasoning" is suggested. In other words, students are expected to compare the two quantities in a ratio. An example given in the standards is, "The ratio of wings to beaks in the bird house at the zoo was 2:1, because for every 2 wings there was 1 beak." Note how the ratio is written, with a colon. Sixth graders also learn the term "unit rate a/b" with a ratio $a:b$ with $b \neq 0$. This language seems complex, but it's easier to understand within an example: "We paid $75 for 15 hamburgers, which is a rate of $5 a hamburger." In other words, the unit rate a/b is a more formal way of making a mathematical comparison.

It will not be a surprise that the standards encourage the use of real-world problems when teaching students about ratios. This might include asking students to figure out unit pricing and constant speed. Examples of what might be asked include: "If it took 7 hours to mow 4 lawns, then at that rate, how many lawns could be mowed in 35 hours? At what rate were lawns being mowed?"

In this grade level, students working with ratios should also learn how to find a percentage of a quantity as a rate per 100—in other words, that 40 percent of a quantity means $^{40}/_{100}$. Converting between parts per 100 and percentages is a key idea in the grade 6 curriculum.

Grade 7

As expected, complexity in using ratios grows in grade 7. Students will now be tasked to work with ratios of fractions, including fractions that are measured in the same type of unit. A typical question for a seventh grader is: "If a person walks $\frac{1}{2}$ mile in each $\frac{1}{4}$ hour, compute the unit rate as the complex fraction $\frac{1}{2}/\frac{1}{4}$ miles per hour." Several steps are needed to arrive at the answer, and seventh graders should be able to persevere to arrive at the correct one.

The concept of proportions, as you can tell, becomes important in grade 7. Students are asked to identify and work with proportional relationships between numbers, whether by testing for equivalent ratios or by graphing on a coordinate plane. Graphing, which many math teachers will show students in the early stages of learning about proportions, has the advantage of visually displaying a straight line if the two quantities are in an even proportion.

Seventh graders also work with proportions by creating equations to express proportion. For example, to solve for the total cost, a student might construct the equation t (total cost) = n (number of items purchased) $\times$ p (constant price). In other words, the total cost of buying baseball cards = the number of card packs purchased $\times$ their constant price per pack.

If this sounds like it might be helpful at home, the Common Core standards think so, too, and emphasize real-world problems for seventh graders. Among the terms that they suggest be introduced are "simple interest, tax, markups, markdowns, gratuities, commissions, fees, percent increase, percent decrease and percent error."

 KEYS TO THE CORE

Notice that middle-school students are tasked with real-world learning in math. Much of what the Common Core suggests in curriculum is rooted in personal financial terminology, not to mention the sorts of skills that all workers in the financial sector will need.

Grade 8

The Common Core standards for math drop "Ratios" as a category in grade 8. Instead, "Functions" is added, which will be discussed at the end of this chapter. However, eighth graders are given short suggestions in the number system subheading. While the directives aren't very long, the idea introduced is important; that is, that eighth graders should learn that numbers are not rational, but that they can be approximated by rational numbers.

Irrational numbers are real numbers that cannot be written as a simple fraction. If you or your child have trouble remembering what an irrational number is, remember that they cannot be written as a fraction, or ratio, thus they are "ir-" (or "not") "ratio." That means that rational numbers can be written as a simple fraction.

Students should understand (the standards say "informally") that every number has a decimal expansion. For rational numbers, that expansion eventually repeats. $\frac{1}{2}$ is a rational number, because it can be written as 1.5. 7.0 is a rational number, since it can be written $\frac{7}{1}$. An irrational number can be written into a decimal, but that decimal never repeats. If you're thinking of *pi* (the symbol for which is π), which begins 3.14159 … you're correct—it's an irrational number! It cannot be expressed as a fraction.

Eighth graders also learn to compare irrational numbers, generally by using the closest approximation in rational form that they can calculate. Students also learn to plot irrational numbers on a line diagram (note: not the same as a graph) and estimate the value of expressions such as π^2.

Expressions and Equations

If your child has been in a school that has followed the Common Core standards in math in prior grades, this section of the standards should seem like a natural progression. Here, students move from working with numbers in problems to working with numbers and variables in equations. It should be noted, however, that some ideas emerge rather abruptly within these standards, and your child may need to rely on their perseverance skills (perhaps with some extra discussion with the teacher) in order to master the new concepts such as *variables*, negative numbers, and functions.

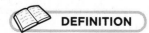 **DEFINITION**

A **variable** is the letter in an algebraic equation, symbolizing what we don't know and are trying to solve for. In the equation $x = 5 - (6 \div 2)$, x is the variable. A problem may have more than one variable.

Grade 6

At the end of fifth grade, most students should have a firm fluency in mathematical skills. Now they'll attempt to use those skills with an algebraic focus. The first step is in learning to write and evaluate numerical expressions that use whole-number exponents. Of course, they'll need to learn what an exponent is: they're those little superscript numbers written to indicate how many times the base number should be multiplied by itself. In the notation 2^3, this means $2 \times 2 \times 2$. 2 is the base number, and the 3 is the exponent. So, sixth graders will learn to write and consider these, although do note that they are not necessarily asked to be fluent in using them.

Sixth graders will also learn to "write, read and evaluate expressions in which letters stand for numbers." These are algebraic equations. Your child might be asked to "subtract y from 5" and rewrite it as $5 - y$.

Students must also be able to identify the parts of an equation, or expression as they are sometimes called in the standards. Necessary vocabulary includes: sum, term, product, factor, quotient, coefficient. Let's review those. A *sum* is the result of adding two or more numbers. In the equation $4 + 5 = 9$, the sum is 9. But that doesn't mean that the sum is always the answer. In the equation $(4 + 5)(3 + 7)$, the sums are 9 and 10, but the answer is 90!

In algebra, the *term* is either a single number, a variable or the numbers and variables multiplied together. In the equation $4x - 8 = 5$, $4x$, 8, and 5 are all terms. The product is when two or more numbers are multiplied together, so in 4×5, the product is 20. Be sure to remember that sum and product are not the same thing!

In algebra, the word *factor* means something slightly different than it did in basic math. Now, *factors* are what you multiply together to arrive at an expression, or what an expression can be broken down into. For example, $(x + 3)(x + 1) = x^2 + 4x + 3$. $(x + 3)$ and $(x + 1)$ are the factors.

The *quotient*, you'll recall, is the answer left after you divide one number by another. And the *coefficient* is the number used to multiply the variable. In the phrase $4x + 3$, the variable is x, of course, so the coefficient is 4.

Sixth graders will use all of the above vocabulary as they begin to solve variables. Some of those problems will involve exponents, and for many of them, students will need to work in the correct order for solving. Your child will probably learn an acronym similar to PEMDAS to remember what order to perform operations in; this means you begin by working within the parentheses, then the exponents, followed by multiplication, division, addition and subtraction.

Let's take a look at an equation to plan how to solve it. Keep in mind, this equation may be more complex than anything your child is assigned in this grade level, but it provides a reminder of what to do.

$$5 + (6 \times 5^2 + 3)$$

First, start in the parentheses, and do the exponent first:

$$5 + (6 \times 25 + 3)$$

Then do the multiplication in the parentheses:

$$5 + (150 + 3)$$

Then the addition in the parentheses:

$$5 + (153)$$

Then the addition outside the parentheses:

$$158$$

Sixth graders will learn that one of the operations they might perform to solve for a variable is to apply the distributive property. For example, the equation $3 (2 \div x)$ can also be expressed as $6 + 3x$. The reverse can be done as well. $24x + 18y$ is also equal to $6(4x + 3y)$. Why bother? Because sometimes the variable can only be found if the equation is distributed in a particular way.

As mentioned above, sixth graders learn to use variables in their problem solving. There is a particular emphasis on the idea that the variable can be a real-world problem that needs solved, such as calculating the maximum speed a car can go before it loses fuel efficiency. This example also speaks to the final portion of this standard for sixth graders. They should also learn to use variables that represent two quantities in a "real-world problem that change in relationship to one another." In other words, two variables are at play in this problem. An example is "In a problem involving motion at constant speed, list and graph ordered pairs of distances and times, and write the equation $d = 65t$ to represent the relationship between distance and time." Note that if the student can arrive at the answer for one of the variables, they will be able to solve for the other as well.

Grade 7

Seventh graders build on the order of operations (remember PEMDAS?) students learned in grade 6. Many may have already begun to work with variables as well, but in grade 7, the standards suggest that this skill definitely be taught. The order of operations is the same when a variable is involved, although, of course, the work is being done to solve for the variable. The goal in such equations is to get the variable alone on side of the equation so that it can be solved. Students are also expected to apply the operations of factoring or expanding this year too. Although factors were introduced in the grade 6 curriculum, factoring may not have been. This is simply breaking down an algebraic expression into the factors:

$2x + 8$ is factored into $2(x + 4)$.

Factoring is the opposite of expanding, as you can see. Please note that so far, all of these operations are only taught with rational coefficients.

Seventh graders are expected to take what they've learned so far in algebraic thinking and be able to solve "multi-step real-life and mathematical problems posed with positive and negative rational numbers in any form (whole numbers, fractions and decimals)." Of course, students will need to work the order of operations correctly, be able to convert between forms (such as inches to feet) and be able to compare what they estimate the answer will be and what they've computed the answer to be. In other words, students should be using their estimating skills to make a reasonable guess at what the answer will be, and use that estimation as a baseline for solving the problem.

 KEYS TO THE CORE

If you're thinking, wait, *negative* numbers? Yep. They're here now, and without much in the way of introduction. A negative number falls before zero on the number scale, which your child should be very familiar with. Negative numbers have a couple of properties worth remembering: when you multiply a negative and a positive number, the result is negative ($-2 \times 6 = -12$). When you multiply a negative number times another negative number, the result is positive ($-2 \times -6 = 12$).

Here's the sample problem the Common Core standards provide, which should give you an idea of the complexity seventh graders will need to persevere through:

> As a salesperson, you are paid $50 per week plus $3 per sale. This week you want your pay to be at least $100. Write an inequality for the number of sales you need to make, and describe the solutions.

As you can see, the emphasis is again on real-world problems, especially situations involving motivational reasons to do math (e.g., having a salary). Also notice that the problem refers to "solutions" indicating that there is more than one acceptable away to arrive at the correct solution. Students are invited to graph the solution set, too, and are sometimes encouraged to walk the teacher through the order of operations they pursued in order to solve the steps of the problem as they show their work for the problem.

Grade 8

The biggest addition to the grade 8 curriculum is that students are now expected work with radicals. A *radical* is an expression that has a square root, cube root or similar. The symbol for square root is: $\sqrt{\ }$. You'll know your child's homework deals with radicals when you see that symbol. In order to understand radicals, we'll need a brush-up on square and cube roots. A *square root* of a number is the value that, when multiplied by itself, gives that number. The square root of 16 is 4, because $4 \times 4 = 16$. A *cube root* is the value that, when multiplied times itself three times, gives that number. For example, the cube root of 27 is 3, because $3 \times 3 \times 3 = 27$. Students will work with roots in their problem solving; a typical problem might ask students to solve for p, when $x^2 = p$. By the end of this grade, they should also understand that $\sqrt{2}$ is *irrational*.

 **DEFINITION**

Remember an **irrational number** cannot be evenly divided into a whole number and be written as a fraction. Pi is the most famous example of an irrational number, but the square root of two is pretty well-known, too.

The advantages of working with radicals should be more apparent to eighth graders. The curricula they're working on in other classes, such as science or social studies, should make clear that being able to write a single digit with a power of 10 is preferable, at times, to writing out a much larger or much smaller number. For example, it is easier to write: Estimate the population of the United States as 3×10^8 and the population of the world as 7×10^9. When dealing with, say, millimeters in seafloor spread, radicals are also much more manageable.

Students in grade 8 also continue to work with graphs, and begin to use the term *slope*—meaning how steep a straight line is—in their work. For example, they might be asked to compare a distance-time graph of a car to a distance-time equation of a train and determine which of the two has greater speed.

Further, eighth graders analyze and solve linear equations and pair of simultaneous equations. Thus, they can solve a linear equation down to one variable (e.g., to solve for x). To do so, they may need to expand expressions into like terms. They're also asked to solve two equations at once, and to recognize when doing so disproves the equations. For example, if given the two equations $3x + 2y = 5$, and $3x + 2y = 6$, the student should not have to solve each before realizing that they cannot both be true, because 5 and 6 are not equal. Eighth graders may be encouraged to graph these equations, so that they can determine if they can both be true.

Lastly, only eighth graders have a set of standards in the common core about functions. The formal definition of a *function* is that it is a special relationship between values, meaning that each of its input values gives back exactly one output value. Your child will learn this concept as $f(x)$, in which x is the value you give it. Sound confusing? Well, it is, a bit. Perhaps it's easier to think of functions as something that is done to a number. Squaring a number, for example, is a function. It's written like this: $f(x) = x^2$. If you put 4 in as x, then: $f(4) = 16$. Notice that the x doesn't have to be a whole number. It could even be an equation, like this: $f(x) = 1 + x - x^2$.

Eighth graders learn to use functions in conjunction with graph work, which helps them to see how the linear functions represented by a table of values and those represented by an algebraic expression determine which function has the greater rate of change. They will also learn how to use functions to model relationships between quantities. However, eighth graders are not asked to write in formal function notation. These standards provide an introduction to using functions but mastery is not expected.

Geometry for Grades 6–8

Along with the algebraic skills students are developing in the middle school years, geometry skills are advancing as well. These tend to build more smoothly that algebraic standards did on existent skills, and most students who are up to speed at the beginning of grade 6 will not have much trouble expanding their skill set in geometrical thinking.

Grade 6

The word "real-world" is once again prominent in grade 6 geometry standards. The expectation is that students understand how to solve for area, surface area and volume without difficulty. They should also be able to work with triangles, special quadrilaterals (that is, four-sided shapes that are not only squares and rectangles) and *polygons* by the end of this grade.

> **DEFINITION**
>
> A **polygon** a two-dimensional (so it is in one plane) shape, with straight sides. The number of sides is not standardized, so squares, triangles, stars and many other shapes are polygons. Circles, however, are not, since they are curved.

Sixth graders will learn and be able to use the formula $V = l \times w \times h$ (that is, volume equals length times width times height) in order to find the volume of right rectangular prisms with fractional edge lengths. A *prism* is a solid object that has two identical ends and flat sides. Prisms are often classified as "square prisms" or "triangular prisms" which simply mean that the object is a square with two identical ends, or a triangle with two identical ends, and so on. Cylinders are not prisms, since one of the sides is not flat. Although prisms are somewhat more complex than previous shapes covered by the standards, note that the formula for finding volume remains the same.

Finally, sixth graders focus on learning how to find the surface area of figures. The Common Core standards suggest that students use computerized or actual nets made up of triangles or rectangles to figure out the surface area of a figure. And, of course, all of the above should be linked to solving real-world problems.

Grade 7

The concept of scale drawing emerges in grade 7. In scale drawing, which you may know as "drawing to scale," students convert the measurements of a much larger object into a smaller drawing in order to understand it, compute any missing figures (such as the side of a cube) and solve problems in which it factors. A student might be given some of the dimensions of a large pyramid, for example, and use a scale of 100 feet to 1 inch in order to draw it. Additionally, students are asked to draw geometric shapes with given conditions (such as a right triangle, say), and to be able to do so freehand, with a rule and protractor and "with technology," which means on a computer or tablet. The ability to work with rulers, protractors, and compasses is expected.

Students in this year should be used to working with prisms. Now they'll also learn about the two-dimensional figures that result from slicing prisms and other three-dimensional figures, as in plane sections from right rectangular pyramids, which result in two-dimensional triangles, or that slicing a cylinder will yield circles.

Speaking of which, circles appear in the standards for the first time in terms of solving for area. Don't be surprised if your seventh grader comes home talking about pi. This year students will learn the formula for the diameter of a circle (2 × the radius of the circle), and for the circumference of a circle (π × diameter of a circle). And don't forget the area of a circle, which is $A = \pi r^2$, or area = 3.14 × radius squared.

KEYS TO THE CORE

Most of us remember that π equals about 3.14. But what is *pi*? It is the number equal to the circumference of any circle divided by the diameter of that circle.

Seventh graders also work with angles in more complex ways, knowing the facts about supplementary (that is, two angles that add up to 180 degrees), complementary (two angles that add up to 90 degrees), vertical, and adjacent angles and being able to write out and solve simple equations for an unknown angle in a figure. These ideas build on what was covered in prior grades, but may introduce new terms for familiar concepts.

Grade 8

Congruence is introduced in grade 8 geometry. Two shapes are congruent when they are exactly the same shape and size. This may require some work on a student's part, to rotate, reflect or translate the shapes until they match. The steps taken to reach congruence may be required in the solving of a problem, and math teachers might require this to be described using coordinates on a graph.

Similarly, eighth graders, when working with triangles much be able to use "informal arguments" (that is, not necessarily formulas or equations) to establish qualities about the angle sum (that is, all three angles in a triangle, added up to 180 degrees) and other angle properties. Much of this is about reasoning—that your child can demonstrate their knowledge about the triangles through discussion based on prior understanding of triangles' properties.

Eighth graders also learn the Pythagorean theorem. This is the familiar formula that reads: $a^2 + b^2 = c^2$. This demonstrates that in a right-angled triangle, the square of the long side, or *hypotenuse*, (c) is equal to the sum of the squares of the other two sides. Students should be able to explain the Pythagorean theorem, as well as demonstrate its usage in both two and three dimensions. Of course, the standards suggest challenging students with "real-world" problems using the theorem.

DEFINITION

The **hypotenuse** is the longest side of a triangle. The hypotenuse is the (c) when employing the Pythagorean theorem.

Eighth graders also continue to solve real-world and mathematical problems involving the volume of cylinders, cones and spheres. The necessary formulas for each are taught.

Statistics and Probability

As you have seen, the Common Core standards in math are determined to teach skills that have bearing on students' future college and career readiness. There is perhaps no area where this is more evident than in the inclusion of statistics and probability in the middle grades. For many parents, the formal study of statistics may not have occurred, if at all, until the upper high school or even college years. But understanding how to work with numbers in ways that help with jobs in science, technology, medicine, sports, and many more fields is a key concern for the common core, so the study of statistics begins in grade 6.

Grade 6

The first Common Core standard for grade 6 in statistics requests that students "develop an understanding of statistical variability." So, they must first learn what a *statistical problem* is, meaning one that anticipates variability in the data that forms the answer. For example, "How old are you?" is not a statistical question; "How old are the students in my school?" is, because there will be a variability in the students' ages.

In understanding statistics, students will need to know several key terms: center, spread, and overall shape. *Center* is used to mean the greatest bunching of answers. In the question above, if half of the students responded that their age was 12, while the other half ranged from age 8 to 14, 12 is a statistical center. (Center is not the same as average.) Note that in a graph of statistical information, it is possible to have more than one center; the students could have been 40 percent 11 years old and 50 percent 12 years old, for example.

The *spread*, as you may have figured out, is that range of ages, specifically how far out they are from the center. A study that includes 6-year-olds will have a larger spread than one that studies only 11-, 12- and 13-year-olds.

Finally, the overall *shape* is the rise and drop of the statistical findings; picture looking at a graph with a line that charts the ages of students and the frequency of some responses. Another way to think of shape is the pattern the data takes. Students also learn that the center of a numerical data set summarizes all of its values, while a measure of the variation describes how its values vary with a single number.

It probably won't be a surprise that learning how to "display" (or graph) numerical data is part of the study of statistics according to the Common Core standards. A number of different types of display are suggested, including dot plots, histograms, and box plots. These sound complicated but are quite simple to grasp when your child is working on them; they will be familiar from media that displays statistics.

Here, too, the standards for math seem to be aligned with scientific study as well. The final standard for working with statistics in grade 6 is to be able to summarize numerical data sets by reporting on the observations (such as noting how many students chose which lunch entrée in the cafeteria), describing the nature of the attribute under investigation (in other words, what is the study about? The frequency students choose a grilled cheese? Or which entrée out of 5 they choose?) and the variability therein. Sixth graders should be able to describe the overall pattern ("Most students chose either pizza or a hamburger.") as well as any striking deviations ("But all of the 12-year-olds chose a salad."). They'll also be asked to find the center and relate that to the rest of the data.

Grade 7

Now that they have some familiarity with statistics, seventh graders will work with great depth in this field. They're asked to begin to use random sampling to draw inferences about a population. The idea of generalizations—that a small portion of the population (the sample) can give a picture of the overall population (the general)—is key here. They'll understand that this is only valid if the sample is representative of the population, and learn to use data from a random sampling to draw inferences about a population. As can be anticipated, the sampling done in a math class will tend to favor mathematical questions instead of questions about social issues or political beliefs. For example, students might be asked to predict the winner of a school election based on randomly sampled survey data. But they'll likely use what they learn about statistics in other courses.

Along with the above, seventh graders will learn to informally compare two populations to infer similarities and differences. Graphing to understand the comparison is also likely. For example, students might be asked to compare the mean height of players on the basketball team and the mean height of players on the soccer team. The thinking is extended to make inferences, predictions, and theories, all informally. For example, the above statistical comparison might lead to an inference about the need for height in basketball over soccer. Remember, an inference is not numerically provable.

Seventh graders also begin to work with probability models. The standards read, "Understand that the probability of a chance event is a number between 0 and 1 that expresses the likelihood of the event occurring." The larger the number is, the more likely an event will occur. Thus, a probability of .001 is a very slim chance of the event happening, whereas the probability of ¾ is much more likely. A probability of .5, or ½, indicates an event that is neither likely nor unlikely.

Given all of that, seventh graders are encouraged to approximate the probability of a chance event by collecting data on the process that produces it, then observing the frequency that it occurs and making a prediction based on the observation. A typical question would read something like this: "When rolling a cube 600 times, predict how often a 3 or 6 will be rolled." Students can collect data by rolling a cube 10, 20, or 50 times to observe the frequency of 3 or 6 appearing. This kind of thinking, in turn, leads to the ability to create probability models, which use observed frequencies of events to generate data for prediction.

All of the data for probability need not be found by personal observation, though. Teachers are also encouraged to have students use organized collections of data, including lists, tables and diagrams. And computer simulations are popular means of data collection, especially for statistical work that might involve medical or archeological data.

Grade 8

By the time they've finished grade 8, students should understand how to work with bivariate data. *Bivariate* means that the data has two variables, such as a study of the sale of ice water based on the temperature outdoors. The two variables are the ice water sales and the outdoor temperature. Students study two variables in hopes of discovering patterns of association between two qualities. For example, students might discover that the warmer it is outside, the more ice water is sold. They also learn to look for clusters (such as ice water selling briskly on a particularly hot day) and outliers (such as a lot of ice water being sold on a day that wasn't very warm at all). Students may even consider this in a linear way, plotting out the two variables and considering them as lines.

Eighth graders may also conduct their own research to look for possible associations in bivariate data. They might survey to find out how many students in their class have a curfew, as well as how many students in the class must call home when school is finished for the day. They could then compare the data to find evidence that those who have a curfew are more likely to have to call home.

How to Support Your Child at Home

Middle school students take great leaps forward in math skills. Supporting their learning at home is no longer a simple as encouraging the practice of mathematical skills, such as adding, subtracting, dividing and multiplying. More than ever, conversation with your child's teachers about how to best support their learning of math at home is key.

Teachers are the best resource for explaining what might be helpful, from workbooks to extra tutoring to computer programs. If your child's teacher offers afterschool practice sessions or tutoring, your child might make it a point to attend. Even students who have done well in basic math can find the wide variety of topics in middle school math baffling. It is the rare child who is not confused by at least one new topic in math.

Pay attention to how your child is completing homework in Math. If they seem to arrive at the correct answer without much work, encourage them to show how they're getting there. Conversely, if they seem to be working through the problem with skill but arriving at the incorrect answer, encourage them to show you the steps they're taking. If you can't find the stumbling block, have them speak to their teacher for help.

The internet has a wide variety of resources for learning early algebra and early geometry. Encourage your child to make use of them for quick reminders. It's especially helpful to have your child explain the concept they just looked up to you; if they can so in a way that you understand, they're on the right track, and are more likely to retain that information.

While the Common Core standards in math repeatedly recommend real-world problem solving, it can be difficult to spontaneously come up with complex problems for your child to solve that make use of their new skills. However, you can more easily discuss how they might go about solving such a problem. For example, you could say, "If we added a fence to the back yard, how much fencing would we need? How would we figure that out?" or "If I only want to spend 15 percent of my monthly income on your birthday party next month, how would I know how much to spend?" It's okay if your child can't come up with the correct answer; the idea is that, talking together, you will help them decide how they would set up the equation if they needed to do so.

It's also helpful to your child if you help them brainstorm appropriate time to use their new skills. Instead of dismissing algebra as an unnecessary skill, ask them why they might need to figure out the square root of a number, or use it in an equation. Discuss together why these skills might be needed. This is particularly helpful if your child is thinking about pursuing a degree or a career that requires this type of skill—they might want to become a researcher, contractor, or nurse, for example.

Geometric thinking is a little more accessible. You can present your child with a food container while you prepare a meal and ask them to calculate the volume of the container. Better yet, have them prepare the meal! The serving of a pie or cake is an excellent opportunity to figure out the diameter, radius and area of a circle. Many schools now celebrate "Pi Day" on March 14 (3/14), and you can add in your own family's celebration, too.

Statistical thinking is often quite captivating to students, providing a way to combine mathematics with social issues and studies. The media often presents the results of surveys; with your child, read up on how the statistics were arrived at, and discuss whether they're accurate and reliable or not. Statistics are far more prominent in our world than we realize; help your student find them in everything from political results to weather reports. Encourage your student to practice their own long-term statistical survey, perhaps by charting the weather over a month, and arriving at the likelihood for snow on a given day.

The Least You Need to Know

- Grades 6–8 present huge leaps in mathematical reasoning and understanding. Most children will find at least some aspect of the work challenging.

- The emphasis moves from mathematical problem solving to more complex tasks, including equation writing and solving variables in algebraic thinking.

- In geometry, high-level thinking is required. Students figure out the area and volume of a myriad of shapes, both two- and three-dimensional.

- Students also work with circles, including finding the radius, diameter, and area of circle (involving pi) for the first time.

- Negative numbers and square roots are introduced.

- Students in grades 6–8 are also introduced to statistics and statistical probability.

The Math Standards for Grades 9–12

Because there is no standard math course pattern in American high schools, this chapter approaches the question of skills in the same way that the Common Core standards do: by skill set. The chapter begins with a section on algebra, but parents should note that this set of standards covers the entirety of algebraic knowledge needed for graduation from high school, which may be covered in one, two, or even three high school courses (Algebra I, II, and III). The same is true for geometry, although it is more likely that students will take only one geometry course in high school. The remaining sections emphasize the other skills the Common Core deems necessary for students graduating high school. Your child may learn these in grades 9, 10, 11, or 12, depending on many factors.

In This Chapter

- How math courses work in American high schools

- Skills specified by the standards for algebra

- The geometry skills that are important in high school

- The number, quantity and functions skills that are key for grades 9–12

- Statistics and probability skills for high schoolers

- How to support your child in learning the standards

The Common Core standards also give some standards for what they call "additional mathematics" for students who want to take advanced courses. These include calculus, advanced statistics (AP Statistics would fall under this title), and discrete mathematics. These standards will be briefly mentioned in sidebars as they appear, with the expectation that relatively few students will learn them in high school.

Understanding Math in High Schools

The vast majority of American high schools sequence high school math courses so that students move through a distinct series of learning experiences in mathematics. A common path is to take Algebra I in grade 9, geometry in grade 10, Algebra II in grade 11, and the option of trigonometry or calculus in grade 12. There are many diversions from this path, however. Some schools, such as those in New York, ask students to take Algebra I their freshman year and Algebra II their sophomore year. Many schools do not require a senior year math course, and some do not require a junior year math course. Some schools are moving toward a math curriculum that is less discrete, offering Mathematics I, II, and III, which combine aspects of all the branches of the field, in the belief that this will make the interconnectedness of the various branches of mathematics more clear.

Gifted, advanced, or honors tracks may have allowed students to take algebra or geometry in middle school, preparing students to take calculus their junior or senior year. Schools may offer advanced placement (AP) courses in calculus, computer science, or statistics, allowing students who qualify to earn college credits while still in high school. High schools may even have an agreement with a local college in order to allow students to attend freshman-level classes while still enrolled in the high school.

Alternately, students who struggle in math may be allowed to repeat a course, take a lower-level course, or participate in an online course in order to improve their skills. At some larger schools, ninth graders could be seated in any one of several available math classes depending on their ambitions, interests, and academic record.

It's vital that as the parent of a high schooler, you find out what courses your child is scheduled to take in high school. If you have questions or concerns, speak with the teacher, principals, or guidance counselor. If your child wants the opportunity to take college classes as a high school student, you'll need to make sure that he or she is on track to do so. The same is true for AP classes.

If you live in a state where some mastery of a subject must be demonstrated before moving on (as in New York's Board of Regents exams), be sure you understand what your child must do, and what the steps will be if he or she is not successful at first, particularly in a course that is a requirement for graduation. A good plan is especially important if your child thinks he may want to study a science (including medicine), math, or computer programming in college. A thorough education in high school math is a must!

Algebra

By the time they complete a formal algebra class, students should understand how to interpret *expressions*. This means both that they should understand how to interpret the expression correctly (which implies that they understand the order of operations taught back in middle school) and that they can manipulate the expression correctly. A high schooler should understand that the structure of the expression $x^4 - y^4$ as $(x^2)^2 - (y^2)^2$ that can be rewritten $(x^2 - y^2)(x^2 + y^2)$.

 **DEFINITION**

> An **expression** is the high school-appropriate term for a record of computation with numbers, symbols that represent numbers (such as x and y), arithmetic operations, exponentiation, and the operation of evaluating a function.

As part of this knowledge, high school algebra students learn to choose the best of the equivalent forms of an expression to use in solving the expression, given a variety of means to do so by their math teacher. And students also learn to derive formulas for a given set of data that allows ratios to be solved. A typical question that would involve this skill is to ask students to calculate mortgage payments. As you can see, the standards' emphasis on real-world skills remains in mathematics, especially now at the advanced level.

High school algebra students learn to perform arithmetic operations on *polynomials*, specifically adding, subtracting, dividing, and multiplying. Note that a polynomial cannot be divided by a variable, so an expression such as $4 \div x$ is will not be part of the work.

 **DEFINITION**

> **Polynomial** is a word that appears frequently in high school math courses. The meaning is found in the root words. *Poly-* means "many" while *-nominal* refers to terms. A polynomial, therefore, is a many-termed expression in which the terms could include exponents, constants, and variables. Terms, you'll remember, are the part of the equation or expression. Here's an example of a polynomial: $3xy + 2x = 7$.

As part of their work with polynomials, the standards suggest that students learn to know and apply the remainder theorem, which allows us to divide polynomials. This allows them to solve problems without intensive long division. The remainder theorem states that when you divide a polynomial f(x) by $x - c$, the remainder will be f(c).

Let's take $2x^2 - 5x - 1$ divided by $x - 3$.

Instead of dividing by $x - 3$, we calculate f(3) and get:

$$2(3)^2 - 5(3) - 1$$

This equals:

$$18 - 15 - 1 = 2$$

Another theory high school students should learn in algebra is the binomial theorem. A binomial is a polynomial with two terms, such as $5x^3 - 4$. The binomial theorem shows what happens when you multiply a binomial by itself, forming a pattern. There are several different ways of teaching this theory, so check with your child's teacher to find out the reasoning they are using in class.

Rewriting rational expressions is not a new idea, but high school algebra students practice doing so. Longer expressions with higher exponents are demonstrated and used. Students should continue to practice inspecting an expression to arrive at a reasonable guess (without actually solving the problem) as well as using long division and theorems to solve the problem. Students may also be introduced to a computer algebra system, especially for more complicated examples. This might involve using a program or application that you can add to your child's computer or tablet at home as well, for extra practice.

High school students should learn to create equations in their algebra classes, according to the Common Core standards. They should be able to write them including just one variable in order to solve problems, and with two or more variables in order to represent relationships between quantities. Using existent formulas in writing equations is encouraged, and students should especially learn to reorganize formulas to arrive at a needed aspect that figures into the formula without changing the properties of the formula. This could mean, for example, rewriting $V = l \times w \times h$ to solve for height instead of volume.

Real-world usage also comes into play. The standards suggest that students be able to write equations that represent constraints and introduce solutions. An example for just such an equation is given: represent inequalities describing nutritional and cost constraints on combinations of different foods. The point in such an equation is not to "solve" the problem but to show the relationship between all of the variables for further consideration.

Another aspect of working with equations that high schoolers should learn is reasoning with equations. To begin with, they should be able to explain the reasoning they will use to solve their equations, another variation on the "show your work" policy that the standards emphasize. As part of this, students should be able to account for any "extraneous solutions" that might arise, such as realizing three steps in that a known theorem will find the solution much more quickly than working through all of the steps.

Solving equations to one variable is expected, as is solving *quadratic equations*. Students may solve quadratic equations by inspection (in other words, recognizing the solution from reading the problem), taking square roots, completing the square, or by using the quadratic formula.

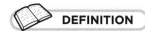

DEFINITION

A **quadratic equation** involves a variable that is squared, such as $2x^2$. Remember, the variable is the letter that is unknown.

Students are now asked to solve systems of equations, which means a set of two or more equations with the same set of unknowns. When solving systems of equations, students must find a set of answers that satisfy all of the equations in the system. Once again, the methods for solving range from inspection to actually solving for the variables.

COLLEGE AND CAREER READINESS

Advanced math students will work in greater fluency with systems of equations. An emphasis using matrix graphing appears in the standards that suggest additional skills in preparation for college, or which will be taught in the first years of college math.

The last standard in algebra returns to an old favorite, solving equations graphically. Now students are expected solve inequalities as well, which are expressions that include the "greater than" or "less than" symbols, or sometimes the "greater than or equal to" and the "lesser than or equal to" symbols. Solving inequalities is very similar to solving equations. An example of inequality is: $5 < 4x$.

High school algebra students should understand that the graph of an equation with two variables is the set of all of the solutions to that equation plotted in the coordinate plane. As can be expected, the standards emphasize that students need to be able to explain all parts of the graph as well as articulate how they'll use it to solve the equation. This includes every kind of equation with two variables they should have encountered: linear, polynomial, rational, absolute value (meaning how far the number is from 0; 6 and -6 have the same absolute value), exponential functions, and *logarithmic* functions.

 **DEFINITION**

> A **logarithm** is the answer to the question, how many of a number do I need to multiply to get another number? For example, how many 2s do I need to multiply to get 16? $2 \times 2 \times 2 \times 2 = 16$. You multiply four 2s to get 16, thus, the logarithm of 16 with a base of 2 is 4.

Geometry

"Interpreting a schematic drawing, estimating the amount of wood needed to frame a sloping roof, rendering computer graphics, or designing a sewing pattern for the most efficient use of material" are all tasks that the Common Core standards for mathematics say require advanced geometry. It's clear that college and career readiness requires a good understanding of the course. The standards hope to support that.

Geometry in high school builds on geometric study in middle school. Students are expected to arrive understanding such terms as angle, circle, perpendicular, point, line, and so on. With that knowledge in hand, they begin their secondary school geometry studies by experimenting with transformations in plane. Congruence is a key idea here; remember that two shapes are congruent if they are the same shape and size, even if they have to be flipped or turned to take up the same space on the plane.

Students will use transparencies, models, and computer software to manipulate two-dimensional shapes, paying particular attention to those that distort distance and angle and those that retain the initial dimensions of shape. Students learn to rotate (that is, turn, usually at a set series of degrees) figures, reflect figures (creating mirror images) and translate figures (to manipulate the shape and/or move it on the plane). Students should be able to draw (using graph paper, tracing paper, or a computer program) a geometric figure that has been transformed if they are also told how it's been rotated, reflected, or translated. Students should also be able to make predictions about the effect such actions will have on the figures.

Congruence of triangles is of particular interest in high school geometry. Whereas prior study often emphasized visualizing and estimating congruency, now students should be able to measure a triangle's sides and angles to demonstrate that they are congruent. A phrase that comes up frequently here is *rigid motion*, which means that if the triangles can be rotated, reflected, and translated, they cannot be altered.

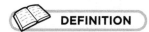 **DEFINITION**

> **Rigid motion** is the action of taking a shape and moving it without changing its shape or size. Rotating, reflecting, and translating shapes are all rigid motions.

There are a number of geometric theorems about congruence that high school students should learn and be able to use. It's helpful to think of these more as properties than as formal equations. For example, students will learn that the measures of interior angles of a triangle will equal 180 degrees, and that the base angles of isosceles triangles are congruent. There are also theorems about parallelograms, including that opposite sides are congruent, as are opposite angles. Knowing these patterns and properties will help students solve geometric problems more quickly as they become shortcuts.

High school geometry students also practice making geometric constructions with a variety of tools and methods. They might use a compass and a straightedge, string, reflective devices, paper folding, and/or computer software for their modeling. An additional twist here is the ability to make the figure of an equilateral triangle, a square, or a regular hexagon inside of a circle.

Moving away from congruence, geometry teachers will likely emphasize similarity as a property. Two shapes that are similar can become congruent, after being resized and possibly, rotated, turned, or reflected. Similarity is especially emphasized in triangles, where the equality of all corresponding pairs of angles and the proportionality of all of the sides means that the given triangles are (formally) similar. Note that we often use the word "similar" in a less formal way than mathematicians but it has a specific meaning for a distinctive quality in math.

As with congruence, there are theorems involving similarity, and your child will learn them in high school geometry. The Pythagorean Theorem, for example, can be used to prove triangle similarity.

There are also trigonometric aspects to similarity. Trigonometry means the study of triangles, so this makes sense. Students may learn more advanced theories that they'll use to solve problems involving right triangles.

COLLEGE AND CAREER READINESS

Students planning to go on to college should note that the standards suggest that advanced geometry students learn to apply trigonometric principles to general triangles (building on how they've learned to work with right triangles).

As they've worked with triangles, so should high schoolers work with circles. There are theorems for the study of circles, particularly on using angles within circles that should be learned. For example, students should know that inscribed angles on a diameter of a circle are right angles. They'll also be expected to find arc lengths and areas of sectors on circles. Arcs are any part of the circumference of a circle, while a sector of a circle is a slice of it; picture a slice of pie.

The standards set up a set of expectations for conical figures. These begin with familiar skills in finding area and diameter, but then build to include deriving the equation of a *parabola*, which in turn allows for the solving of the area of a cone.

DEFINITION

A **parabola** is a special kind of curve, shaped like an arch. Parabolas often appear in graphing work, but are not formally named and used in the standards until high school.

Working with graphs, high school students should learn to use coordinates to prove simple geometric theorems algebraically. Here, the skills from algebra and geometry combine. The extensive use of graphing in algebra is now used to answer questions in geometry, such as computing the perimeter of a polygonal shape through the use of graphing coordinates.

The standards have not forgotten volume, either. High school geometry students should be able to explain volume formulas and use them to solve problems. Notice the emphasis on "explain" again here; knowledge of the formulas isn't enough, nor is being able to calculate using them. Students should be able to articulate what the formulas are based on and why they work. This includes the formulas for cylinders, pyramids, cones, and spheres.

COLLEGE AND CAREER READINESS

Working with parabolas gets more complex in college-prep or college courses. Students will work with ellipses and hyperbolas. Students are also tasked with more complex work in volume formulas, including Cavalieri's principle.

Finally, the last set of standards for geometry challenge high school students to use geometric shapes, their measurements and their properties to describe objects. This means that students will make connections between—you guessed it!—the real world and the shapes in their classroom, by comparing the human torso to a cylinder, for example. They'll also learn to use *density* in area and/or volume in modeling (such as including persons per square mile). And they'll work on using modeling to solve design problems, such as modeling a bridge that minimizes construction costs or fits in an uneven landscape.

Number, Quantity, and Functions Skills

Exponents and rational exponents form the first set of standards in these areas. Rational exponents are often actually the root of a number. $2^{1/2} = \sqrt{2}$. Students will learn to work with rational exponents and rewrite them into more familiar regular exponents. Note that rational exponents are often called fractional exponents

Similarly, students will learn the properties of rational and irrational numbers. Specifically, they'll cover why the sum or product of two rational numbers is rational; that the sum of a rational number and an irrational number is irrational; and that the product of a nonzero rational number and an irrational number is irrational.

Also, *complex numbers* are an important part of high school math. Most high school students will only dip their toes into working with complex numbers, but the Common Core standards do give a series of directives for advanced, college-bound students working with complex numbers, most of which involve calculating with them. However, the standards do suggest that all high school students learn to solve quadratic equations with real coefficients but that result in complex solutions.

 **DEFINITION**

A **complex number** is a combination of a real number and an imaginary number, which gives a negative result when squared.

Moving on to functions, students once again build on what they have already mastered in middle school classes. The more formal study of functions begins with learning how to notate functions correctly, as well as to recognize that sequences can be functions.

With the emphasis on practical skills that comes with the standards, students are tasked with interpreting functions that arise in application in terms of the context in which they are used. Being able to graph functions correctly continues to be an important skill, and students are also asked to calculate and interpret the average rate of change of a function over a specified period of time. Writing functions is mentioned, too. The kinds of functions that a student should be able to graph and/or write include linear, quadratic, square roots, cube roots, polynomial functions, exponential functions, and logarithmic functions.

Students will also learn to build functions, meaning finding the function that describes a relationship between two quantities. For example, a student might build a function that shows the relationship between the temperature in the atmosphere as a function of height, and the height as a function of time, and the connection between the two. They'll also work on building new functions from existing functions, particularly in finding the inverse of an existent function. Do note that all of these tasks with functions occur in algebra and geometry classes, too; it's very likely that your child will learn to use functions in those classes.

COLLEGE AND CAREER READINESS

Advanced, college-bound students and their teachers will be interested in investigating the Common Core standards for working with vectors. The entirety of the section on vectors is marked for advanced students, so it is not covered here. More complex work in building new functions is also part of the advanced math standards.

Moving on from functions, high school math students will work on linear, quadratic, and exponential models, constructing and comparing them. Again, these skills are tied to both algebra and geometry. Context is a major consideration with this area of the standards. Students are asked to consider the context of the problems they've been assigned and keep it in mind when building models. Keep in mind, accuracy in some contexts is far more important than in others.

The last set of standards in this section cover trigonometric functions. Here, students are asked to work with the unit circle, which means a circle with a radius of 1. The unit circle can be used to better understand the properties of triangles, and students will learn to use it to do so. They'll also work with "periodic phenomena," a term that we most likely would use to think of a wave pattern. Amplitude, frequency, and midline are all considered in this area. Finally, in trigonometry, students are supposed to learn the Pythagorean identity, using it to find the measurements of triangles.

COLLEGE AND CAREER READINESS

For early college or advanced high school math students, the study of trigonometric functions goes deeper, including understanding the use of special triangles and addition and subtraction formulas for sine, cosine, and tangent.

Statistics and Probability

The final section of Common Core standards for math in grades 9–12 deals with statistics and probability. Your child could end up taking an entire class in statistics, or encounter them only in a political science class. No matter where they pop up, the standards for learning go into greater depth than you probably expected. The study of statistics at the high school level has advanced and deepened quite a bit in the last decade, and the standards want to continue that trend.

High school students should be able to "summarize, represent and interpret data on a single count or measurement variable" according to the first standard. This harks back to what has already been learned in prior grades. Students should be able to plot and graph statistics, compare the center and spread, interpret differences in the center and spread and to use standard techniques of working with data in order to fit the set into a normal distribution, allowing the estimation of population percentages. Students should also understand when the data cannot be used in a standard way and be able to explain why. The same is true for two categorical and quantitative variables and students will also learn to interpret linear models, and work with them—especially on computers.

KEYS TO THE CORE

Note the frequency with which the standards encourage the use of computers. A computer or tablet and a graphing calculator may be seen as essentials in your teenager's classroom.

Going further into working with statistics, high school students should be challenged to understand and evaluate random processes that underlie their statistical experimentation. This refers back to the fact that statistics are based on a random population sample. Testing their statistical processes is important. The standards suggest that teachers pose questions such as, "A model says a spinning coin falls heads up with the probability 0.5. Would a result of 5 tails in a row cause you to question the model?"

Making inferences from such thinking is also a key skill. Students are also encouraged to justify their conclusions, both in their observations, but also by using sample surveys (that is, testing another random sampling) and experimenting. The ability to generate and compare another data set to the original experiment is key.

At the high school level, working with probability continues to grow more complex. Students learn about independent and conditional probability, as well as how to determine each. Conditional probability measures the probability of an event given that another event has occurred. For example, students might consider and calculate the likelihood of a tsunami occurring if a volcano has erupted. Taking this probability and presenting it on a graph or chart is part of this skill, as is the ability to correctly estimate the probability before solving for it. The standards also ask that students be able to express probability in "everyday language and situations" with the example, "Compare the chance of having lung cancer if you are a smoker with the chance of being a smoker if you have lung cancer."

COLLEGE AND CAREER READINESS

Students looking to take statistics classes in college may wish to look over the advanced standards offered in the Common Core in this area. These emphasize using probability to make decisions and to evaluate the outcomes of decisions made. It's worth noting that many doctoral programs in all fields require at least one statistics class.

How to Support Your Child

Higher level math is challenging for many students. It is here more than at any other level that the standards' insistence on perseverance and precision is needed. Students must be precise at every step of their problem-solving to arrive at the correct answer, but the amount of steps required, not to mention the challenge of thinking through how to solve a problem, require perseverance. Homework cannot be rushed. Although your teen may have more obligations than ever before, between a job, relationships, and afterschool activities, making homework a priority will send the message that dedication is required in order to understand math. You may even want to suggest that your child do her homework with a friend or in a group of classmates, turning what can be a solitary struggle into a communal effort.

Make sure your child has the proper tools for completing math homework. This might include graphing paper, protractors, compasses, rulers, a graphing calculator or even a tablet computer. Don't underestimate the power of a good set of pens and pencils, too. Drawing and graphing is a big part of high school math, and a great way to engage students who like to use their hands.

Talking with your child's teacher often falls by the wayside in high school, and, of course, it's important that students begin to take personal responsibility for success in school. But maintaining good communication with teachers, even in high school, is a worthwhile endeavor. At the very least, your child's teacher should be able to provide a syllabus or other kind of overview of the course early on in the school year, allowing you to follow along with the class. Many high schools have a parents' night in the fall, which is a great time to meet your child's teachers and let them know that academic success is important to you. Attend parent-teacher conferences, and follow up with teachers about issues that you hear about during the conferences. Keep in touch throughout the year.

Take advantage of other outlets for math skills that your student's school offers. There might be a math club, or even a competitive math team, which your teenager may find enjoyable. Online resources still abound, and students may find books, movies, articles or even plays about famous mathematicians to be inspiring and intriguing. The play *Doubt* and the movie *A Beautiful Mind* are just two examples.

As mentioned at the beginning of this chapter, schools now often offer a variety of ways to advance in studies, from honors classes to AP courses to college classes. Discuss with your child what he or she will need to do to be ready for college or a career after high school, and work together to make sure such opportunities are taken advantage of. Taking an AP class, for example, often combines the best of college and high school with the opportunity to work directly with a supportive teacher in a small classroom, while also possibly earning college credit. Others may enjoy the opportunity to take a college class and try on that life before committing to it. And some students would prefer to enjoy high school as high school, without extra pressures.

If you feel you will not understand your child's math homework enough to be of help, you may want to talk with your child's teacher about how you can get up to speed. But don't underestimate how helpful you can be simply by listening to your child's description of what the problem is asking and how they'll go about solving it. A great deal of higher level math is about setting up the problem correctly, and less about computation. You can listen, ask questions, and speak up when you're not sure he's on the right track.

Finally, if your job or volunteer work requires mathematical or statistical thinking, you can engage your teenager in helping you. Those who work in construction, for example, might ask for help with geometric figuring, while those who work in public policy could possibly use a hand with statistical surveying. The point is not to overload your student with extra work, but to show how math, even advanced math, still has practical uses.

The Least You Need to Know

- The standards for math in grades 9–12 look at subjects instead of grade levels.

- The basics of algebra and geometry are covered, including standards that would be taught in Algebra I and II.

- Statistics and probability are an important part of the standards at this level, and grow in complexity.

- The standards include topics such as modeling that most likely will be taught in algebra and geometry.

- The emphasis continues to be on real-world problems and the use of computers and appropriate software is also suggested.

- There are a number of standards that are suggested for advanced high school or early college students. The majority of high schoolers will not need to know them before graduation, and quite possibly not in college either.

- Keeping in touch with your child's teacher is important, even in upper grades. Discuss your child's post-high school plans so you can prepare for them together.

Assessments, Implementation, and Moving Forward

This section looks at where the United States is today, four years after the Common Core began to be implemented in schools. You'll learn about the impact the standards have had, including some bumps in the road and the lessons that were learned. You'll also read about the assessments that will be used to measure learning based on Common Core standards and the different companies that create these tests. The section wraps up with a look at the next steps for implementation of the Common Core standards.

Common Core Assessments

If you have a school-age child, you're no doubt aware of the many standardized tests that are now part of the education landscape in the United States. There has been much debate over the validity of these assessments, particularly when student performance is tied to federal funding. Many parents and educators are concerned that "teaching to the test" has become the norm in classrooms, as teachers feel pressured to do whatever is necessary to raise test scores.

The Common Core does not eliminate the need for testing, but its champions hope that the emphasis on critical thinking and problem solving will result in assessments that give a more accurate picture of student achievement. New approaches to testing that focus on process rather than rote memorization help to align assessments to the way students are learning in class. New assessments that give students the ability to apply their knowledge by answering open-ended

In This Chapter

- The difference between current assessments and those aligned with the Common Core

- The computer skills will students need for new assessments

- Who creates the assessment materials and how they are administered

- How to help your child prepare for the new assessments

questions, manipulating and creating diagrams, and using evidence to support their reasoning give a more accurate picture of a student's skills than a strictly multiple-choice test.

This chapter will cover how standardized tests have been traditionally administered and what kinds of changes you can expect to see in assessments aligned to the Common Core.

A Brief History of Standardized Tests

Standardized tests have been administered in the United States since World War I, when the results were used to assign servicemen to various positions. In 1926, the SAT was the first of our current modern assessments to hit the scene. By the late 1940s, it was the standard that most universities used as a gauge for acceptance.

 DID YOU KNOW?

The earliest version of the SAT took 90 minutes and consisted of 315 questions on vocabulary, basic math, and fill-in-the-blank analogies like (grass:field::_____:desert).

The process of standardized testing was streamlined in 1936 with the invention of the automatic test scanner. This accomplished one of the primary goals of standardized testing, which was to be able to assess and score a large number of participants in a short amount of time. In 1959, the ACT test was developed to compete with the SAT. It covered a more comprehensive set of subjects including English, math, science, and later, history. The ACT is considered to lean more toward the content knowledge side, while the SAT tends to favor logic and reasoning.

Historically, except for primer versions of each, the ACT and SAT test have been relegated to a student's junior and senior year of high school, respectively. Most states have had a standardized achievement test for elementary, middle, and junior high grade levels going back to the 1970s or early 1980s. It wasn't until No Child Left Behind was enacted in 2001 that states were required to implement standardized testing in almost all grade levels to measure and track *academic achievement* and *academic growth* of students.

 **DEFINITION**

Academic achievement measures a student's academic performance at one specific time and compares a student's performance to a standard.

Academic growth measures the student's academic progress over an amount of time, usually from year-to-year, and compares a student's performance to his or her previous performance.

With the development of new standards, a new assessment arrived soon after. Common Core is no different. Because the Common Core standards are so different from most previous state standards, the new assessments that align to them will be unlike what states previously have had in place. Some states are choosing to create their own assessments to align with the standards, but there are also national groups that are developing new testing formats designed to be more engaging and adaptive.

How Common Core Assessments Are Different

For the most part, standardized assessments have been of one type: a multiple choice test that provides a range of answers from which students choose. This style of testing worked with the standards many states had in place prior to the Common Core, because they focused on memorizing facts and formulas to answer *what* questions.

The Common Core promotes more *why* and *how* questions through critical thinking and problem solving. It is difficult, if not impossible, to challenge a student to think critically on a multiple choice test. The Common Core demands new and different ways of assessing performance.

Written Answers

The Common Core puts a great deal of emphasis on writing at every grade level. Although most states have had a standardized writing assessment in place for several years, it is usually a standalone test that only evaluates writing. Most Common Core assessments integrate writing into the test as a way to evaluate a student's ability to support ideas and answers with evidence. For example, a student may still be asked a multiple choice question, but they might be required to support the answer they chose with evidence from a text within the test. So the student is not just assessed on their ability to choose the correct answer, but they are also assessed on their ability to provide reasoning to their decision.

Students may also be asked to read a passage and then write short answers to questions related to the passage. Instead of 20 multiple choice questions about a passage, there might be four *constructed response* questions that take longer to answer.

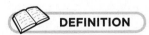 **DEFINITION**

Constructed response questions require the student taking the test to provide their own answer without the aid of any choices.

Students might be required to revise and rewrite a poorly-written paragraph. They could also be given new information to include into the paragraph.

Beginning in grade 3 and up, students could be given information or a text to read and asked to complete *performance tasks* like writing a persuasive argument. Students in grades 3 and 4 could be given two texts to integrate into the performance task, and high school students could be asked to incorporate up to five sources in their responses.

 **DEFINITION**

> **Performance tasks** direct a student to a certain outcome by posing a question, asking the student to make a comparison, or asking student to form a relationship between two ideas. The student must apply previous knowledge and acquired skills to accomplish the task

Most of the new Common Core assessments will be computer-based, so students could be given source material to read, view, or listen to and then asked a series of higher-order thinking questions about the material. Students would have to analyze the information and give supporting evidence in their answers. In another section of the test, students could be asked to write a persuasive essay over these same materials where they must provide claims, counterclaims, and evidence as required in the Common Core ELA standards.

Multi-Step Problem Solving

There are noticeable differences in Common Core math assessments as well. Students will still be asked to solve simple equations, but they will also be asked apply their knowledge to real-world problems, sometimes applying the answer from the simple equation. Instead of choosing an answer from multiple choices, students will be required to key in their answer. This dramatically reduces the chance that a student can guess at a correct answer by selecting a provided choice.

There are also performance tasks in math assessments that are multi-step problems. Students receive a point value for a problem based on the steps that are correctly completed, with the majority of the points given for the correct answer to main equation. Subsequent points would be awarded for application of the answer in follow-up questions. For instance, a student might be asked to solve an equation based on a word problem, and then asked to create a chart or graph to help explain the answer. They might also be asked to type an explanation of how they arrived at the answer.

How Common Core Assessments Are Administered

Most of the new assessments aligned to Common Core will be administered online through a computer or tablet device. Depending on the assessment, students will have a combination of texts to read, videos to watch, or audio recordings to listen to as resource material to answer questions.

This media capability is a quantum leap from the paper test booklets most students used in the past. With the ability to move between the text and the questions, a student can be required to answer a question and then highlight, copy, and paste words, phrases, or passages that provide supporting evidence for their answer. This aligns with Common Core anchor standards for literacy. The media capabilities also allow developers of the assessment to include video clips and possibly websites as sources of information that the students may draw from to support their claims in essays or short-answer responses.

 DID YOU KNOW?

The answer is yes and no. The computer will score many of the items, but flesh and blood human beings will have to score some portions where students are writing short answers or essays.

In order for students to use an online assessment platform seamlessly and naturally, they must begin learning computer literacy skills and keyboarding skills early in their education. If students are not competent at manipulating items on a computer or tablet and minimally competent at typing by grade 3, then the assessment becomes a test of their computer skills rather than a test of their academic knowledge and skills. Along with basic word-processing skills, students must also learn to manipulate graphs and spreadsheets.

Another difference in an online platform is that unless a school has a one-to-one computer to student ratio, all students in a grade may not take the assessment at the same time, as they would with a paper-and-pencil version. Test developers understand that infrastructure and equipment might be a challenge. One option for addressing this is using a rolling schedule that allows small groups of students to take the test at different times. In most states, the state-required standardized assessments are administered at the end of the school year in kindergarten through eighth grade and at the end of a course in high school. So end-of-course exams depend on whether a high school is on a block schedule, in which courses end each semester, or a year-long schedule.

Assessment Vendors

There are three major assessment vendors that have developed or are in the process of developing what has been termed by some as the "next generation" in assessments. Each vendor has a slightly different slant, but ultimately they each create testing material that aligns very closely to the standards. It is highly likely that if your child is in a state that has adopted the Common Core standards, they will be assessed using one of these vendors. Because the standards are consistent from state to state, the vendors don't have to create state-specific tests. If your child is being assessed using "Vendor A" and your nephew in another state is also being assessed using "Vendor A," then they are taking the exact same assessment. If you are interested in learning which assessment your state has adopted, that information can be found on your state's Department of Education's website.

PARCC

PARCC stands for Partnership for Assessment of Readiness for College and Career. It is supported by a group of states that joined forces to create online math and ELA assessments that align to Common Core standards. PARCC tests are fixed form, which means the questions don't adapt based on a student's answer to a previous question. The tests are designed to measure a student against grade-level expectations. In this way, test results indicate whether a student is at grade level and on the correct trajectory to college and career readiness.

Prior to this type of testing, the only real way to gauge if a student was on track to graduate college and career ready was by taking the ACT or SAT during their junior and senior years. This is a little late to find out if your child is ready for opportunities after graduation. The PLAN test, which is an early version of the ACT, and the PSAT, which is an early version of the SAT give a somewhat clearer picture of a student's readiness. However, they are still not given until after a student is out of elementary and middle school. In contrast, if a grade 3 student does poorly on the assessment, parents and teachers will know that student needs additional support to get back on track to college and career readiness.

 DID YOU KNOW?

More information on the PARCC assessment can be found at parcconline.org, including a list of the participating states and sample question items.

Smarter Balanced Assessment Consortium (SBAC)

The Smarter Balanced Assessment Consortium is usually just referred to as Smarter Balanced. It is also a group of states that have come together to develop an assessment that aligns with Common Core. It will be an adaptive-form assessment. This means that when a student answers a question, the computer generates two more questions based on their answer. In this way, if a student keeps getting a correct answer, the difficulty will increase. If a student misses a question, the difficulty will decrease. The theory behind this type of assessment is that teachers can see if students are working ahead or behind their current grade level. This assessment will be implemented for the first time in the 2014-2015 school year.

 DID YOU KNOW?

More information on Smarter Balanced can be found at smarterbalanced. org, including a list of the participating states and practice items.

ACT Aspire

The ACT Aspire is a partnering company to ACT. The assessment offers multiple question formats such as constructed-response, selected-response, and technology-enhanced items. The big selling point of ACT Aspire is that they have the benefit of aligning to their sister company ACT, and that they offer *interim assessments* and classroom level assessments.

 **DEFINITION**

Interim assessment is a form of assessment used by educators to evaluate the learning progress of students. This type of assessment is used to guide instruction in preparing students for an end-of-year standardized test.

According to ACT Aspire, it will be offered in a paper-and-pencil version indefinitely as long as adopters of the test need this option. This differs from PARCC and Smarter Balanced, which both have a pencil-and-paper option now, but have hinted this might be for a limited time. However, it is unlikely that schools in the United States will be giving anything but online standardized tests after 2018, whether a state is using Common Core standards or not.

 DID YOU KNOW?

More information on ACT Aspire can be found at discoveractaspire.org.

How to Help Your Child Prepare

Because there is so much emphasis placed on standardized test performance, many parents are very concerned about doing as much as possible to ensure that their children do well. It's important to keep in mind that all the things you do to foster your child's education will ultimately help them on assessments. Reading to and with them, engaging them in conversations about what they're learning, and applying critical thinking to real-world situations are the best ways to instill the skills your child will need to be successful. However, there are a few things you can do specifically to help your child prepare for assessments.

Technological Literacy

One of the first things is to support your child in their technological literacy. If you have a computer or tablet at home, start teaching them at an early age how to use a mouse and keyboard for basic functions. There are literally thousands of educational games out there for children of all ages, and these are a good way for young children to begin gaining familiarity with computer technology and equipment. Kids in today's generation are born into a culture of technology, so they pick up the basic skills very quickly.

Keyboarding skills will become important, especially starting in grade 3. If you do have a computer or tablet at home, the earlier you can expose your child to correct keyboarding form the less likely he or she will be to develop bad habits. There are a multitude of free online programs in a game format, or you could purchase inexpensive keyboarding tutorial software.

Practice Resources

Both PARCC and Smarter Balanced offer practice tests within grade bands, such as grades 3–5 ELA, to help parents and students familiarize themselves with this type of testing platform. These practice tests are not intended to prepare students with content or academic skills, but rather to help them see what kinds of questions will be asked and what computer literacy skills, such as drag and drop, will be required. Both groups offer these practice tests free on their websites.

ACT Aspire also offers practice tests, but they incorporate items from all grade bands. For example, the math practice test has items for grade 3 through early high school. This practice test gives students limited exposure to the types of questions they will have in their grade, but it does provide a good overview for parents, educators, and policymakers as to the format Act Aspire will use.

The Least You Need To Know

- Most standardized assessments are transitioning to an online format, including those aligned to Common Core.

- Students will need to learn computer literacy skills and keyboarding skills early in their education.

- Unlike traditional standardized tests, assessments aligned to the Common Core rely on written answers and multi-step problems rather than multiple-choice questions.

- The three primary assessment vendors that supply schools with assessments aligned to the Common Core are PARCC, Smarter Balanced, and ACT Aspire.

- Parents and students can explore these new assessment through practice items on each of the respective websites.

Implementation of the Common Core

In 2015, most states that have adopted the Common Core standards will begin their fourth year of implementation. There was no implementation formula given to states, so some states experienced hiccups in implementing the standards where others did not. However, as educational initiatives go, this is the largest scale in which states have worked independently toward a common goal and produced positive results with their own plans for implementation.

In this chapter, lessons learned from implementation of the standards will be discussed as well as what needs to happen in states for the Common Core to have the impact the developers intended. There will also be a look at the perception educators in K-12 and higher education have of the standards.

In This Chapter

* What states and districts have learned from implementing the Common Core standards

* How educators view the Common Core standards

* How the adopting the Common Core affects higher education

* What needs to happen for the Common Core to be successful

The Opportunity for Sharing

One of the positive aspects of having common standards is that states can see what is or is not working around them to help direct their own work. Before Common Core standards, states did not have the ability to do an apples-to-apples comparison of *best practices*. It was often challenging to replicate work that seemed to be getting results in another state because the content or grade level expectations might not align. For example, it would be like an ice hockey player trying to learn how to improve his skills by going to watch a field hockey game. The basic concepts might be the same, but the nuances of each sport are quite different.

 **DEFINITION**

Best practice is a term that is used to describe an instructional strategy that has proven to get positive results. It is often used when describing training strategies or new resource materials for the classroom.

The fact that over forty states are all working through implementation brings a great deal of sharing of ideas to the table on a scale that has not been possible before. Teachers from different states who meet at conferences or professional development training feel a sense of camaraderie with one another because of the instructional practices they share through Common Core standards. This has not only linked veteran teachers but new teachers as well. It has also created a space for the sharing of ideas and resources. In the past, a teacher might pose a question on an online forum about a grade 6 math standard, and the responses would be limited to teachers in that state. Now this same teacher could theoretically draw on the collective insight of teachers from across the country, all of whom could bring a different perspective on how to teach the standard.

This is one of the key things to remember about the standards. States that have adopted Common Core are not clones of each other. Rather, states that have adopted Common Core are operating from the same foundational skills at each grade level, which allows teachers from all over the country to share information and learn from each other. In fact, there are jobs being created just to manage the massive amounts of online information about Common Core best practices that have been shared by teachers. This type of sharing across states can only lead to more opportunities for improvement and support.

Implementation Lessons Learned

In talking with people involved in the implementation process across the country, several lessons have emerged. The greatest one seems to be the importance of communication at the beginning of implementation. Before the implementation of the Common Core, many state standards changed on a regular basis, and there was rarely much effort to explain the changes to the public. For this reason, most state leaders assumed that the same approach would work when introducing the Common Core.

Many state leaders also believed that these standards were not only an improvement on existing standards, but they also brought a level of consistency among states that was invaluable. With all this in mind, they did not see the need to "sell" the concept of Common Core standards to the public at large because the concept of the standards made so much sense. They were not prepared for the public backlash against the Common Core, fueled largely by misleading or incorrect information.

The results of this miscalculation have been massive communication efforts by states to inform the public exactly what Common Core is, why the state adopted the standards, how classrooms will look different, and more recently what new assessments for the standards might look like.

The Importance of Parent Engagement

One benefit of this experience is that states and districts have become more focused on engaging parents and explaining new education initiatives or reforms that may be taking place at the state of district level. Every Common Core conference, seminar, or training I have been a part of the past two years as either a participant or presenter has had some kind of session on parent engagement. States and districts are going above and beyond to find new ways to reach parents and to communicate the importance of the implementation changes that come with the Common Core. For the first time, districts of every size are hiring communications directors, which was previously a role found only in large urban districts.

Many schools and school districts have hosted parent or community nights to give an overview of the Common Core standards, as well as offering an opportunity for parents to ask questions they may have. Some districts are creating parent toolkits that contain materials that give information on Common Core and the assessments to go with them. Some of these resources also discuss the myths that surround the Common Core and explain how classrooms and homework may look different so that parents are not caught off guard. Some districts or schools even have websites dedicated to explaining the standards and the implementation process, as well as the assessments that accompany them. Ultimately, however, if you have questions you can't get answered through the resources provided by your child's school, it's always a great idea to discuss your questions with your child's teacher or principal.

TAKE CARE

Communication to parents has always been an ongoing challenge for states when implementing any new initiative. Departments of Education are usually limited to sharing news through the internet or major newspapers in the state, so they rely heavily on school districts to pass along information that is important for parents to know.

Slow and Steady May Not Be Best

Most states implemented the standard in a gradual progression through grade levels starting in kindergarten through grade 5 one year, grades 6 through 8 the next year, and grades 9 through 12 the third year. New assessments aligned to the standards will follow for most states in the 2014-2015 school year. This gradual implementation model is different from the way states typically transition to new standards, which is usually a wholesale change for all grades in one year, or sometimes standards are only changed in elementary school or high school. As mentioned in chapter 4, some leaders have questioned in hindsight if implementing so slowly and deliberately resulted in too long of an adjustment period, allowing time for opposition to the standards to develop. Some have voiced that a "ripping the Band-Aid off" approach might have been more effective.

The Need for Common Core Materials

Another issue that some schools and districts faced in the early stages of implementation was a lack of textbooks or commercial instructional materials supporting the teaching of the standards. One of the prevalent myths is that there are "Common Core" textbooks written by the developers of Common Core; however, there has been a deliberate stance taken by the Common Core State Standards Initiative that no commercial materials will be created under this entity. This left the purchase or creation of curriculum materials up to the districts.

TAKE CARE

Remember, Appendix B in the Common Core standards gives a list of example texts that meet the complexity standards for each grade level. It is not a required, or even suggested, reading list.

In reality, the standards lend themselves to teacher-created materials and lessons much more than pre-made worksheets, workbooks, or what has historically been used as a textbook. If school districts had been overly reliant on pre-made materials or textbooks as part of their curriculum, then it was a challenge to implement the standards with no commercial materials as instructional aids.

More Public Input

One positive aspect to the opposition to Common Core is that it has encouraged some parents and other stakeholders to get more involved in what is going on in their school district. Schools and school districts are trying to be very cognizant of the fact that you can't be too transparent when dealing with school academic issues, so many districts have revamped their textbook and curriculum committees to include more parents and local stakeholder groups. This is in an effort to make sure the public has input on textbook selection so that materials are reflective of the local values of the community surrounding the school.

 TAKE CARE

Remember that the standards are what students are expected to learn. The curriculum is the textbooks, materials, and instructional practices used to teach the standards.

The Need for Technology

The cost of upgrading the technology infrastructure in schools has also been a topic of debate in some states. States that are choosing to adopt new online assessments to align with Common Core standards must meet minimum technology readiness requirements in their schools. This is approximately a 1 to 6 ratio of computers to students, and schools must also have high speed internet.

Some school districts have argued that requiring this type of technology upgrade puts an undue financial burden on schools and diverts funds from other needs. Others argue that these upgrades should be made regardless of a change in assessment platforms because technology is such an important aspect of our culture, as well as college and career readiness.

 DID YOU KNOW?

The average American spends a little over two hours a day interacting with a computer and smartphone, and the average American household spends 17 percent of their monthly budget on technology-related expenses.

It should be noted that three of the major Common Core assessment providers, PARCC, Smarter Balanced, and ACT Aspire will offer paper-and-pencil versions of their assessments during the transition period from paper to completely online. PARCC has guaranteed the first year will have a paper-and-pencil version, with the possibility of a second and third year. Smarter Balanced will offer a paper-and-pencil version for the first three years of the transition, and ACT Aspire has not yet published the time frame to which the paper-and-pencil version will be limited.

Assessment Results

New York and Kentucky have created the Common Core assessments for their states and were the first in the country to administer a completely Common Core-aligned assessment. Kentucky, the first state to adopt Common Core, administered its test in the 2011-2012 school year, and New York administered its assessment in the 2012-2013 school year. Both states saw significant drops in their state-wide student achievement. However, this was an expected outcome for which both states prepared the public through aggressive communication plans.

Both states correctly assumed students would find the new assessments challenging, since the new tests had much higher expectations. In the minds of the state leaders, this higher expectation on the assessment aligned with the higher expectations for the way students were learning in class. It should also be noted, however, that Kentucky did see slight improvement the next year it administered its assessments.

Most of the other states that have adopted Common Core will begin using completely aligned assessments in the 2014-2015 school year. It should be noted that some of these states have chosen to delay accountability for students and teachers on the scores from these tests for one to two years. This has stemmed some of the opposition around the standards. It has also been applauded by teacher unions across the country as an acknowledgement that a small amount of grace should be extended to educators during a time of transition. The National Education Association has been a supporter of Common Core standards from the beginning, although it has taken issue with implementation of the standards in some states, arguing that teachers lacked sufficient training or resources to adequately implement the standards. By delaying accountability for assessment results, some states have extended an olive branch to their state union affiliates in an effort to help mitigate some of the challenges teachers have faced with implementation.

Educator Perceptions

Educators have overwhelmingly supported the concept and intent of the Common Core standards, but some have had problems with the quality of implementation in their state or the available resources in their state. In states that tie student scores on standardized tests to a teacher's evaluation, teachers have opposed accountability for their students' scores on the first or second administrations of Common Core-aligned tests. Some educators have argued that since states are acknowledging there will be a drop in student scores, there needs to be a grace period for accountability until students become more familiar with the standards, how they are taught, and how they are assessed.

Concern About Technology

Some educators also argue that student computer skills are an issue, since many of the new Common Core-aligned assessments are administered online. It's not just a matter of having the computers and infrastructure to take the assessments, it is also a matter of students having the necessary computer literacy skills and keyboarding skills to take the assessment in an unencumbered way. Some educators worry assessments such as these become more a test of a student's computer competency skills and typing proficiency than an assessment of their content knowledge and problem solving abilities. To address this issue, schools must incorporate classes for basic computing skills and keyboarding into the curriculum at the primary grades.

KEYS TO THE CORE

In order to meet the keyboarding requirements necessary to accomplish the grade 4 task of typing one page in a single sitting, a student will need to type about 300 words. At 25 words per minute, they will be typing for fourteen minutes without a break.

The flipside of the technology argument is a strong belief of many educators that these types of skills should be incorporated into the curriculum regardless of a change in assessment. To many educators, online assessments and the ability to use computers seamlessly in the learning process are a necessary component of preparing students to be college- and career-ready.

Worry About Parent Backlash

Some teachers also feel pressure from frustrated parents. As discussed in previous chapters, some of the new approaches that focus on critical thinking and problem solving can be unexpected and challenging for parents. As a result, the teacher may become the target for the parent's frustration. This is a hard pill for teachers to swallow, since they know the student is working at a higher level than before. This is why it is more important than ever to communicate regularly with your child's school. It is also important to attend parent/teacher nights or open house events as much as possible to get an accurate picture of the type of learning that is going on in classrooms and how to support this learning.

The Effect on Higher Education

Higher education institutions were also affected by the adoption of the Common Core. In states that have adopted the standards, teacher preparation programs must adapt their courses to match instructional practices that can support Common Core standards. This has required training for many college professors of education, who do not have personal experience teaching to the Common Core standards

One of the positive aspects to this is that college professors are attending trainings side-by-side with public school educators. In many states, this connection through professional development has strengthened the relationship between higher education and K-12 education. This has also led some teacher preparation programs to focus more on the practical components of teaching and less on the theoretical. States have started looking at the effectiveness of teacher preparation programs by analyzing the test data of their graduates in the first five years of their career after graduation. State-supported colleges and universities are especially under the microscope to evaluate the effectiveness of their programs. This means that the training future teachers receive must align as much as possible with the work being done in the field.

The Role of Administrators

As states develop teacher evaluation systems that are more rigorous, administrators who must perform the evaluations need to have a good working knowledge of the Common Core standards and the instructional practices that support them. Without an understanding of the instructional shifts that have taken place with the implementation of the standards, principals and other administrators will find it very challenging to give good feedback to teachers after observing them.

DID YOU KNOW?

Forty-one states recommend or require that a teacher's evaluation include multiple measures to get a more complete analysis of a teacher's performance. No state uses standardized test data alone as the sole measure of teacher performance and effectiveness.

With the role of the principal becoming more of an instructional leader rather than a building manager, teachers are increasingly looking to them for instructional support and to provide professional development opportunities that are relevant to the needs in the school. States like Tennessee have undertaken large-scale administrator training programs that help foster a good understanding of the standards and how to support their implementation. These trainings were geared toward helping to equip principals, curriculum supervisors, and superintendents in supporting implementation at the school and district level. This is another deviation from most changes in standards in the past. It is usually only the teachers who receive training when new standards are adopted. The idea of including principals, curriculum supervisors, and superintendents in the training process signals an ownership of the standards at a new level.

Despite some of the implementations snags along the way and the residual challenges, such as new assessments, that have accompanied the standards, educators have been some of the most vocal advocates in favor of the standards. The Common Core seems to have a unifying effect for teachers who believe the standards will truly help their students succeed.

TAKE CARE

If you hear something negative about the Common Core, make sure to analyze whether it is specific to the standards themselves or something attributed to the standards.

Moving Forward

The political nature of the Common Core discussion seems to increase on a weekly basis. This has become a disheartening distraction for educators as they try to keep moving forward with the teaching the standards. If you look at it from the teacher's perspective, it becomes a mixture of alarm and discouragement to think that four years of training, classroom shifts, and student progress might be derailed by political lines in the sand, especially when most of these discussions and challenges to the Common Core are coming several years after the fact.

The political issues surrounding Common Core seem to be the only thing that could derail the continued implementation. States are seeing increased gains in student achievement and preparation for college and career readiness, but there seems to be little of the discussion geared around this. The further discussions drift from the emphasis on students and student learning, the more red flags should go up about the true nature of the conversation. Many educators who support Common Core standards use the simple argument of asking, "What is plan B if we don't use Common Core standards?" For many states that have adopted Common Core standards, the alternative would be going back to standards that had them ranked in the bottom twenty percent of the nation or back to a differing mix of standards that had the United States falling well behind other countries on international math, science, and language assessments.

Importance of Sound Curriculum

It has been discussed earlier that control of curriculum decisions are made at the local level. This means that as Common Core is implemented, schools and school districts must have strategies in place to vet materials to make sure they support Common Core standards with fidelity. Just because it has a "Common Core" sticker on it, doesn't necessarily mean it supports the standards. Some education resource companies have tried to capitalize on the mad dash by some states, school districts, and schools to purchase classroom materials. As educators become savvier to the instruction of the standards, they should also become more discerning in the materials they choose as well.

Altering the Standards

The ability of states to choose whether or not to adopt the Common Core and the level of local control once they do is both a blessing and a curse. Because the states chose independently to adopt the standards, there is no governing body to make sure that the standards are implemented with fidelity, that assessments align to the standards, or that the standards are kept intact in each state.

As previously mentioned, states that adopt the Common Core are free to add additional standards (up to 15 percent) at each grade level if they chose to do so. However, altering or removing just one of the standards is a violation of the trademark and copyright agreement of the developers of the Common Core. Though they do not have Common Core materials or textbooks, the developers are adamant about protecting the stair-step progression that allows the standards to build on each other from year to year. To remove even one standard undermines future learning and skills that are dependent upon that standard.

If a state does alter or remove a standard, who calls them out on it? The answer is: no one. Although the developers of the Common Core or one of the consortiums involved with assessment development might address this departure, there is no one with the authority to bring a state back into 100 percent alignment to the standards. Again, this shows the freedom to adopt the standards and the freedom to choose not to adhere to them completely. Although removing or altering standards would defeat the purpose, that freedom exists nonetheless.

Some states that wish to settle some of the political turmoil around the standards continue to tinker with the idea of modifying the standards to make them more tailored to their specific needs. However, it would be a challenge to determine which standards to remove or alter since the Common Core attempts to narrow the focus of foundational skills to a manageable amount at each grade. The developers of Common Core are also quick to acknowledge that the standards are the "minimum" learning expectations at each grade level. If a state chooses to add additional material for student to go beyond these minimum expectations, they have the freedom to do this. This is a much preferred alternative to tinkering with the standards just for the sake of rebranding.

For some states that had felt they had high standards before Common Core, adding the percent to the standards makes much more sense than removing or altering standards. This keeps consistency, while also allowing states to include concepts they feel are beneficial to their students. Again, it is important to remember that Common Core standards are the minimum expectations, not the maximum. For some states, the minimum is still much higher than what they previously had in place. For other states, the Common Core provides an opportunity to expand from these foundational skills to a level that challenges all students to grow academically.

Continuing Professional Development

Ongoing training for educators is also a must to see the standards succeed. Many educators have become comfortable with the higher expectations of Common Core and they can start refining their instruction to really capitalize on the rigor and skills they have to offer. In other words, teachers are at the point in the learning curve where it's not just about figuring out how to teach the standards; they are now positioned to teach them better. This is not only because teachers are becoming more familiar with the standards, but also because students are adapting to the increased expectations. The students who started their academic careers with Common Core are showing success as well. In most states, those students will be entering grade 3 in the fall of 2014. As the first cohorts of students make their way up the grade levels each year, the academic strength of each class should be evident, and it should appear as a foundational upwelling.

When I was an assistant football coach, our team wasn't the greatest in the world. As a matter of fact, our record was pretty dismal a couple of years in a row. One of the other assistant coaches was constantly telling us: "We just need to hang on a few more years. Help is on the way." He was referring to a group of students in the middle school who were exceptional athletes. His belief in these students proved true—five years later, that group of young men led the team to a number two ranking in the state. I use this real-life analogy as an example of the hope that many educators see in Common Core standards. There is a belief that every year the cohorts of students who started in kindergarten with Common Core standards will be the first of many students that are graduating with academic skills and knowledge that prepare our students for success at unprecedented levels.

DID YOU KNOW?

The rate that human knowledge doubles is approximately every 12 months. This is up from every 25 years in 1947. This means that students who started kindergarten under Common Core standards will see human knowledge double at least 13 times by the time they graduate. That gives a whole new meaning to learning critical thinking, problem solving, and research skills versus trying to memorize as much information as possible.

The Least You Need To Know

- One of the most important lessons to come out of the implementation of the Common Core is the importance of parent engagement and communication.

- Student test scores will likely drop during the first year or two of implementation due to increased expectations, but this is not an indication of a decrease in learning.

- Most educators support the standards, but there are concerns about implementation and adequate teaching materials.

- Challenges to Common Core continue to become more political rather than academic.

Next Steps for Parents

If you are a parent and have chosen to read this book, then it is evident you are interested in learning more about your child's classroom experience and how to support him or her in being as successful as possible. Keep in mind that you do not have to be an expert in education standards or instructional practices to support your child. A crucial part is simply building a relationship with your child's school. This, above all, will help you understand the best ways to create an environment at home that supports the type of learning taking place in the classroom.

The information in this chapter will prepare you to have an informed, productive conversation with your child's teacher, whether your child is in elementary, middle, or high school. Begin this dialogue at the start of the school year, and continue it throughout the year.

In This Chapter

- The importance of building a relationship with your child's teachers and school

- How to handle frustration over challenges at school

- Focusing on effort rather than grades

- A review of how to best support your child from kindergarten through high school

- The goal of college and career readiness

Building Relationships with the School

As a parent, it is critical that you understand the expectations of your child's teacher. Do not rely on the student as the only conduit for all information coming from the school. Take advantage of back-to-school events, open house nights, and parent/teacher conference nights to meet teachers and get specific information on how to support your child.

However, don't limit your interactions to just these events. Ask teachers early on what form of communication they prefer and stay in contact with them. Most teachers use email in order to have an ongoing discussion without the difficulty of coordinating a phone call. This also helps keep a running record of the dialogue so that the student's progress can be monitored and a clearer picture of where a student needs help can be obtained.

 **TAKE CARE**

If you have major concerns or are looking for in-depth advice from the teacher on how to support your child at home, make a special appointment. Parent nights, back-to-school events, and open houses are not structured for this type of conversation. By making a specific appointment, you and the teacher will be able to have a longer, more focused conversation.

Unfortunately, many times a parent/teacher interaction is limited to issues related to poor academic performance or behavior problems. If you establish a relationship with your child's teachers early on, it will be much easier to navigate the negative waters when they arise. For example, you might ask the teacher to contact you when your child does well on an assignment so that you can see the standard the teacher is trying to get your child to reach.

Continue the Dialogue

It is also important to continue to engage your child's teachers even as they get older and move into middle and high school. For some reason, parent engagement seems to decline as students get older. I saw this year after year when I was a principal at an elementary school and later a high school. In the elementary school, the halls would be crowded with parents on the parent/teacher nights or open house nights, but when we had parent/teacher nights at the high school, only a few parents would attend.

This may be because parents feel that their role as an academic support diminishes as students get older, especially as the academic work may go beyond a level of comfort for adults who have been out of school for a while. However, it is important to maintain a strong relationship with the school and specifically the teachers in order to keep a solid academic environment at home. This also lets your child know that you are still part of the process of supporting his or her learning and are not only called upon when there is a problem.

Don't Be Afraid to Ask Questions

If you have questions or concerns, it is better to address them early on rather than until the next parent/teacher night or other school-sponsored event. Teachers would much rather address problems before they get to a point of frustration that is too overwhelming for the student to overcome. If your child is struggling and you don't understand how to do the work as the assignment asks, have the teacher give you some guidelines or examples of questions you can ask your child to help direct their work. You can help facilitate the process by leading your child through broader questioning that is similar to the way they are directed in class. These questions are not about giving the student the answer as much as giving the student direction to come to the answer themselves.

 DID YOU KNOW?

Many teachers use text alert systems to send texts to parents in order to keep them in the loop regarding upcoming tests, assignments, or events. Check with your school or teacher about signing up for this option.

Emphasizing Effort over Grades

A good way to keep your child motivated and make sure they are doing their best is to emphasize the effort they have given to an assignment rather than the grade they receive after they turn it in. If you focus on the effort, you can encourage your child when they might struggle through some of the material.

Prepare for Setbacks

As the standards become more challenging and expectations are increased, it is only natural that some students might struggle when they begin working with the Common Core standards. This is especially true in the middle and high school grades. I have seen many parents become frustrated when their child who had been getting high grades suddenly begins bringing home lower scores. This is alarming to some parents who might not be used to their children being challenged at school.

The higher expectations of the Common Core can be especially difficult for students in middle school and high school who did not start their academic career with the standards. For some students, it is the equivalent of being thrown to the deep end of the pool to learn how to swim. Most states have taken steps to support these students through intervention and remediation programs, but it still does not negate the fact that some students might initially struggle with Common Core standards until they become acclimated to the higher expectations and rigor the standards support.

Find Growth in the Struggle

As a parent myself, I know it can be frustrating when your child's grades drop. This is not an uncommon phenomenon in classrooms that have implemented Common Core standards. There is often a small dip in scores when students encounter the standards the first time. The good news is that patience usually pays off, and students become accustomed to the higher expectations and start scoring at the same level as they had in the past.

The even better news is that your child is probably growing more academically than they ever have before. Researchers have found that there is increased growth in the struggle. The more students have to work for answers, the more they are engaging their cognitive abilities. It may be easier on both the student and teacher memorize a list of facts and figures and apply it later on a test, but if this is the only type of learning students are doing, they are not being pushed outside their comfort zones. Using problem-solving techniques and participating in critical thinking activities are where real growth takes place.

Don't worry if your child struggles a little with his or her work. It's not good for them to be continually frustrated, but it is good to challenge them to think about answers and work for solutions. This will take patience from both you and your child. There will be nights around the kitchen table when everyone might become fed up with homework. Try to keep your own frustration in check. If your child sees you reacting in a negative way, they will see that as an excuse to be negative about their homework. Homework time is rarely fun, but it doesn't need to be viewed by your child as a horrible time they dread each evening. Try to make it as lighthearted as possible, and remember that struggling a little through content and growing academically is a much better than breezing through busy work.

 **TAKE CARE**

Even though it may take a great deal of patience and a good poker face on your part, don't let you child see you become frustrated with their homework. Acknowledge that it's a challenge for both of you, and think about guiding questions that might lead your child to the answer. Don't be afraid to call in support if needed. Contacting a classmate might do the trick, or using a free homework hotline. If you have exhausted all resources, write the teacher a note and ask for guidance so you and your child will understand specifically what is being asked.

Reviewing Your Child's Work

As parents, we are used to helping our children with their homework, or at the very least, we're used to being asked, "Is this right?" as they wave a paper in front of our faces. To be honest, there may be times when you can't answer that question. Sometimes it's not about knowing the right answer as much as it is being able to ask guiding questions that lead a child to assess their own work. Your child's teacher should be able to provide a set of guiding questions at the beginning of the year to ask in order to support your child. Also, if you need to send a note to the teacher asking for help, be specific in your details so the teacher can also be specific in the response. Let the teacher know at which point you and your child got stuck.

Supporting Your Child from Kindergarten through High School

Studies have shown that academic success is strongly tied to parental involvement. Demonstrate to your child that education a priority by taking an active role in their schooling and reinforcing the skills they are learning in the classroom. This doesn't mean piling on extra worksheets or forcing your child to read textbooks during summer vacation. There are many learning opportunities that occur naturally in your daily life.

Kindergarten to Grade 2

The first years of your child's academic career are arguably the most important. It is during this time that students learn foundational skills that will be used the rest of their lives. Since the Common Core standards build on each other like stairsteps from year to year, it is critical that students find success in kindergarten through second grade, and your support as a parent is an important part of the process.

The most effective activity you can do at this age to invest in your child's success is carve out a dedicated time each evening for reading to your child and listening to your child read. Asking questions during the reading and also encouraging your child to pose their own questions is an easy but valuable way to make the time support the skills they are learning in class.

It is also important to emphasize writing and to have them periodically produce writing that relates to their life. This can be as simple as writing thank-you notes or a short description of a picture they drew. Some parents mistakenly think that "writing" means an essay, when really, at this age, you just want them in the habit of integrating writing into their lives, in addition to what they are doing in class.

Math is a little more of a challenge to support at home, but there are some foundational skills you can reinforce with minimal frustration for you or your child. Having your child count objects around you while in the car or in a restaurant, then taking away or adding objects to the total is an easy way to get them thinking about addition and subtraction. You don't have to set up written problems to get them thinking about number value and relationships.

 TAKE CARE

Your behavior will quickly set the tone for your child's perception of math at this age, so make sure your child understands you are supportive of learning math concepts, even if you're unfamiliar with some of the methods your child may be learning.

The other important concepts at this age to talk about are measurement, time, and money. You don't have to carry around a ruler to support measurement, but you can use do simple things like asking how many spoon lengths is the edge of the table to get them thinking about the concept of measurement. You can also point out time changes on a clock and have your child time something while you are waiting somewhere or driving down the road. To get your child more familiar with money, have him or her count the change in your pocket or discuss the price of items in your shopping cart. None of these activities have to be mentally strenuous. The point is to give attention to math as part of their lives, not to create lessons every time you walk down the grocery aisle.

When trying to support literacy or math at home, ultimately, your child's teacher is the most valuable resource at your disposal during these years. As him or her what you can do to specifically support the instruction they are providing in class. Keeping an open line of communication with the teacher not only helps you stay informed on ways to support your child, it also shows your child at an early age you value what they are doing at school.

KEYS TO THE CORE

Even though it might not be the most popular move with your child, ask the teacher what you can do over the summer to support your child in maintaining the skills they have learned that year. It doesn't have to be a nightly activity, but once a week or every other week finding a fun way to do a "review night" will help support your child in retaining the skills he acquired the year before.

Grades 3–5

Third grade through fifth grade is where you will see your child start reading more complex texts and writing a great deal more. Your child will be asked more and more to give their opinion and justify it with evidence. When you read together, have your child explain their thinking as they answer questions you pose. Also, continue to have your child do informal writing. Encourage them to practice reasoning and justification by writing a letter explaining why they should be allowed to do a special activity or buy something they want.

In math, it might be worth your time to invest in a grade-appropriate workbook or software for a computer or tablet. Skills in this grade band become increasingly complex, so it's not as easy to support your child's learning by counting sugar packets at the restaurant. Use a math workbook sparingly but consistently so it doesn't seem like a punishment. You could have your child do one problem before they watch their favorite show or while you are waiting for an appointment. New math software programs usually incorporate the skills being taught in a fun way, so create a "math time" where your child gets a minute of watching their favorite show or playing a video game for every minute they spend on their math software.

The main idea at this age is not to make afternoons seem like an extension of school, but to consistently integrate short learning opportunities into your routines. Reading for twenty minutes each evening, writing a note once or twice a week, and occasionally playing some math games on the computer creates a mindset and environment of showing your child your home values education.

KEYS TO THE CORE

One way to encourage your child to apply the skills they have learned is to have them identify concepts within activities they enjoy to keep doing those activities. For example, as long as they can find a math concept such as geometric shapes, patterns, or the use of addition or subtraction by characters every three minutes, they can keep watching a show. The same concept could be applied to video games.

Grades 6-8

In English/language arts, you child will be doing a lot of speaking, reading, and writing that supports arguments they make based on evidence, and they will also start researching on their own. Students in these grades also start incorporating the skills they are learning in ELA into other subject areas such as social studies and science. Discuss their favorite books and take an interest in what they are writing by reading what they produce in class. This will show them you value the skills they are acquiring.

The math skills your child is learning in these grade bands become more complex and integrate more real-world scenarios into the problems. It is not uncommon for a student to become frustrated with at least one mathematical concept at this time, so don't get discouraged if this does occur. Take advantage of any before or after school academic support that may be offered, and stay in consistent communication with your child's math teacher.

This is a great age to start discussing future plans your child may have after high school and how the skills they are learning now will support those plans. Visit college campuses or even tour manufacturing plants to start planting the seeds of career awareness.

KEYS TO THE CORE

This is the age students start to discuss what they want to do "when they grow up." Have them research a career they are interested in and see where math concepts might be used in this job.

Grades 9–12

Your child will be applying their literacy skills across subject areas and conducting more and more individual research to produce their own written perspective, with appropriate evidence. Historical documents and technical texts become more of a focus, so visiting museums and historical sites will support the learning they are doing in class.

Many students find higher level math challenging, but there are a great deal of problem-solving and critical-thinking skills supported through the math standards in high school for which students can find real-life application. For some reason, parental involvement at school seems to decline when students reach high school, but this is as important a time as ever to maintain a good line of communication with your child's math teacher. Make sure you attend parent nights or open house events and discuss with your child's math teacher the way you can best support the learning taking place in class. Your child's math teacher can help connect you with supplemental resources and additional academic support programs provided by the school. The main thing is to be involved enough to catch any struggles your child may have so they don't get too frustrated and throw up their hands.

As your child progresses through high school, help them refine their career interests and start making long term goals for what they would like to do after graduation. Nothing has to be set in stone, and it is likely the goals will change regularly, but the important thing is to have your child thinking long term and understand the skills they are learning have an application in college or a career.

 KEYS TO THE CORE

Keep a consistent place where homework can be done without distractions of other people in the house or a TV in the background. Keeping a drawer stocked with supplies also shows the importance you give to homework at your home.

Keeping the End in Mind

One of the most important things to keep in mind is that this is a long-term process in which each part builds on the previous parts. The concepts your child is learning about in third grade are actually preparing them for fourth grade work, which in turn prepares them for fifth grade work and so on. This means each concept is important in the process of preparing your child for the ultimate goal of college and career readiness after high school graduation. In a very real sense, the work your child is doing in third grade is preparing them for work at the end of high school.

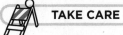

TAKE CARE

In the end, your child will look to you to set the tone for how important school is and the skills that are acquired there through all grade levels. If nothing else, sit at the kitchen table reading a book while your middle schooler or high schooler does their homework. Being present shows that you value time for learning.

I have used the term "college and career ready" a million times throughout this book, but what does that really mean? It's not so much about a specific path as it is equipping your child to have options and opportunities when they graduate. It means that the skills they possess allow them to choose from any path instead of being limited to one path. The object of Common Core is not to produce a worker drone or even a student destined for college. The object is to instill in students the skills and knowledge they need to be able to choose without limitation from all options before them.

The Least You Need To Know

- As a parent, you have the right and responsibility to ask talk to your child's teacher to better understand how they are learning.

- You will never know if you don't ask. Don't be afraid to get clarification on what and how your child is learning if you need it.

- Your child's grades may initially drop when he or she begins working with the Common Core, but it will be worth the long-term success.

- Being "college- and career-ready" means your child will be equipped with the skills to choose any path after graduation.

Frequently Asked Questions

Q: What are the Common Core State Standards?

A: The Common Core State Standards are a set of college and career readiness standards that will be taught from kindergarten through grade 12. The standards are written for English language arts and mathematics and have been voluntarily adopted by 43 states in the United States. They were designed to ensure that all students who graduate high school are fully prepared to take introductory college courses for credit or to enter the workforce.

Q: What is the goal of the Common Core State Standards?

A: The overarching goal of the Common Core State Standards is to ensure that American students are able to meet college and career expectations. The standards were created to help prepare students for success in an ever-growing global economy by providing them with rigorous content and an opportunity to apply higher-order thinking skills to real-world applications.

Q: Who led the development of the Common Core State Standards?

A: The development of the Common Core was led by state governors through their organization, the National Governors Association Center for Best Practices (NGA) and by the education commissioners from the Council of Chief State School Officers (CCSSO). Education experts, teachers, administrators, and parents from across the country also provided input.

Q: Were teachers involved in the creation of the Common Core State Standards?

A: Yes. Teachers always played a part in the development of the standards. From the drafting process to the implementation process, teachers continually provided professional feedback. Teachers served on the original feedback and work groups for the English language arts and math standards, and each of the major teacher organizations (The National Education Association, American Federation of Teachers, National Council of Teachers of English, and National Council of Teachers of Mathematics) were responsible for putting together teacher feedback groups to offer constructive thoughts on the standards. Also, during the drafting process, teachers were asked to become members of state teams that discussed the drafts. During the final two public comment periods, many other teachers were able to offer their insight on the Common Core State Standards.

Q: How do the Common Core State Standards compare to the previous state standards?

A: The Common Core standards were developed by studying the standards and expectations of the world's highest-achieving countries and by building on the best state standards that could be found in the United States. Research on what students need to know to be able to successful for their college studies and careers was studied thoroughly to create the best and most practical standards for students. No state was asked to lower their standards. The Common Core State Standards only provide more focused, evidence-based goals that will help students across America become ready for post-high school life.

Q: Why are the Common Core State Standards important?

A: Unlike previous standards which varied from state to state, the Common Core State Standards allow a unity among states to ensure equity for all students. States are now able to use the same kinds of tools such as textbooks, assessments, and other teaching materials, which helps ensure students can compete academically with their peers from all over the nation, regardless of where they live. The consistency of the high standards also helps to provide clear expectations for all teachers and students on what knowledge and skills will be necessary for students to have to achieve success after graduation.

Q: What evidence and criteria were used for the development of the Common Core State Standards?

A: Evidence to support the creation of the standards came from a variety of sources. Developers studied academic research and looked carefully at survey feedback from business leaders across the nation who identified many of the necessary skills that students will need to enter college or the workforce. They also used assessment data such as scores from the National Assessment of Educational Progress (NAEP) to determine the framework needs in the subject of English language arts. Comparisons to high-performing countries and states were made, and information from the Trends in International Mathematics and Science (TIMSS) showed that the "traditional" math curriculum had to become more focused in order to promote better student performance.

There were also specific criteria necessary for guiding the development of the Common Core State Standards. Developers looked for standards that were evidence- or research-based. They needed to be practical and realistic for use in the classroom and allow for students to be able to apply higher-order thinking and problem-solving skills. Also, the standards needed to be clear and consistent across all states. It was important for the Common Core to be aligned with college and career readiness expectations and to become an improvement to what most states were currently using.

Q: What role did international benchmarking play in the development of the Common Core State Standards?

A: Before the development of the Common Core, international assessments such as the Programme for International Student Assessment (PISA) and Trends in International Mathematics and Science Study (TIMSS) began to show a vast difference between the standards of high-performing countries and those of the United States. In order to improve the U.S. education system, the standards from top-performing nations were consulted during the development of the Common Core State Standards.

Q: What subject areas are included in the Common Core State Standards?

A: At the time of publication, there are only Common Core State Standards for English Language Arts and math.

Q: Why are the Common Core State Standards only for English language arts and math?

A: These two subjects were chosen for the Common Core because they are the two main areas upon which students will build skill sets that bridge to other subject areas. Learning to write, read, speak, listen, and use language effectively are valuable tools for helping students become college- and career-ready in a variety of disciplines. The literacy standards available for history, science, and technical subjects are meant to be supplemental and do not replace current standards.

Q: Will other subject areas be creating Common Core State Standards in the future?

A: At this time, the two organizations behind the development of the Common Core, the NGA and the CCSSO, are not working on the creation of standards in other academic areas. However, there are other organizations across content areas like world languages and arts that are working to produce more aligned and rigorous standards. Science standards called Next Generation Science Standards are in the process of being produced by major science organizations.

Q: What supports are being provided to teachers to help them ensure that students are prepared to reach the new goals established by the Common Core State Standards?

A: Because the Common Core is a state-led initiative, any decisions on the implementation process have been made by state and local education leaders. This has allowed for state leaders to take the best approach for their systems and to provide the specific supports their teachers will need to help students become successful in mastering the standards. Corestandards.org is a website that can link readers to a state-by-state implementation guide concerning the new standards and supports being offered to teachers across the nation.

Q: Do the Common Core State Standards dictate how teachers must teach?

A: The standards are just specific lists that establish what students should learn, but they are not a curriculum for teachers to follow. Because teachers know what works best in their classrooms and can use instructional strategies targeted for their individual students, how a teacher teaches is up to his or her discretion. Many schools will partner to train their teachers on how to best help students reach the standards.

Q: Will the NGA Center and the CCSSO be creating common instructional materials and curricula?

A: No. The Common Core State Standards are not curriculum, nor do they call for the use of any particular curriculum. States that adopt the standards may work toward finding or developing their own instructional materials that align with them, but as always, teachers are still free to develop their own lesson plans and choose their own materials. As more states begin their journey into implementation, many publishers around the nation are beginning to try to develop new resources for helping teach these shared standards.

Q: How will the Common Core State Standards be assessed?

A: A new generation of assessments is being developed to give meaningful feedback on how students are doing building the necessary skills to become college- and career-ready. There are two major state-led consortia, the Smarter Balanced Assessment Consortium (Smarter Balanced) and Partnership for Assessment of Readiness for College and Careers (PARCC) that are working to create relevant assessments. Most of the states have chosen to participate in one of these consortia. To determine your state's assessment consortium, visit your state's education website.

Q: How do the more rigorous standards affect English language learners and students with disabilities?

A: The training involved with preparing teachers to deliver the Common Core State Standards is full of collaborative opportunities where professionals can share best practices and real-life experiences. This dialogue is what helps teachers work to improve the strategies they present in the classroom and can lead to an improved ability to serve students with diverse needs. It is important to note that the standards do include resources for applying the standards that will help teachers successfully reach these groups of students. These resources can be found on the Common Core State Standards website (corestandards.org) under the "Resources" tab.

Q: If the standards in our schools are raised, doesn't that mean more students will become frustrated and lead our schools to higher drop-out rates?

A: It is not more likely that students will drop out of school. Though there are a variety of factors that lead students to drop out, research supports the idea that most students want to be challenged in school. There is data that shows approximately 7 out of 10 students who drop out say that they were not motivated or challenged to work hard in school and that they probably would have worked harder if higher academic expectations had been placed on them.

Q: When do the new standards take effect?

A: Most states began implementation in 2010 with a gradual progression that included additional grade levels each year. For example, in year one, an elementary school might implement just the kindergarten through grade 3 standards. Then in the second year, they would include the standards for grades 4 and 5. Your state should have its implementation timeline on the department of education website.

Q: Is there a required reading list for the English language arts standards?

A: No, there is not a list of required reading provided in the standards. However, the Common Core State Standards does provide a list of sample texts to help teachers navigate what text complexity is appropriate for various grade levels. There are exemplar texts that are suggested to help teachers meet the high demands of reading required for the standards and that offer teachers new possibilities. Ultimately, though, what is read in the classroom is decided by the teacher.

Q: Does the Common Core favor informational texts over literature?

A: The Common Core State Standards are designed to have students reading more informational texts. Previous standards gave students a limited exposure to these types of texts, and experts agree that when students get into college or a career, most of their reading will be of informational texts. There are still many literature standards across the grade levels where students will be able to enjoy high-quality literature. The standards specify that by high school, 70 percent of what students read should be informational and 30 percent should be literature, but that split applies across all subject areas, not just English.

Q: Do the math standards cover all key math topics in the proper sequence?

A: The challenge with having 50 different sets of standards in the past was that states covered different topics at different times or in different grade levels, especially in math. The Common Core State Standards have created a coherent math progression that will help students build a fundamental "number sense" and the ability to apply mathematical knowledge to real-world situations. There is a flexibility within the standards that will allow advanced students to study harder topics earlier, such as having an eighth grade student study algebra.

Q: How will the Common Core State Standards affect higher education?

A: If the Common Core is successful in its goal to make students more college ready, there will be an impact on higher education institutions in the United States. As many as one-third of college students begin their coursework by having to take remedial classes, but if the standards succeed, students should arrive better prepared and with less need for remedial work. Also, having been prepared to handle rigorous work, students will come to college with a better ability to handle the more difficult work; thus possibly increasing college graduation rates.

Q: Does the implementation of the Common Core require schools to have more technology?

A: Outside of adopting the Common Core State Standards, schools have been ever-increasing their usage of technology in an effort to keep students engaged and to allow students easy access to information. Some of the assessments being created to align to the Common Core are online assessments, which may cause some districts to have to update or maintain internet speeds. Also, many of the standards themselves do support the use of technology, so whenever it is appropriate, the use of technology should be integrated into the teaching and learning process to provide students with the best access to information or experiences they need to become prepared for success in college and career.

Q: What data will be collected on students?

A: Student information and educational records are private and are protected by federal law through the Family Educational Rights and Privacy Act (FERPA). Personally identifiable information cannot be legally sold or even released without parental consent. Most states collect some student information through their standardized assessments; however, the federal government does not have access to the student-level information housed in state data systems. Common Core is not some mechanism for collecting student data for the federal government. Also, there will be no further collection of data related to the assessment other than that already authorized by current federal law.

Q: Was the Common Core mandated by the federal government?

A: The Common Core was not a mandate of the federal government. In fact, there are about four states that have chosen to not adopt the standards. Because President Obama voiced his approval for the Common Core and because the federal government put stimulus money into building standardized tests that were aligned to the Common Core, many people have been under the impression that these standards were federally mandated. This is simply not true. Common Core was a state-led initiative.

Q: If the states chose to adopt these standards, why are people getting so riled up over them now?

A: Even though the Common Core State Standards were adopted by states, the adoption did not require approval from state lawmakers. In most states, state agencies, boards of education, or chief education officers for the state gave approval for the Common Core. This means that many parents and community members feel as though the general public did not have a say in the process or that they heard about the standards far too late for them to provide feedback. There have been controversies in some of the states that adopted the Common Core, but most states have fully implemented the standards and have been teaching them for several years.

Q: Who will manage the Common Core State Standards in the future?

A: The Common Core will continue to remain in the hands of each state. Adoption of the standards or any necessary revisions will continue to be a part of the voluntary decision process. The NGA and CCSSO will continue to be the leading organizations involved with decision-making. Federal funds will never be used to develop or revise Common Core standards, and any changes that may be made will have to be made based on research and evidence.

Q: How much will it cost states to implement the Common Core State Standards?

A: Costs for implementing the standards will vary from state to state. The costs associated with implementation are typically those for training teachers, buying curriculum materials, changing assessments, and providing professional development. However, these are normal costs on which most states spend significant amounts of money as it is. The value in having consistency across the states is that it allows an opportunity for some cost-saving through the using of open source technology. States can share materials and other resources via the internet.

Q: Do other countries do this?

A: Some countries do, but not all. The United States gives an unusual amount of control over public schools to the local education agency, which makes it hard to compare to other nations. There are many developed nations that have national educational standards, and the half of the highest performing nations on the PISA exam do have national standards.

Q: How will we know if all of this is working?

A: It will take a few years of transition time to determine if the Common Core is working as planned. Supporters of the standards say that improvement should be measured by increased college and career readiness for high school graduates as well as by American students' results on international tests like the PISA.

Q: How does the Common Core support a stronger economy?

A: American students are growing up in a global economy and a mobile society. With military families moving frequently, technology jobs becoming increasingly mobile, and the competition for careers moving internationally, students are faced with learning new skills to adapt to this kind of society. The current job market has approximately 25,000 unfilled jobs (in each state alone) for highly skilled workers, and it's become a focus to help students build the critical skills they need to be competitive in the job market. Reports indicate that our nation has jobs, but lacks qualified applicants. One of the goals of the Common Core is to allow students to build those real-world skills, making them career-ready.

Q: How will the Common Core improve the quality of our education?

A: The Common Core State Standards are designed to ensure real understanding. With the Common Core, teachers are responsible for covering fewer standards, allowing them to go deeper into the material. Students are able to actually master the material instead of having just a surface-level awareness of basic facts. Learning becomes more hands-on with a focus on what students will actually use in real life. Also, the standards emphasize learning fundamentals that students can use as building blocks for understanding deeper concepts and critical thinking. The consistency of common standards makes it possible for teachers across the nation to collaborate and learn from one another as professionals. Lastly, having consistent and high expectations for all students gives educators a clear picture on what the expectations are. Expectations across states become similar and allow educators to judge what students are truly learning.

Q: Should I talk to my child's teacher about Common Core?

A: Yes. It is always a good idea to communicate with your child's teacher and stay involved in his or her education. Ask the teacher about learning expectations and help create a plan that will help your child be successful. Teachers across the nation are continuing to receive training on the Common Core State Standards and can provide valuable feedback to helping you understand what is going on in the classroom.

Q: **What is the difference between "Common Core" and "Common Core-aligned"?**

A: It is actually a big difference. The authors of the Common Core State Standards do not publish or endorse any kind of textbooks, materials, or curriculum that may be available. However, publishers of these items are still able to produce educational products and label them as "Common Core-aligned."

Q: **Who is for the Common Core standards? Who is against them?**

A: While this question cannot be answered definitively, it is interesting due to the controversy that appears to surround the standards. Most of the organized opposition comes from conservative groups who are wary of the federal government playing a role in education and who feel standardizing education is an overreach and attempt to control the schooling of children. However, there are high-profile conservatives like former Arkansas Governor Mike Huckabee and former Florida Governor Jeb Bush who strongly support the Common Core. Many large teachers' unions support the use of the Common Core standards, but not all have fully backed the implementation process. It appears that most survey results find that teachers and administrators currently teaching the standards to students find them to be beneficial and an improvement for students.

Glossary

academic achievement   Measures a student's academic performance at one specific time and compares a student's performance to a standard.

academic growth   Measures the student's academic progress over an amount of time, usually from year to year, and compares a student's performance to his or her previous performance.

addends   The numbers that are added together. In the equation $5 + 6 = 11$, 5 and 6 are the addends.

advanced searches   Research done using digital libraries and search engines on the internet to conduct searches in scholarly journals beyond a basic Google search. These digital libraries often require a fee the school pays each year in order to access information in journals specific to subjects like science or history.

anchor standards   The broader concepts in English and Language Arts that support college and career readiness when students graduate. The basic skills needed to master these concepts are introduced in Kindergarten and build on each other like a stairstep each year until graduation.

best practice   An instructional strategy that has proven to get positive results. The term is often used to describe training strategies or new resource materials for the classroom.

close reading   The practice of reading and rereading a text that is at the appropriate level of complexity to gain deeper meaning and comprehension by analyzing key words, phrases, and how ideas unfold.

college- and career-ready   A student who graduates high school and can enter college or a career training program without having to take remedial courses that don't count toward his or her degree.

complex number   A combination of a real number and an imaginary number, which gives a negative result when squared.

composite number   A whole number that can be divided by at least one other number besides itself and 1. 4 is the first composite number.

consortium   A group of states that have banded together to produce a Common Core-aligned assessment. Joining forces lowers the individual cost of assessment development for each state and allows student scores to be compared across multiple states.

constructed response   A question type that requires the student taking the test to provide their own answer without the aid of any choices.

cosine   A term used in right triangles to represent the length of the adjacent side divided by the hypotenuse.

curriculum   The textbooks, materials, instructional techniques, and other resources used to teach standards.

decodable words   The words that follow regular spelling patterns.

decode   To translate a printed word into a sound.

expression   The high school-appropriate term for a record of computation with numbers, symbols that represent numbers (such as x and y), arithmetic operations, exponentiation and the operation of evaluating a function.

feedback groups   Experts from around the country who would review draft portions of the standards as the work teams wrote them and make recommendations to help guide the work teams.

fluency   The ability to read a grade-appropriate text with purpose, expression, and understanding.

high-frequency words   The words that appear most often in printed materials. For example, the words *I*, *and*, and *the* make up 10 percent of the English words in print.

hypotenuse   The longest side of a triangle. The hypotenuse is the (c) when employing the Pythagorean Theorem.

implementation   The term used to represent the plan for training educators on how to teach the standards, assess the standards, and provide materials to teach the standards.

informational text   A specific kind of nonfiction that is used to present or explain information. Examples include articles, speeches, instructional manuals, or memoirs.

interim assessment   A form of assessment used by educators to evaluate the learning progress of a student. This type of assessment is used to guide instruction in preparing students for an end-of-the-year standardized test.

irrational number   A number that cannot be evenly divided into a whole number and be written as a fraction. Pi is the most famous example of an irrational number, but the square root of two is pretty well-known, too!

logarithm   The answer to the question, "How many of a number do I need to multiply to get another number?" For example, how many 2s do I need to multiply to get 16? $2 \times 2 \times 2 \times 2 = 16$. I multiplied 4 of the 2s to get 16, thus, the logarithm of 16 with a base of 2 is 4.

mean   Another word for average. In statistics, when people speak about the mean of a set of data, it's the average of the data.

memorandum of understanding   A document that individuals or groups sign to show they are committed to a cause. It is usually not legally binding and does not involve money. It is often used as a formal agreement on a plan or process for a project or partnership.

parabola   A special kind of curve, shaped like an arch. Parabolas often appear in graphing work, but are not formally named and used in the standards until high school.

performance tasks   Tasks that direct a student to a certain outcome by posing a question, asking the student to make a comparison, or asking the student to form a relationship between two ideas. The student must apply previous knowledge and acquired skills to accomplish the task.

polygon   A two-dimensional (so it is in one plane) shape, with straight sides. The number of sides is not standardized, so squares, triangles, stars, and many other shapes are polygons. Circles, however, are not, since they are curved.

primary source   A document that was written during the time being studied.

prime number   A whole number greater than 1 that cannot be divided by any number except itself and 1. 2 and 3 are prime numbers.

quadratic equation   An equation that involves a variable that is squared, such as $2x^2$. Remember, the variable is the letter that is unknown.

rhombus   Aa four-sided shape in which all sides have the same length. All opposite angles in a rhombus are equal. We often think of a rhombus as diamond-shaped, although a right-angle square is technically also a rhombus.

rigid motion   The action of taking a shape and moving it without changing its shape or size. Rotating, reflecting, and translating shapes are all rigid motions.

rigor   A term that typically describes a level of instruction or instructional materials that challenges students to the fullest extent of their learning abilities rather than a middle-of-the-road approach.

secondary source   A document that was written after an event occurred and provides a secondhand account, perspective, or analysis.

sine   A term used in right triangles to represent the length of the opposite side divided by the hypotenuse.

special exception   The term used for a process or substance that doesn't act in a typical way. For example, when dry ice is continually heated, it doesn't melt into a liquid and then turn into a gas as regular ice does. Instead, it sublimates, or turns directly from a solid into a gas when heated.

standards   The clearly defined statements of the knowledge and skills students should have at each grade that prepares them for the next grade.

syllables   The units of sound that are the building blocks of words. For example, the word *dog* has one syllable and the word *water* has two syllables. Segmenting syllables means to break a word into its sound parts, such as *wa|ter* and *beau|ti|ful*. Blending syllables means to pull together sound parts to make a word, such as *sur* + *prise* = *surprise*.

text complexity   The measure of how challenging reading materials are. To determine text complexity, teachers consider the knowledge needed to understand the context of what is being read, the length and complexity of words and sentences, and how motivated and interested the student is to read the text.

variable   The letter in an algebraic equation, symbolizing what we don't know and are trying to solve for. In the equation $x = 5(6/2)$, x is the variable. A problem may have more than one variable.

whole numbers   Positive integers of any denomination: 0, 1, 2, 3 …. Whole numbers cannot be negative or fractional. Whole numbers do not use a decimal.

work teams   The two groups created for math and ELA to write the Common Core standards. They wrote draft portions of the standards and then submitted them to feedback groups for review.

Examples of Complex Texts

Using appropriately complex texts at each grade level is one of the most critical aspects for success with the Common Core as well as successful preparation for pursuits after high school.

Unfortunately, determining text complexity is not an absolute science. There are many factors to consider, including the level of background knowledge and contextual information needed to understand a text, the length and complexity of words and sentences, and the interest and motivation of the reader. Software programs that analyze the words and sentences in a text can be helpful in determining text complexity, but it is more nuanced than just quantifying long words and complex sentences.

The following examples of appropriately complex texts for kindergarten through grade 12 come from Appendix B on the Common Core State Standards website (corestandards.org/assets/Appendix_B.pdf). They provide an idea of the kind of text your child should be reading at each grade. Visit this site for more information and examples of complex texts.

Kindergarten

"As I Was Going to St. Ives"
Anonymous

> As I was going to St. Ives,
> I met a man with seven wives,
> Each wife had seven sacks,
> Each sack had seven cats,
> Each cat had seven kits,
> Kits, cats, sacks, and wives,
> How many were going to St. Ives?

Grade 1

"Mix a Pancake"
Christina Rossetti

> Mix a pancake,
> Stir a pancake,
> Pop it in the pan;
> Fry the pancake,
> Toss the pancake—
> Catch it if you can.

Grade 2

"Stopping by Woods on a Snowy Evening"
Robert Frost

> Whose woods these are I think I know.
> His house is in the village though;
> He will not see me stopping here
> To watch his woods fill up with snow.
>
> My little horse must think it queer
> To stop without a farmhouse near
> Between the woods and frozen lake
> The darkest evening of the year.
>
> He gives his harness bells a shake
> To ask if there is some mistake.
> The only other sound's the sweep
> Of easy wind and downy flake.
>
> The woods are lovely, dark and deep,
> But I have promises to keep,
> And miles to go before I sleep,
> And miles to go before I sleep.

Grade 3

"Afternoon on a Hill"
Edna St. Vincent Millay

> I will be the gladdest thing
> > Under the sun!
> I will touch a hundred flowers
> > And not pick one.
>
> I will look at cliffs and clouds
> > With quiet eyes,
> Watch the wind bow down the grass,
> > And the grass rise.
>
> And when lights begin to show
> > Up from the town,
> I will mark which must be mine,
> > And then start down!

Grade 4

"Casey at the Bat"
Earnest Lawrence Thayer

> The outlook wasn't brilliant for the Mudville nine that day;
> The score stood four to two with but one inning more to play.
> And then when Cooney died at first, and Barrows did the same,
> A sickly silence fell upon the patrons of the game.
>
> A straggling few got up to go in deep despair. The rest
> Clung to that hope which springs eternal in the human breast;
> They thought if only Casey could but get a whack at that—
> We'd put up even money now with Casey at the bat.
>
> But Flynn preceded Casey, as did also Jimmy Blake,
> And the former was a lulu and the latter was a cake;
> So upon that stricken multitude grim melancholy sat,
> For there seemed but little chance of Casey's getting to the bat.

But Flynn let drive a single, to the wonderment of all,
And Blake, the much despis-ed, tore the cover off the ball;
And when the dust had lifted, and the men saw what had occurred,
There was Johnnie safe at second and Flynn a-hugging third.

Then from 5,000 throats and more there rose a lusty yell;
It rumbled through the valley, it rattled in the dell;
It knocked upon the mountain and recoiled upon the flat,
For Casey, mighty Casey, was advancing to the bat.

There was ease in Casey's manner as he stepped into his place;
There was pride in Casey's bearing and a smile on Casey's face.
And when, responding to the cheers, he lightly doffed his hat,
No stranger in the crowd could doubt 'twas Casey at the bat.

Ten thousand eyes were on him as he rubbed his hands with dirt;
Five thousand tongues applauded when he wiped them on his shirt.
Then while the writhing pitcher ground the ball into his hip,
Defiance flashed in Casey's eye, a sneer curled Casey's lip.

And now the leather-covered sphere came hurtling through the air,
And Casey stood a-watching it in haughty grandeur there.
Close by the sturdy batsman the ball unheeded sped—
"That ain't my style," said Casey. "Strike one," the umpire said.

From the benches, black with people, there went up a muffled roar,
Like the beating of the storm-waves on a stern and distant shore.
"Kill him! Kill the umpire!" shouted someone on the stand;
And it's likely they'd have killed him had not Casey raised his hand.

With a smile of Christian charity great Casey's visage shone;
He stilled the rising tumult; he bade the game go on;
He signaled to the pitcher, and once more the spheroid flew;
But Casey still ignored it, and the umpire said, "Strike two."

"Fraud!" cried the maddened thousands, and echo answered fraud;
But one scornful look from Casey and the audience was awed.
They saw his face grow stern and cold, they saw his muscles strain,
And they knew that Casey wouldn't let that ball go by again.

The sneer is gone from Casey's lip, his teeth are clenched in hate;
He pounds with cruel violence his bat upon the plate.
And now the pitcher holds the ball, and now he lets it go,
And now the air is shattered by the force of Casey's blow.

Oh, somewhere in this favored land the sun is shining bright;
The band is playing somewhere, and somewhere hearts are light,
And somewhere men are laughing, and somewhere children shout;
But there is no joy in Mudville—mighty Casey has struck out.

Grade 5

"A Bird Came Down the Walk"
Emily Dickenson

A Bird came down the walk—

He did not know I saw;
He bit an angleworm in halves
And ate the fellow, raw.

And then he drank a dew
From a convenient grass,
And then hopped sidewise to the wall
To let a beetle pass.

He glanced with rapid eyes
That hurried all abroad—
They looked like frightened beads, I thought—
He stirred his velvet head —

Like one in danger; cautious,
I offered him a crumb,
And he unrolled his feathers
And rowed him softer home

Than oars divide the ocean,
Too silver for a seam,
Or butterflies, off banks of noon,
Leap, plashless, as they swim.

Grade 6

"O Captain! My Captain!"
Walt Whitman

> O Captain! my Captain! our fearful trip is done;
> The ship has weather'd every rack, the prize we sought is won;
> The port is near, the bells I hear, the people all exulting,
> While follow eyes the steady keel, the vessel grim and daring:
> But O heart! heart! heart!
> O the bleeding drops of red,
> Where on the deck my Captain lies,
> Fallen cold and dead.
>
> O Captain! my Captain! rise up and hear the bells;
> Rise up—for you the flag is flung—for you the bugle trills;
> For you bouquets and ribbon'd wreaths—for you the shores a-crowding;
> For you they call, the swaying mass, their eager faces turning;
> Here Captain! dear father!
> This arm beneath your head;
> It is some dream that on the deck,
> You've fallen cold and dead.
>
> My Captain does not answer, his lips are pale and still;
> My father does not feel my arm, he has no pulse nor will;
> The ship is anchor'd safe and sound, its voyage closed and done;
> From fearful trip, the victor ship, comes in with object won;
> Exult, O shores, and ring, O bells!
> But I, with mournful tread,
> Walk the deck my Captain lies,
> Fallen cold and dead.

Grade 7

"The Railway Train"
Emily Dickenson

> I like to see it lap the miles,
> And lick the valleys up,
> And stop to feed itself at tanks;
> And then, prodigious, step

Around a pile of mountains,
And, supercilious, peer
In shanties by the sides of roads;
And then a quarry pare

To fit its sides, and crawl between,
Complaining all the while
In horrid, hooting stanza;
Then chase itself down hill

And neigh like Boanerges;
Then, punctual as a star,
Stop—docile and omnipotent—
At its own stable door.

Grade 8

Excerpt "Give Me Liberty or Give Me Death"
Patrick Henry

They tell us, sir, that we are weak; unable to cope with so formidable an adversary. But when shall we be stronger? Will it be the next week, or the next year? Will it be when we are totally disarmed, and when a British guard shall be stationed in every house? Shall we gather strength by irresolution and inaction? Shall we acquire the means of effectual resistance by lying supinely on our backs and hugging the delusive phantom of hope, until our enemies shall have bound us hand and foot? Sir, we are not weak if we make a proper use of those means which the God of nature hath placed in our power. The millions of people, armed in the holy cause of liberty, and in such a country as that which we possess, are invincible by any force which our enemy can send against us. Besides, sir, we shall not fight our battles alone. There is a just God who presides over the destinies of nations, and who will raise up friends to fight our battles for us. The battle, sir, is not to the strong alone; it is to the vigilant, the active, the brave. Besides, sir, we have no election. If we were base enough to desire it, it is now too late to retire from the contest. There is no retreat but in submission and slavery! Our chains are forged! Their clanking may be heard on the plains of Boston! The war is inevitable—and let it come! I repeat it, sir, let it come.

It is in vain, sir, to extenuate the matter. Gentlemen may cry, Peace, Peace—but there is no peace. The war is actually begun! The next gale that sweeps from the north will bring to our ears the clash of resounding arms! Our brethren are already in the field! Why stand we here idle? What is it that gentlemen wish? What would they have? Is life so dear, or peace so sweet, as to be purchased at the price of chains and slavery? Forbid it, Almighty God! I know not what course others may take; but as for me, give me liberty or give me death!

Grades 9-10

Excerpt "The Odyssey"
Homer

> Sing to me of the man, Muse, the man of twists and turns
> driven time and again off course, once he had plundered
> the hallowed heights of Troy.
> Many cities of men he saw and learned their minds,
> many pains he suffered, heartsick on the open sea,
> fighting to save his life and bring his comrades home.
> But he could not save them from disaster, hard as he strove—
> the recklessness of their own ways destroyed them all,
> the blind fools, they devoured the cattle of the Sun
> and the Sungod blotted out the day of their return.
> Launch out on his story, Muse, daughter of Zeus.
> Start from where you will—sing for our time too.
>
> By now,
> all the survivors, all who avoided headlong death
> were safe at home, escaped the wars and waves.
> But one man alone …
> his heart set on his wife and his return—Calypso,
> the bewitching nymph, the lustrous goddess, held him back,
> deep in her arching caverns, craving him for a husband.
> But then, when the wheeling seasons brought the year around.
> That year spun out by the gods when he should reach his home,
> Ithaca—though not even there would he be free of trials,
> even among his loved ones—then every god took pity,
> all except Poseidon. He raged on, seething against
> the great Odysseus till he reached his native land.

Excerpt "Candide, or the Optimist"
Voltaire

In the country of Westphalia, in the castle of the most noble Baron of Thunder-ten-tronckh, lived a youth whom Nature had endowed with a most sweet disposition. His face was the true index of his mind. He had a solid judgment joined to the most unaffected simplicity; and hence, I presume, he had his name of Candide. The old servants of the house suspected him to have been the son of the Baron's sister, by a very good sort of a gentleman of the neighborhood, whom that young lady refused to marry, because he could produce no more than threescore and eleven quarterings in his arms; the rest of the genealogical tree belonging to the family having been lost through the injuries of time.

The Baron was one of the most powerful lords in Westphalia, for his castle had not only a gate, but even windows, and his great hall was hung with tapestry. He used to hunt with his mastiffs and spaniels instead of greyhounds; his groom served him for huntsman; and the parson of the parish officiated as his grand almoner. He was called "My Lord" by all his people, and he never told a story but everyone laughed at it.

My Lady Baroness, who weighed three hundred and fifty pounds, consequently was a person of no small consideration; and then she did the honors of the house with a dignity that commanded universal respect. Her daughter was about seventeen years of age, fresh-colored, comely, plump, and desirable. The Baron's son seemed to be a youth in every respect worthy of the father he sprung from. Pangloss, the preceptor, was the oracle of the family, and little Candide listened to his instructions with all the simplicity natural to his age and disposition.

Master Pangloss taught the metaphysico-theologo-cosmolonigology. He could prove to admiration that there is no effect without a cause; and, that in this best of all possible worlds, the Baron's castle was the most magnificent of all castles, and My Lady the best of all possible baronesses.

"It is demonstrable," said he, "that things cannot be otherwise than as they are; for as all things have been created for some end, they must necessarily be created for the best end. Observe, for instance, the nose is formed for spectacles, therefore we wear spectacles. The legs are visibly designed for stockings, accordingly we wear stockings. Stones were made to be hewn and to construct castles, therefore My Lord has a magnificent castle; for the greatest baron in the province ought to be the best lodged. Swine were intended to be eaten, therefore we eat pork all the year round: and they, who assert that everything is *right*, do not express themselves correctly; they should say that everything is *best*."

Grade 11

"Economic Bill of Rights"
Franklin D. Roosevelt

It is our duty now to begin to lay the plans and determine the strategy for the winning of a lasting peace and the establishment of an American standard of living higher than ever before known. We cannot be content, no matter how high that general standard of living may be, if some fraction of our people—whether it be one-third or one-fifth or one-tenth—is ill-fed, ill-clothed, ill-housed, and insecure.

This Republic had its beginning, and grew to its present strength, under the protection of certain inalienable political rights—among them the right of free speech, free press, free worship, trial by jury, freedom from unreasonable searches and seizures. They were our rights to life and liberty.

As our nation has grown in size and stature, however—as our industrial economy expanded—these political rights proved inadequate to assure us equality in the pursuit of happiness.

We have come to a clear realization of the fact that true individual freedom cannot exist without economic security and independence. "Necessitous men are not free men." People who are hungry and out of a job are the stuff of which dictatorships are made.

In our day these economic truths have become accepted as self-evident. We have accepted, so to speak, a second Bill of Rights under which a new basis of security and prosperity can be established for all—regardless of station, race, or creed.

Among these are:

> The right to a useful and remunerative job in the industries or shops or farms or mines of the nation;

> The right to earn enough to provide adequate food and clothing and recreation;

> The right of every farmer to raise and sell his products at a return which will give him and his family a decent living;

> The right of every businessman, large and small, to trade in an atmosphere of freedom from unfair competition and domination by monopolies at home or abroad;

> The right of every family to a decent home;

The right to adequate medical care and the opportunity to achieve and enjoy good health;

The right to adequate protection from the economic fears of old age, sickness, accident, and unemployment;

The right to a good education.

All of these rights spell security. And after this war is won we must be prepared to move forward, in the implementation of these rights, to new goals of human happiness and well-being.

America's own rightful place in the world depends in large part upon how fully these and similar rights have been carried into practice for our citizens.

Resources

Achieve the Core
achievethecore.org
A relevant site for teachers or parents, it provides assessment questions, sample lesson plans, and ready-made professional development modules for helping achieve success while teaching the Common Core.

All Things Common Core
allthingscommoncore.com
This site links readers to various blog topics related to the CCSS.

Association for Supervision and Curriculum Development
ascd.org/ASCD/pdf/siteASCD/publications/policypoints/PolicyPoints_Common_Core_State_Standards.pdf
This link will take direct users to an article by the ASCD, and education advocacy group, that looks at many of the myths versus facts associated with the Common Core.

Benchmarking for Success
corestandards.org/assets/0812BENCHMARKING.pdf
A resource put out jointly by the NGA and CCSSO, this document explains the need for ensuring that American students receive a world-class education.

College and Career Readiness
act.org/commoncore/pdf/FirstLook.pdf
A report put out by ACT, this document details a first look on how students perform on the ACT since studying under the Common Core. Its findings support the idea that the CCSS are making students more college- and career-ready through the testing gains shown across the nation.

Common Core 360
schoolimprovement.com/products/common-core-360/
This site contains videos, resources, and lesson plans that are useful to educators who want to successfully implement the Common Core. This site also contains links to blogs where people are giving input on many topics related to the standards.

Common Core Standards App
itunes.apple.com/us/app/common-core-standards/id439424555?mt=8
This link will take you to a downloadable application for Apple or Android devices. The app puts all the Common Core standards at your fingertips and enables you to search standards quickly and easily by either subject matter or grade level.

Common Core State Standards Initiative
corestandards.org
The official site for the Common Core State Standards, which has been designed to allow users to explore the Common Core. It features a history of the standards, frequently asked questions, and a state-by-state guide to examining the standards.

Common Core Toolkit
p21.org/storage/documents/P21CommonCoreToolkit.pdf
This 48-page guide includes a framework for twenty-first century skills and offers an overview of the Common Core as well as resources necessary for those beginning implementation. Likely valuable for districts or states working toward Common Core implementation, it has short explanations on what that should look like in action.

Council of Chief State School Officers
ccsso.org
Dedicated to one of the major groups behind the Common Core State Standards initiatives, this site will allow browsers to find out more about the people who first advocated for the standards.

Engage NY
engageny.org)
This New York Common Core website is a tool for educators or parents interested in learning more about the standards. It delivers implementation and assessment resources as well as a family guide that helps to explain the CCSS.

Literacy Design Collaborative
ldc.org
This site provides a research-based framework and set of tools and resources for teachers looking to design literacy-rich lessons across the content areas. LDC supports the Common Core and the continued mission to provide rigor in the classroom.

National Governors Association
nga.org/cms/home.html
The NGA was one of the first major groups to play a role in the development of the Common Core. This site will answer questions about who was involved and may be a resource about what to expect from the standards.

National Math + Science Initiative
nms.org/Resources/CommonCoreOpenResources.aspx)
This site from the National Math + Science Initiative gives a list of free, open resources that are available for users interested in exploring more about the Common Core. The resources address a variety of topics such as diversity, higher education, curriculum, and instruction.

National PTA
pta.org
For anyone whose child's school is associated with the National PTA, this website gives parents resources for helping their children be successful with the Common Core. It includes tips on communicating between home and school and offers suggestions for helping parents reinforce the standards at home.

NEA Today
neatoday.org/2013/05/10/six-ways-the-common-core-is-good-for-students/
This article from the National Education Association shares perspectives from educators who feel that the Common Core standards are good for students. It examines six reasons why most teachers feel these standards are the best options for reaching students.

PBS Learning Media
pbslearningmedia.org
This site allows users to browse the standards and find teaching and learning resources to support them. Users can search by content or grade level for specific resources.

The Mathematics Common Core Toolbox
ccsstoolbox.com
Coordinated by the CCSSO and the NGA, this site helps users promote rigorous learning in mathematics classrooms by providing instructional materials based on the Common Core. It also provides an explanation for the progression and learning trajectories of the mathematics standards.

The Teaching Channel
teachingchannel.org
This site requires a user login, but it offers more than 150 videos that explain implementation of the Common Core. It also contains videos of teachers demonstrating Common Core-aligned lessons.

TN Core
tncore.org
Another state devoted to Common Core implementation, Tennessee has put together a site that explains how the standards will affect teaching. It provides resources across the disciplines to help with the teaching or assessing of the Common Core.

Work Teams and Feedback Groups

This appendix lists the members of the work teams and feedback groups that were involved in the development of the Common Core State Standards. It is important to note the geographic and professional diversity of the people involved in the process to fully understand the "group effort" from the state level that went into developing the standards.

Mathematics Work Team

Beth Aune
Director of Academic Standards and P-16 Initiatives
Minnesota Department of Education

Deborah Loewenberg Ball
Dean, School of Education
University of Michigan

Nancy Beben
Director, Curriculum Standards
Louisiana Department of Education

Sybilla Beckmann
Professor of Mathematics
University of Georgia

Stacey Caruso-Sharpe
Mathematics Teacher, Lynch Literacy Academy
Board of Directors, New York State United Teachers Vice President, American Federation of Teachers

Diana Ceja
Teacher on Assignment
Garey High School
Pomona, California

Marta Civil
Professor
University of Arizona

Douglas H. Clements
SUNY Distinguished Professor
University at Buffalo
Department of Learning and Instruction,
Graduate School of Education

Thomas Coy
Public School Program Advisor
Arkansas Department of Education

Phil Daro
America's Choice and Strategic Education
Research Partnerships

Ellen Delaney
Associate Principal
Spring Lake Park High School
Spring Lake Park, Minnesota

Susan Eddins
Faculty Emerita, Illinois Mathematics and
Science Academy Educational Consultant

Wade Ellis
Mathematics Instructor, Retired
West Valley College

Francis (Skip) Fennell
Professor, Education Department
McDaniel College
Past-President, NCTM

Bradford R. Findell
Mathematics Initiatives Administrator
Ohio Department of Education

Sol Garfunkel
Executive Director
COMAP, the Consortium for Mathematics
and Its Applications

Dewey Gottlieb
Education Specialist for Mathematics
Hawaii Department of Education

Lawrence Gray
Professor of Mathematics
University of Minnesota

Kenneth I. Gross
Professor of Mathematics and Education
University of Vermont

Denny Gulick
Professor of Mathematics
University of Maryland

Roger Howe
William Kenan Jr. Professor of Mathematics
Yale University

Deborah Hughes Hallett
Professor of Mathematics
University of Arizona
Adjunct Professor of Public Policy
Harvard Kennedy School

Linda Kaniecki
Mathematics Specialist
Maryland State Department of Education

Mary Knuck
Deputy Associate Superintendent
Standards-Based Best Practices
Arizona Department of Education

Barbara J. Libby
STEM Director
Office for Mathematics, Science and
Technology/Engineering
Massachusetts Department of Elementary
and Secondary Education

James Madden
Professor of Mathematics
Louisiana State University

Bernard L. Madison
Professor of Mathematics
University of Arkansas

William McCallum
Math Work Team Leader
Mathematics Head
Department of Mathematics
University of Arizona
Senior Consultant to Achieve

Ken Mullen
Senior Mathematics Program Development
Associate
ACT

Chuck Pack
National Board Certified Teacher (NBCT)
Mathematics Department Chair
Mathematics Curriculum Coordinator
Tahlequah Public Schools District
Board of Directors, Oklahoma Education
Association

Becky Pittard
National Board Certified Teacher (NBCT)
Pine Trail Elementary School
Volusia County Schools, Florida

Barbara J. Reys
Lois Knowles Distinguished Professor of
Mathematics Education
University of Missouri–Columbia

Katherine Richard
Associate Director, Mathematics Programs
Lesley University

Deb Romanek
Director, Mathematics Education
Nebraska Department of Education

Bernadette Sandruck
Professor and Division Chair of Mathematics
Howard Community College
Columbia, Maryland

Richard Scheaffer
Professor Emeritus
University of Florida

Andrew Schwartz
Assessment Manager, Research and
Development
The College Board

Rick Scott
P-20 Policy and Programs
New Mexico Department of Higher
Education

Carolyn Sessions
Standards and Curriculum Projects
Coordinator
Louisiana Department of Education

Laura McGiffert Slover
Vice President, Content and Policy Research
Achieve

Douglas Sovde
Senior Associate, Mathematics
Achieve

Sharyn Sweeney
Mathematics Standards and Curriculum
Coordinator
Massachusetts Department of Elementary
and Secondary Education

Mary Jane Tappen
Deputy Chancellor for Curriculum,
Instruction and Student Services
Florida Department of Education

Mark Thames
Assistant Research Scientist
School of Education
University Michigan

Patrick Thompson
Professor of Mathematics Education School
of Mathematical and Statistical Sciences
Arizona State University

Donna Watts
Coordinator for Mathematics and STEM
Initiatives
Maryland State Department of Education

Kerri White
Executive Director of High School Reform
Oklahoma State Department of Education

Vern Williams
Mathematics Teacher
H.W. Longfellow Middle School
Fairfax County, Virginia

Hung-Hsi Wu
Professor Emeritus of Mathematics
Department of Mathematics
University of California–Berkeley

Susan Wygant
Mathematics Specialist
Minnesota Department of Education

Jason Zimba
Professor of Mathematics and Physics
Bennington College
Student Achievement Partners

Mathematics Feedback Group

Richard Askey
Professor Emeritus of Mathematics
University of Wisconsin–Madison

Hyman Bass
Samuel Eilenberg Distinguished University
Professor of Mathematics and Mathematics
Education
University of Michigan

Elaine Carman
Middle School Math Instructional Specialist
Department of Science, Technology,
Engineering and Mathematics
Office of Curriculum, Standards and
Academic Engagement
New York City Department of Education

Andrew Chen
President
EduTron Corporation

Miguel Cordero
Secondary Math Instructional Specialist
Department of Science, Technology,
Engineering and Mathematics
Office of Curriculum, Standards and
Academic Engagement
New York City Department of Education

Linda Curtis-Bey
Director, Department of Science,
Technology, Engineering and Mathematics
Office of Curriculum, Standards and
Academic Engagement
New York City Department of Education

John A. Dossey
Distinguished University Professor Emeritus
of Mathematics
Illinois State University

Scott Eddins
Tennessee Mathematics Coordinator
President,
Association of State Supervisors of
Mathematics (ASSM)

Lisa Emond
Elementary Math Instructional Specialist
Department of Science, Technology,
Engineering and Mathematics
Office of Curriculum, Standards and
Academic Engagement
New York City Department of Education

Karen Fuson
Professor Emerita
Northwestern University

Sandra Jenoure
Early Childhood Math Instructional
Specialist
Department of Science, Technology,
Engineering and Mathematics
Office of Curriculum, Standards and
Academic Engagement
New York City Department of Education

Tammy Jones
Content Editor
Tennessee Standards Committee

Suzanne Lane
Professor, Research Methodology Program
School of Education
University of Pittsburgh

Fabio Milner
Director, Mathematics for STEM Education
School of Mathematical and Statistical
Sciences
Arizona State University

Jodie Olivo
Grade 5 Teacher
Nathanael Greene Elementary School
Pawtucket School Department
North Providence, Rhode Island

Roxy Peck
Associate Dean and Professor of Statistics
College of Science and Mathematics
California Polytechnic State University, San
Luis Obispo

John Santangelo
New England Laborers'/Cranston Public
Schools Construction and Career Academy,
American Federation of Teachers,
Rhode Island Federation of Teachers and
Health
Professionals, Cranston Teachers' Alliance

Wilfried Schmid
Professor of Mathematics
Harvard University

Ronald Schwarz
High School Math Instructional Specialist
Department of Science, Technology,
Engineering and Mathematics
Office of Curriculum, Standards and
Academic Engagement
New York City Department of Education

Matthew Ting
Mathematics Instructional Coach
Los Angeles Unified School District

Uri Treisman
Professor of Mathematics and of Public
Affairs
Executive Director
Charles A. Dana Center
University of Texas at Austin

W. Stephen Wilson
Professor of Mathematics
Department of Mathematics
Johns Hopkins University

English/Language Arts Work Team

Marilyn Jager Adams
Research Professor
Department of Cognitive and Linguistic
Sciences
Brown University

Marcia Ashhurst-Whiting
Language Arts Literacy Coordinator
Division of Educational Standards and
Programs
New Jersey Department of Education

Sorel Berman
English Teacher, Retired
Brookline High School
Brookline, Massachusetts

Katherine Bishop
National Board Certified Teacher (NBCT)
Exceptional Needs Educator
Putnam City Public Schools
National Education Association
Oklahoma City, Oklahoma

Dana Breitweiser
English Language Arts Curriculum
Specialist
Arkansas Department of Education

David Buchanan
Project Manager, ESE Performance
Standards Project
Office of Humanities
Center for Curriculum and Instruction
Massachusetts Department of Elementary
and Secondary Education

Paul Carney
Coordinator of Ready or Not Writing and
Step Write Up programs for the Center for
College Readiness
English Instructor
Minnesota State Community and Technical
College

David Coleman
President
Student Achievement Partners

Patricia D'Alfonso
English/Language Arts Specialist/Coach
West Warwick Public Schools
West Warwick, RI

Janet Davis
Point Professional Development Advisor
Los Angeles Unified School District

Matthew Davis
Director, Reading Program
Core Knowledge Foundation

Steve Delvecchio
Librarian
Seattle, Washington

JoAnne T. Eresh
Senior Associate for English Language Arts
Achieve

Jan Freeland
Middle and Secondary English Language
Arts Supervisor
Middle and Secondary Standards
Louisiana Department of Education

Sally Hampton
Senior Fellow
America's Choice and Strategic Education
Research Partnerships

Juley Harper
ELA Education Associate
Curriculum and Instruction
Delaware Department of Education

Joel Harris
Director
English Language Arts Curriculum and
Standards, Research and Development
The College Board

Bobbi Ciriza Houtchens
U.S. Department of Education Teaching
Ambassador Fellow (2009)
Teacher and English Language Facilitator
Arroyo Valley High School
San Bernardino, CA

Michael Kamil
Professor, Language Learning and Policy
Stanford University School of Education

Valerie Kinloch
Associate Professor, Literacy Studies
School of Teaching and Learning
Ohio State University

Karen Klinzing
Assistant Commissioner
Minnesota Department of Education

Susan Lafond
National Board Certified Teacher (NBCT)
in English as a New Language (EAYA ENL)
Assistant in Educational Services
New York State United Teachers

Carol D. Lee
Professor of Learning Sciences and African
American Studies
Northwestern University President
American Educational Research Association

David Liben
Liben Education Consulting L.L.C.

Meredith Liben
Liben Education Consulting L.L.C.

Cheryl Liebling
Director, Office of Literacy
Massachusetts Department of Elementary
and Secondary Education

James Marshall
Associate Dean of Academic Programs
Professor of Language and Literacy
Education
University of Georgia

Margaret McKeown
Senior Scientist Learning Research and
Development Center
Clinical Professor, Instruction and Learning
School of Education
University of Pittsburgh

Nina Metzner
Senior Test Development Associate
in Language Arts
ACT

Louisa Moats
Moats Associates Consulting, Inc.

Laura Mongello
Vice President, Product Development
The Quarasan Group, Inc

Sandra M. Murphy
Professor Emerita
University of California, Davis

Jim Patterson
Senior Program Development Associate in
Language Arts
ACT, Inc.

Anthony Petrosky
Professor of Education and English
Associate Dean for Academic Program
School of Education
University of Pittsburgh

Julia Phelps
Director of Curriculum and Instruction
Massachusetts Department of Elementary
and Secondary Education

Susan Pimentel
ELA Work Team Leader, English Language
Arts
Senior Consultant to Achieve

Donlynn Rice
Administrator of Curriculum, Instruction,
and Innovation
Nebraska Department of Education

Ricardo Rincón
Sunrise Elementary Teacher
University of Phoenix Faculty and Mentor
National ELL Training Cadre

Tracy Robertson
English Coordinator
Virginia Department of Education

Kari D. Ross
Reading Specialist
Division of School Improvement
Minnesota Department of Education

Petra Schatz
Educational Specialist
Language Arts, Instructional Services
Branch
Office of Curriculum, Instruction, and
Student Support
Hawaii Department of Education

Diana Senechal
Author
ELA and ESL certified
New York State

Timothy Shanahan
Professor of Urban Education
University of Illinois at Chicago

Miriam Soto-Pressley
Elementary Teacher
American Federation of Teachers
ELL Cadre Committee
Hammond, Indiana

Laura McGiffert Slover
Vice President, Content and Policy Research
Achieve

Charon Tierney
Language Arts Specialist
Minnesota Department of Education

Vince Verges
Executive Director
Test Development Center
Florida Department of Education

Elaine Weber
Consultant
Macomb ISD, Michigan

Susan Wheltle
Director, Office for Humanities, History and
Social Science
Center for Curriculum and Instruction
Massachusetts Department of Elementary
and Secondary Education

Karen Wixson
Professor of Education
University of Michigan

English/Language Arts Feedback Group

Mark Bauerlein
Department of English
Emory University

Gina Biancarosa
Assistant Professor of Special Education
College of Education
University of Oregon

Sheila Byrd Carmichael
Education Policy Consultant

Erika Cassel
National Board Certified Teacher (NBCT)
Humanities Teacher
Central Kitsap Junior High

Barbara R. Foorman
Francis Eppes Professor of Education
Director
Florida Center for Reading Research
Florida State University

Juley Harper
ELA Education Associate, Curriculum and
Instruction
Delaware Department of Education

George Kamberelis
Wyoming Excellence Chair of Literacy
Education
College of Education
University of Wyoming

Deborah D. Perry
Director of K-12 English Language Arts
Arlington, Massachusetts Public Schools

Cheryl M. Scott
Professor
Department of Communication Disorders
and Sciences
Rush University Medical Center

Doranna Tindle
Instructional Performance Coach
Friendship Public Charter School
Clinton, Maryland

Marc Tucker
President
National Center on Education and the
Economy

Arlette Ingram Willis
Professor
University of Illinois

Index